Suffren versus Hughes describes the fascinating but relatively little-known naval campaign between Britain and France for mastery of the Indian Ocean in the closing years of the War of American Independence. It is effectively the third volume of a trilogy recording the history of the Royal Navy during this period, the earlier volumes being *Crisis at the Chesapeake* (2021) and *From Ushant to Gibraltar* (2022).

The contest for control of the sea was crucial to the maintenance of Britain's position in India. It was played out against the political, economic and military background created by the impact of the British East India Company upon the complex system of the various dynasties that ruled India and competed amongst themselves for advantage.

Britain and France sent out squadrons of ships of the line which were at various times nearly equal in strength. In the course of their hard-fought campaign, these fought five battles, none of which produced the decisive victory which each sought.

This campaign was remarkable not just for the strategic and tactical questions which it raised, but also for the light it shed on the characters and abilities of the respective commanders. Sir Edward Hughes and Pierre-André de Suffren were very different men, who brought to their commands contrasting approaches to the particular problems of naval warfare of the eighteenth century. Hughes was a very typical product of the traditions of the Royal Navy, a patient and careful exponent of all that he had learned from his training and experience. Suffren, on the other hand, was untypical of French admirals of the period; he was bold, aggressive and innovative, and impatient of the stately conventions of sea battles of the period.

Each of them had extremely difficult problems to overcome, in addition to the fact that they were operating many thousands of miles from home, which meant that orders reached them months after they were first issued. Hughes faced considerable difficulties in his relationship with the various presidencies of the East India Company which ruled British India at this time. Suffren, on the other hand, who conducted the campaign for the most part without any effective base, was frequently badly let down by some of his captains, while the performance of his squadron demonstrated that the French navy was far less efficient than the British. For both men, a central problem was obtaining supplies, as well as that of effecting repairs to their ships, some of which were extremely badly damaged during the battles which they fought.

The two men had a very considerable respect for each other. However, while the life and career of Suffren has generated a huge literature, principally among French historians, that of Hughes has passed relatively unnoticed. Both men, though, deserved well of their countrymen for what they were able to achieve.

Quintin Barry is a retired solicitor and employment judge. He has also held a variety of offices in both public and private sectors including the NHS and local radio. Following a lifelong interest in history, he is the author of a number of books on military and naval history. These include an acclaimed two volume history of the Franco-Prussian War of 1870–1871, a history of the Austro-Prussian War of 1866, and the first modern history of the Russo-Turkish War of 1877–1878. He has made a particular study of the life and career of Helmuth von Moltke. Among his recent naval books are: *Far Distant Ships: The Blockade of Brest 1793-1815*, *Crisis at the Chesapeake: The Royal Navy and the Struggle for America 1775-1783*, and *From Ushant to Gibraltar: The Channel Fleet 1778-1783*.

Suffren versus Hughes

War in the Indian Ocean 1781–1783

Quintin Barry

Helion & Company

Helion & Company Limited
Unit 8 Amherst Business Centre
Budbrooke Road
Warwick
CV34 5WE
England
Tel. 01926 499619
Email: info@helion.co.uk
Website: www.helion.co.uk
Twitter: @helionbooks
Visit our blog at http://blog.helion.co.uk/

Published by Helion & Company 2024
Designed and typeset by Mach 3 Solutions Ltd (www.mach3solutions.co.uk)
Cover designed by Paul Hewitt, Battlefield Design (www.battlefield-design.co.uk)

Text © Quintin Barry 2024
Illustrations © as individually credited
Maps by George Anderson © Helion & Company 2024
Cover: The Battle of Cuddalore, 1783, oil on canvas by Robert Dodd, courtesy, James L. Kochan Collection, Wiscasset, Maine.

Every reasonable effort has been made to trace copyright holders and to obtain their permission for the use of copyright material. The author and publisher apologise for any errors or omissions in this work, and would be grateful if notified of any corrections that should be incorporated in future reprints or editions of this book.

ISBN 978-1-804513-39-2

British Library Cataloguing-in-Publication Data.
A catalogue record for this book is available from the British Library.

All rights reserved. No part of this publication may be reproduced, stored in a retrieval system, or transmitted, in any form, or by any means, electronic, mechanical, photocopying, recording or otherwise, without the express written consent of Helion & Company Limited.

For details of other military history titles published by Helion & Company Limited, contact the above address, or visit our website: http://www.helion.co.uk

We always welcome receiving book proposals from prospective authors.

Contents

List of Illustrations and Maps		vi
Preface		vii
Acknowledgements		viii
1	Pierre André de Suffren	9
2	Hughes	26
3	India in 1780	33
4	Hyder Ali	44
5	D'Orves	51
6	Johnstone	57
7	Preparations in France	63
8	Porto Praya	70
9	The Cape of Good Hope	83
10	The Capture of Trincomali	89
11	Sadras	98
12	Provedien	114
13	Negapatam	130
14	The Madras Committee	146
15	Trincomali	155
16	Winter	170
17	Bussy	179
18	Cuddalore	187
19	Conclusion	204
Appendix: The Two Squadrons 1782–1783		212
Bibliography		215
General Index		217
Index of Ships		220

List of Illustrations and Maps

Illustrations

Pierre André de Suffren (1729-1788). (Anne S.K. Brown Collection)	9
Louis XVI, King of France. (Anne S.K. Brown Collection)	15
The Marquis de Castries. (Public Domain)	24
Vice Admiral Sir Edward Hughes, 1786, mezzotint by Jones after Reynolds. (Anne S.K. Brown Collection)	27
Hyder Ali, 1762. (Anne S.K. Brown Collection)	43
Sir Eyre Coote. (Public Domain)	48
Lord Macartney, Governor of Madras. (Public Domain)	89
Sir Richard King. (Public Domain)	108
Suffen meeting Hyder Ali. (Public Domain)	148
Sir Richard Bickerton. (Public Domain)	151
Tipu Sultan. (Public Domain)	181

Maps

India in 1780.	34
The Carnatic.	41
The Battle of Porto Praya.	71
The Battle of Sadras.	100
The Battle of Provedien.	116
The Battle of Negapatam.	134
The Battle of Trincomali.	157
Cuddalore, 13-15 June.	197
Cuddalore, 16-17 June.	200

Preface

Exiled with Napoleon Bonaparte to Saint Helena, Emmanuel, comte de Las Cases, wrote of Pierre André de Suffren: 'Monsieur de Suffren had genius, originality, great ardour, strong ambition, a will of iron … Very tough, very strange, extremely egotistical, hard to get along with, a bad comrade, he was loved by none but admired and appreciated by all.'[1] Napoleon, who had not been very lucky in his admirals, mourned the fact that Suffren had not lived in his time, and that he could not find someone of his kind. He would, he said, have made him his Nelson, and affairs would have taken a very different turn. The life and career of Suffren has inspired an enormous literature, principally among French historians, most of whom rate him among the most outstanding of French naval leaders.

His opponent during the fierce campaign of 1782–1783 in the Indian Ocean, Sir Edward Hughes, has not enjoyed such a remarkable reputation. A typical product of the Royal Navy, embodying all its traditional virtues, he was a patient and conservative naval leader, whose tactical and strategic approach was instinctively defensive. His relatively unglamorous career has inspired no biographies, and he remains one of Britain's lesser-known commanders. While there has almost invariably been a ship in the French Navy bearing Suffren's name, the Royal Navy has never possessed a vessel named after Hughes, not least because it has had so many much more distinguished names to choose from. But Hughes was a patient, competent leader who, like Suffren, overcame very considerable difficulties. Both men deserved well of their countrymen.

This book is a history of the contest between the two men, which was fought out over five battles, concentrated in a period of less than 16 months. It is, in effect, the third volume of a trilogy recording the history of the Royal Navy in the latter years of the American War of Independence. The two previous volumes were *Crisis at the Chesapeake* and *From Ushant to Gibraltar*, both also published by Helion.

---

1 Emmanuel Las Cases, *Mémorial de Sainte Hélène* (Paris: Editions Garnier Freres, 1961), vol.II, p.524.

Acknowledgements

I should like to record my thanks to my editors Robert Griffith (in respect of this, the third volume of a trilogy concerning the Royal Navy during the War of American Independence), and Andrew Bamford (in respect of the first two volumes) for their patient and thorough work. My thanks go also to: my publisher, Duncan Rogers, for his continuing and unwavering support; to George Anderson for preparing the maps; to Sotheby's for permission to use the cover image of the Battle of Cuddalore painted by Robert Dodd; to Laurence Townsend and Katie Proctor for their IT support; and to my wife Diana and my family for their patience during the writing of this book and all the others that have gone before.

1

Pierre André de Suffren

Pierre André de Suffren was born on 29 July 1729 into a well-established aristocratic family in Provence. His father, Paul de Suffren, was Seigneur of Saint Tropez, as well as of Richeboiss and La Mole, and had in 1721 become Marquis de Saint Cannat. Two of his brothers were Knights of Malta serving in the Royal Comtois Regiment. He and his wife, Marie-Hieronyme de Bruni de la Tour d'Aigues, who came from another noble Provençal family, had nine surviving children, of whom Pierre André was the third boy. He was born in the family's winter house in the small market town of Saint Cannat, on the Marseille-Aix road.[1]

Suffren's father, despite his illustrious titles, was not wealthy; two of his daughters entered a convent, and he decided that his two youngest sons should emulate his brothers and enter the Order of St John, a traditional calling for the younger sons of the French aristocracy. The boys could enter the Order as children. These decisions, however, did not indicate a particular devotion to the church; as one of Suffren's biographers observed, they were prompted solely by the need to make provision for the children of a large family.[2]

The boys would assume their duties as Knights of the Order at the age of 18 on their formally professing the priestly vows of chastity, poverty, and obedience to the head of the Order. It was a statutory requirement that they serve in the fleet at Malta. The Grand Master, Raymond Despuis, granted Suffren and his brother, who were aged eight and seven respectively, the privilege of entry to the Order on 23 September 1737.

Pierre André de Suffren (1729-1788). (Anne S.K. Brown Collection)

---

1   Roderick Cavaliero, *Admiral Satan* (London: I.B. Tauris, 1994), p.4.
2   J.B. de la Varende, *Suffren et ses ennemis* (Paris: Flammarion, 1948), p.19.

Suffren grew up with a great love for the Provençal countryside and always spoke with a Provençal accent. He had an especially profound affection for his cousin Marie-Thérèse de Perrot de Seillans, three years older than him, who married just before he went to Malta to make his profession as a knight. Widowed young, Marie-Thérèse and he had a lifelong correspondence, although sometimes, wishing to give her his news, his letters to her were scarcely distinguishable from the despatches which he sent to the Minister of Marine.[3]

The young Suffren would grow up with a remarkable appetite for food, amounting to gluttony:

> A passion for the red hot pilaus and bouillabaisses of his native Provence followed him round the world, and he could happily shovel into his mouth curries that reduced his fellow mariners to tears. His appetite was gargantuan and, like many meridionals, he ran quickly to fat. But it did not diminish his energy. Indeed his sweating bulk was able to cope with the torrid tropical summer better than thinner men from northern parts.[4]

William Hickey, a young Calcutta lawyer who had been captured by Suffren aboard an East Indiaman, wrote in his memoirs a famous description of Suffren as he appeared in 1782:

> Of bizarre dress and figure … He looked more like an English butcher than a Frenchman of consequence. About five feet six inches in height, very corpulent, with little hair on the top of his head but more on the sides and back. Although quite fat, he used neither powder nor pomade, wore no curls and had a short queue three or four inches long tied with an old bit of twine … He was wearing a pair of old shoes from which the straps had been cut, and unbuttoned trousers … Stockings of cotton or yarn and not of the cleanest hung over his legs… A linen shirt, completely soaked with sweat.[5]

At the age of 14, Suffren was sent to the naval college for *gardes-marines* at Toulon, run by the Society of Jesus. The training was, however, sketchy at best, and many years later Suffren wrote scathingly of its inadequacy in the education of naval officers:

> It is charlatanry of the worst kind to persuade the Ministry that a boy who knows his two books by heart at 14 years old is best suited to be either a sailor or a fighter … At the moment, with a false certificate and three geometry teachers well paid by the parents … a boy of 12 can become a *garde-marine*. At 14 he has forgotten everything, is made an *enseigne*, knows

---

3 Cavaliero, *Admiral Satan*, p.6.
4 Cavaliero, *Admiral Satan*, p.6.
5 Philippe Masson, 'Pierre-Andre de Suffren de Saint-Tropez' in Jack Sweetman (ed.), *The Great Admirals* (Annapolis: Naval Institute Press, 1997), p.184.

nothing about how to command or that is not in his nature, and learns nothing more.⁶

When he arrived at the naval college, Suffren soon discovered that however glorious might be his antecedents among the families of the Midi, they were by no means outstanding when compared to those of many of his fellow pupils. He was proud of his ancestry but had to put up with the fact that the navy was full of Bretons and Normans; the Bretons especially were apt to look down on those from Provence. Frequently the sons of sea officers who were members of the *Grand Corps de la Marine*, they were brought up to believe that they had a particular entitlement, and Suffren deeply resented them.⁷ La Varende suggests that soon after he arrived in Malta he fought a duel with a Breton who called him an olive merchant; Cavaliero, on the other hand, is inclined to doubt the truth of this legend. It is, though, not inconsistent with what is known of Suffren's fierce pride in his family.

He was to take part in his first naval action as a *garde-marine* in the battle of Toulon in 1744, aboard the *Solide*, 64, as part of the French fleet under *Lieutenant-général des Armées Navales* Claude Élisée de Court de La Bruyère. At this time Spain was at war with Britain, but France had remained, for the moment, neutral. A Spanish squadron had been blockaded in Toulon by a British fleet under Vice Admiral Thomas Mathews. In February, the Spanish commander decided to put to sea escorted by the French fleet, which sailed with strict instructions designed, if possible, to avoid firing the first shot against the British. Mathews, a haughty and insensitive individual, was on particularly bad terms with Rear Admiral Richard Lestock, the commander of his rear division. Resentful of his treatment by Mathews, Lestock chose to apply literally the current fighting instructions, which meant that his division fell overnight some seven or eight miles away from the main body of the fleet.

When this came up with the enemy – the French were leading the Spanish at this time – Mathews, in the *Namur* and Cornewall, the commander of the *Marlborough*, both 90-gun ships, attacked the Spanish centre, but in the result were largely unsupported. The Spanish flagship, the 114-gun *Real Felipe* was badly mauled, but both British ships were seriously damaged; the *Marlborough* was particularly hard hit, being dismasted, and her captain was killed. Meanwhile the leading British division of 10 ships, under Rowley in the *Barfleur*, faced the whole of the French fleet of 16 ships together with two Spanish ships. Rowley resolved to attack de Court's flagship, the *Terrible*, 78. Part of Rowley's division remained out of range and when de Court, determined to come to the aid of the *Real Felipe*, attacked with his whole fleet together, Rowley conformed to this movement, as did Mathews, who now shifted his flag to the *Russell*, 80. Both fleets lay to for the night. The next day they were further apart, and although Lestock made some effort to pursue the Allied fleet, Mathews recalled him. The consequence of this indecisive battle was disastrous for the British navy. Eleven captains faced a court martial, and many were cashiered.

---

6   Regine Pernoud, *La Campagne des Indes: Lettres inédites du Bailli de Suffren* (Mantes: Petit Mantaise,1941), p.66.
7   La Varende, *Suffren et ses ennemis*, p.25.

Lestock himself faced a court martial, but he was acquitted on all the seven charges brought against him. Mathews, who came to trial in 1746, was cashiered on the grounds of several breaches of duty.[8]

Suffren's experience of this battle left a profound impression on his mind. It seemed to him that the lesson to be learned there had been that Mathews and Cornewall had done the right thing in attacking the Spanish centre so that the ships following, being the rest of the British centre division and Lestock's division, could break through the Spanish line and destroy it. Their failure to do so left him convinced of the importance of launching an attack on the enemy that was capable of being decisive, and also as to the defects of a slavish adherence to the doctrine of the line.

During the following three years Suffren spent a great deal of time at sea, crossing the Atlantic on three occasions, and learning his trade to much greater effect than he had done at the naval college. In 1745, aboard the *Pauline*, he was present in an action off Martinique when the British Vice Admiral Isaac Townsend captured or drove onshore a large part of a valuable convoy intended to reinforce the French forces in the West Indies. The following year, now serving in the *Trident*, Suffren took part in the unsuccessful attempt to recapture Cape Breton.[9]

In 1747 Suffren and his brother made their solemn profession as Knights of Malta in the Grand Priory of Aix. That autumn Suffren joined the *Monarque*, 74, part of the squadron under *Chef d'Escadre* Marquis de l'Etenduére of eight ships of the line and one armed merchantman, which sailed as an escort to a convoy of 250 transports bound for Canada. Ten days later the squadron was intercepted by Rear Admiral Edward Hawke, with 14 ships of the line. Hopelessly outnumbered, de l'Etenduére ordered the convoy to scatter, accepting that he must sacrifice his squadron to save the convoy, and prepared to meet the enemy's attack.

The ensuing battle was another crucial element in the young Suffren's naval education. It began at 11:30 a.m., when the *Neptune*, *Fougueux*, *Severn* and *Monarque* were attacked by 11 British ships of the line to windward and four to leeward. Their position was hopeless, but they put up a fierce resistance, as one by one they struck their colours, with the *Monarque* surrendering at 3:00 p.m. Two of the French ships escaped, both badly damaged; these were the *Tonnant* and the *Intrepide*. With the capture of the *Monarque*, Suffren passed into captivity, but many years later, looking back at the battle, he described it as 'one of the most glorious battles ever to be fought at sea.'[10] While a prisoner of war, Suffren was mortified by the arrogance which he encountered at the hands of his captors, and he remained bitterly hostile to Britain for the rest of his life.

When the war ended, Suffren was promoted to the rank of *enseigne*. He next went to Malta, for if he was to progress in his career as a Knight of St John he must complete his 'caravans.' Ashore, this meant escorting caravans of pilgrims. At sea, it involved undertaking cruises aboard Maltese vessels, six months in a galley and 12 months aboard a sailing ship. Here again, Suffren encountered the contempt of the

---

8   John Creswell, *British Admirals of the Eighteenth Century* (London: George Allen and Unwin, 1972), pp.67–78.
9   Sir John Knox Laughton, *Studies in Naval History* (London: Longmans Green, 1887), p.95.
10 Ruddock F. Mackay, *Admiral Hawke* (Oxford: Clarendon Press, 1964), p.78.

Bretons for the Provençals, who were known as *mocos*. In 1748 the Maltese navy was integrated with that of France, but the Knights of Malta continued in the service; in 1755 there were 50 still so engaged, a number which four years later had risen to 73.[11]

Suffren completed his required service in Malta and return to France, where in 1755 he was appointed to the *Dauphin Royal*, 74, one of a squadron under *Chef d'Escadre* Comte Dubois de la Motte sent out to Canada that spring. There was, as yet, no formal declaration of war between Britain and France; but this mission proved to be ill-fated, encountering a British squadron under Vice Admiral Edward Boscawen, which captured two ships of the line; the *Dauphin Royal* narrowly escaped the same fate before reaching safety in Louisbourg.[12] His next appointment was as a lieutenant aboard the *Orphée*, 64, and in her he took part in the action fought by the fleet under *Chef d'Escadre* Marquis de la Galissonière against Admiral John Byng off Minorca on 20 May 1756. The French commander's object was to cover the expeditionary force on the island under the Duc de Richelieu. Byng, unfortunately for him, followed closely the fighting instructions and formed a line of battle, but his rear was too far behind, and in the course of the engagement his van was badly damaged. Ultimately, he broke off the action; the French captured Minorca, and Byng duly faced the court martial which had its fatal outcome.

In January 1758 Suffren joined the *Océan*, 80, flagship of the squadron commanded by *Chef d'Escadre* Comte de La Clue; frustratingly, it was blockaded in Cartagena, and until the British squadron left the station to refit it was unable to put to sea. When he was able to do so, La Clue sailed for Toulon, only for it to be blockaded again, this time by Boscawen. The original intention was that he should, when he was able to escape, sail to Brest and pick up a convoy for Canada. In due course Boscawen left the station to refit at Gibraltar, and it was decided that La Clue's squadron should form part of a fleet under *Vice-Amiral du Ponant* Comte de Conflans to cover an invasion of England, and he sailed in August, hoping to slip through the Gibraltar Straits unobserved. However, he was spotted by a British frigate, and Boscawen put to sea in pursuit. Five of La Clue's squadron became detached and went on to Cadiz. The remaining seven were no match for Boscawen's 14, and on 17 August were overwhelmed after putting up a fierce resistance. Aboard the *Océan*, Suffren commanded the guns of the upper battery. The flagship, with three others ran into Lagos Bay, where two of them were taken and the *Océan*, which with the remaining ship had run aground, was burned to the waterline. For a second time Suffren became a prisoner of war. He was soon exchanged, having given his parole, but as a result was unemployed against Britain for the remainder of the war.[13]

Instead, he was engaged in operations against the pirates of the western Mediterranean. In the following years he commanded a number of vessels, including two xebecs, the *Caméléon* and the *Singe*, in which he gained valuable experience in handling these fast and manoeuvrable warships. Also serving in these operations was another Provençal, François-Joseph-Paul de Grasse, alongside whom he fought against the Moroccan corsairs based on El Arraich, an operation which went

---
11 Cavaliero, *Admiral Satan*, p.13.
12 Lawton, *Naval Studies*, p.97.
13 Cavaliero, *Admiral Satan*, pp.15–16.

disastrously wrong. In 1767 Suffren was given command of the frigate *Union*, but he was becoming disenchanted with his lack of progress in the French navy, and in the following year went back to Malta, where he took command of the galley *San Nicola*. This was not a particularly useful career move but, thwarted in his hope of promotion in the French navy, he next sought the post of captain general of the Maltese fleet. Largely a sinecure, it brought with it promotion to the rank of Knight Grand Cross. However, in the event, in 1772 Suffren was appointed to the command of the French 26-gun frigate *Mignonne* with, at last, the rank of *capitaine de vaisseau*.

The *Mignonne* was sent to cruise in the Levant, but in fact saw no action. Nevertheless, Suffren was glad to be at sea again, and in his final report to the Minister he wrote: 'Only long cruises can make good crews. The English keep their ships on regular service for years at a time and are way ahead of us in this respect.'[14] In August 1774 there was a change at the head of the Ministry of Marine, when Antoine de Sartine, who had been *lieutenant-général de police* in Paris, was appointed to a post in which he quickly succeeded in making a very decided impression.

During the decade which followed the end of the Seven Years War the French navy had undergone a substantial revival. The Duc de Choiseul, Louis XV's chief minister, saw the need to reconstruct France's navy if it was ever to avenge its defeat in the war which had been ended in 1763 by the Treaty of Paris. He appealed to national pride to supplement government spending on new warships, an appeal which was enormously successful. At the same time he introduced administrative reforms which substantially increased the navy's efficiency, including the rebuilding of the great naval ports of Brest and Toulon, and the remodelling of the corps of cadets which produced aspiring officers. He did not, though, succeed in overcoming the attitude of social superiority with which those of noble origin (the *rouges*) regarded the rest (the *bleus*). Among the noble officers, there was a strong sense that they were the equal of their superiors, which was seriously harmful to discipline. Admiral James quoted a passage from the work of Onésime-Joachim Troude, the French naval historian, who wrote of the situation under Louis XV's successor:

> Under Louis XVI the intimacy and fellowship existing between the chief and subordinate led the latter to discuss the orders which were given to him. Admiral, captain, officers, midshipmen, ate together; everything was in common. They 'thee'd-and-thou'd' each other like chums. In handling the ship, the inferior gave his opinion, argued; and the chief, irritated often preferred to yield rather than make enemies.[15]

Sartine's predecessor, de Bruyne, had also introduced a number of administrative reforms, which were, though, much less successful. He did, however, establish an annual squadron of evolution which undertook a number of training cruises, giving the crews of the ships involved valuable experience in ship handling, gunnery, and

---

14 Georges Lacour-Gayet, *La marine militaire de France sous le regne de Louis XVI* (Paris: Honore Champion, 1905), p.460.
15 Admiral W. James, *The British Navy in Adversity* (London: Longmans, Green and Co., 1933), p.80.

signalling. This innovation was continued by Sartine, although at first on a rather small scale; in 1775, when commanded by *Capitaine de Vaisseau* Luc Urbain du Bouëxic de Guichen, it only involved four frigates and eight smaller vessels. In the following year, *Chef d'Escadre* Louis-Charles du Chaffault led a squadron of three ships of the line, seven frigates and a number of smaller vessels.[16]

During the cruise of the squadron of evolution in 1775, Suffren had been in command of the frigate *Alcmène*. In 1777 he at last achieved his ambition to command a ship of the line, when he was appointed to the *Fantasque*, 64, and took part in the cruise of that year under the command of *Capitaine de Vaisseau* Comte de Barras, which took place in the Mediterranean. Suffren was pleased with his ship's performance, which proved to be better than he had expected. Barras originally led two 74s, three 64s and two frigates on the cruise, but by the end of the year his force had grown to 12 ships of the line, a reflection of the steadily deteriorating international situation.

Louis XVI, King of France.
(Anne S.K. Brown Collection)

A crucial step towards the outbreak of war was taken by the signing of a commercial treaty between France and the United States of America. This recognition of American sovereignty ultimately made war with Britain inevitable, though for the moment neither side was ready for immediate hostilities. It was clearly not far off, though, and the appointment of *Vice-Amiral* Comte d'Estaing, to the command of the fleet at Toulon showed clearly that the outbreak of war was imminent. D'Estaing sailed from Toulon on 13 April 1778 with his flag in the *Languedoc*, 80. He was under orders for North America, and Suffren's *Fantasque* formed part of his fleet of 12 ships of the line.

There was a good deal of uncertainty at the British Admiralty about d'Estaing's destination, which was increased by the French fleet's inordinately slow passage; it took 33 days to reach the Straits of Gibraltar from Toulon, and another 52 days to reach North America. It was delayed in mid-Atlantic by d'Estaing's insistence on carrying out a series of exercises. D'Estaing had come to the navy from the army, where he had a reputation for boldness and personal courage. Taken prisoner while

---

16 E.H. Jenkins, *A History of the French Navy* (London: Macdonald and Jane's, 1973), p.147.

serving in India in 1759, he was released on parole, and thereafter went to sea in a French East Indiaman. Promoted to *lieutenant général* in the army in 1762, he was also given the naval rank of *chef d'escadre*. In 1763 he was formally transferred to the navy with the rank of *lieutenant general des armées navales*, the equivalent of a British vice admiral, and became governor of the Leeward Islands.[17] It was soon to become apparent, however, that while not at all lacking personal courage, one of his chief characteristics as a naval commander was that of extreme caution.

By the time that d'Estaing finally reached landfall in North America the British had, so far as they could, been able to prepare to meet him. The withdrawal from Philadelphia and the Delaware estuary had been completed, and Vice Admiral Lord Richard Howe's fleet, significantly weaker than that of d'Estaing, was safely ensconced in New York harbour behind the shallow bar of Sandy Hook. The channel there was no more than 23 feet deep; d'Estaing's heaviest ships drew 25 feet, and when he arrived there, the pilots sent to him by George Washington refused to attempt it. Suffren, in the *Fantasque* and François Hector d'Albert de Rioms in the *Sagittaire*, 50, were all for making the attempt, but d'Estaing ruled it out. There is some evidence that the estimates of the depth may have been inaccurate; on 22 July a fresh north-east wind coincided with a spring tide to give the greatest possible depth of water in the channel, which might then have been practicable, but d'Estaing would not chance it, and withdrew.[18]

D'Estaing, once he had shaken off the vessels sent after him by Howe to monitor his movements, now made for Narragansett Bay, anchoring off Rhode Island on 29 July. Next day he sent Suffren in the *Fantasque* with d'Albert de Rioms in the *Sagittaire* to force their way into the bay. On 5 August they worked their way up the Western channel, into the upper bay, and they were followed by two more ships of the line that entered the channel. The senior British naval officer, seeing that the escape of the British ships from the bay was now impossible, gave orders that they be burned, while five transports were sunk to impede further progress by the French.[19] These operations cost the British five frigates, two sloops and some galleys, as well as the transports. Suffren sailed in as close as he dared to identify the burning hulks, and to allow his crew to enjoy 'a spectacle which would have been more satisfying had we run any danger.'[20]

On 9 August Howe, with a somewhat stronger force then he had had at New York, appeared and anchored off Port Judith. D'Estaing recalled the ships of his fleet, and as quickly as he could put to sea to engage Howe who, not having the weather gauge, retired. The fleets manoeuvred cautiously. On the morning of 11 August, as d'Estaing was preparing to close, the weather changed dramatically, and a violent gale blew up, scattering the ships. Both fleets suffered damage, but the French more seriously and ultimately, after further manoeuvres, d'Estaing retreated to Boston to refit. By now the ships of Vice Admiral John Byron's squadron, sent across the

---

17 Cavaliero, *Admiral Satan*, pp.31–32
18 Captain A.T. Mahan, *Major Operations of the Navies in the War of American Independence* (London: Sampson Low Marston, 1913), p.68.
19 Mahan, *Major Operations*, pp.69–70.
20 Cavaliero, *Admiral Satan*, p.33.

Atlantic to reinforce Howe but themselves scattered in bad weather, had arrived to give Howe the numerical superiority. D'Estaing was not prepared to put to sea to break the blockade which the British now established; Suffren, remembering La Clue's experience in 1759, chafed at the inaction, observing that the enemy 'leave us little hope of undertaking any major enterprise.'[21] He suggested that he and d'Albert could take two frigates to prey upon the Newfoundland fishing fleets, but d'Estaing refused to move. His secret orders, unknown to both the Americans and his own captains, were to sail to the West Indies if he lost local superiority, and when on 2 November a storm blew Byron off station, he decided that the time had come to go. He put to sea on 4 November, heading for Martinique.

Shortly before the outbreak of war, the British government had prepared a plan to seize the French held island of Saint Lucia and had ordered Howe to detach a squadron under Commodore William Hotham to convoy 5,000 troops for service in the West Indies. With two 64s, three 50s and some smaller vessels, Hotham sailed on the same day as d'Estaing. The two forces steered parallel courses, each being unaware of each other's movements.

Meanwhile the French, once war had broken out, had themselves not been idle in the West Indies, sending a force from Martinique in September 1778 to capture the British island of Dominica. Although it had been strongly fortified, its garrison was inadequate to hold it against a determined assault. Its capture was important to the French, because they now held an unbroken chain of four islands: Guadalupe, Dominica, Martinique, and Saint Lucia.

The new British commander in the Leeward Islands, Rear Admiral Samuel Barrington, had been ordered to remain at Barbados until Hotham's convoy arrived, so there was little that he could have done about Dominica. He sailed briefly as far north as Antigua, before returning to Barbados to wait for Hotham. The latter, as well as d'Estaing, had run into a violent gale off Bermuda; then, on 25 November, one of Hotham's convoy fell into the hands of d'Estaing, who thus learned of the British movements. Reckoning that the enemy convoy was heading for Antigua, d'Estaing made his way there but he had guessed wrong, and after cruising off the island for 48 hours he sailed to Fort Royal in Martinique, where he arrived on 9 December. Hotham meanwhile had continued to Barbados, where he arrived on 10 December.

Barrington wasted no time. With his own two ships of the line and Hotham's squadron and convoy, he sailed at once from Barbados to Saint Lucia, anchoring in the Grand Cul-de-Sac on 13 December. The French governor retreated inland into the hills, and British troops were soon digging in around the Carénage harbour.

By the evening of 14 December, the British held the shoreline from Point La Vigie to the southern point of the Carénage, as well as the town of Morne Fortunée. Barrington intended to move his transports into the Carénage, but he was prevented from doing so by d'Estaing's arrival that evening. The transports, some 50 or 60 in number, were hastily moved inside the line of warships, which he anchored across the mouth of the Grand Cul-de-Sac. At the northern end of his line he posted the *Isis*, 50, to prevent the enemy from passing around it, supported by three frigates. His

---

21 Cavaliero, *Admiral Satan*, p.34.

flagship, the *Prince of Wales*, 74, anchored at the southern end of the line; between it and the *Isis* there were five more vessels.[22]

The next day, d'Estaing stood in to the island, and finding Barrington's squadron in its position determined on an attack. This, however, consisted only of passing down the British line from north to south, firing at long range. That afternoon he tried again, but the cannonade was still ineffectual. Frustrated, he resolved to land the 7,000 troops that had accompanied him, and he put them ashore in a small bay to the north of Point La Vigie. On 18 December these troops launched an attack on the British earthworks. With d'Estaing at their head they launched three assaults, all of which were driven back with considerable loss.

Out at sea Suffren had been watching these operations with mounting fury, and that evening he wrote to d'Estaing to appeal for a more effective naval assault, which would involve re-embarking the troops that had been put ashore:

> In spite of the little effect of the cannonade of 15 December, and the unfortunate setback sustained by our troops, we can still be successful. But the only means of achieving this is vigorously to attack the enemy squadron. In view of our superiority, their earthworks would be of no effect if we lay them on board and anchor at the top of their anchor buoys. If we delay, they may escape, slip away under cover of darkness, leaving the troops to cover their retreat, and if we have weather again like the night before they would fly away. As it is, our ships being unmanned they can neither sail nor fight. What happens if Admiral Byron comes? What will our ships do without crews or general? Their defeat will mean the loss of both the colony and the army. Let us destroy the squadron. The garrison would then have to surrender – if Byron comes after, he will please us very much.[23]

This was altogether too bold a scheme for d'Estaing to countenance. In the event he did re-embark his men and withdrew to a position out of harm's way in the hope of a change of wind that might enable him to resume his attack. This occurred on 24 December, and he stood in again. Barrington, however, had warped his ships closer in, so that his flanks were better supported by additional earthworks that had been erected and in which he placed heavy guns, and where the wind reached his line less certainly. Confronted by this situation, d'Estaing abandoned his projected attack and, on 29 December, returned to Martinique. The French troops that had remained on the island surrendered on the following day.[24]

In Martinique, Suffren was contemptuous of his commander's lack of aggression, and he was beginning to regret that his return to the navy had, after all, not led to any satisfactory conclusion. Thinking that he might have been better off with the Knights in Malta, he wrote to the Grand Master on 3 January 1779: 'The wretched events that I have witnessed are enough to increase my regret at being so far from your Highness. Could I only drive them from my mind … They have shown how

---

22 Mahan, *Major Operations*, p.102.
23 Lacour-Gayet, *marine militaire*, pp.188–189.
24 Mahan, *Major Operations*, p.104.

dangerous it is to put someone in command of a squadron who is not a sailor and is never likely to be one.'25

D'Estaing's opponents shared Suffren's contempt for his performance; Governor Burtt of Saint Kitts wrote sardonically to Barrington to observe that 't'would be a thousand pities if his most Christian Majesty lose such a subject. I will not prostitute the word and call him officer. I shall never expect to see the art of war written by this Count.'26

D'Estaing, however, believed that from Martinique he could wage an effective war of attrition against the British in Saint Lucia. This, though, was an objective that was unattainable once Byron arrived there in January with 10 ships of the line and assumed overall command. For several months, there was little activity of note; both sides received further reinforcements, the latest to arrive bringing the French strength at Martinique to a point at which it was somewhat superior. Suffren's opinion of d'Estaing did not improve, as he made clear in a series of letters to his cousin. On 5 January he wrote from Martinique that 'our campaign has been a series of vicissitudes some lucky, some unlucky and some stupid. In my 35 years of service I have seen plenty, but never so many. One cannot imagine the foolish manoeuvres we have undertaken, the foolish and treacherous advice that has been given.' He went on to regret not having stayed in Malta. A month later, after Byron had joined Barrington, he wrote that they were awaiting the arrival of a squadron from France which would bring the two fleets almost to parity, but he reckoned that the strategy to be followed would be like that of an Italian comedy, fencing aimlessly. In March, he reflected that led differently, they would have been laden with glory and riches, but had achieved neither. On 2 April he wrote again, sadly observing that the truth was that d'Estaing did not know what to do and had neither the will nor ability to do it even if he did.27

This miserable period came to an end when at the beginning of June 1779 Byron left Saint Lucia to escort a large convoy out into the Atlantic, and while he was beating back to the Leeward Islands *Chef d'Escadre* Jean Guillaume Toussaint Picquet, Comte de la Motte, slipped into Fort Royal with further reinforcements. This gave d'Estaing 25 ships of the line, and he was finally moved to do something with them. He sent an expedition to seize the small island of Saint Vincent, and then on 30 June sailed from Fort Royal with his whole fleet to the British island of Grenada, which he reached on 2 July. That evening, he put his troops ashore, and within two days the garrison of the island capitulated. Thirty richly laden merchant men were also taken.28

At dawn on 6 July, Byron appeared, with 21 ships of the line, a frigate, and a convoy of 28 vessels carrying troops and equipment. When his arrival was reported, the French fleet, which was anchored in no sort of order in St George's Bay, raised anchor with instructions to form a line of battle in order of speed – that is, not in

---

25 Cavaliero, *Admiral Satan*, p.38.
26 D. Bonner Smith (ed.), *Letters and Papers of the Hon Samuel Barrington* (London: Navy Records Society, 1937), p.241.
27 Lacour-Gayet, *marine militaire*, pp.464–466.
28 Mahan, *Major Operations*, p.105.

their usual stations. Suffren, in the *Fantasque*, was the first to be ready, and led the fleet out of the bay, steering north-west on the starboard tack. Byron was under the impression that d'Estaing had no more than 16 of the line with him. The British fleet was sailing southwards, on the port tack, and three of his ships were in a group somewhat ahead of the rest. These were the *Sultan*, 74, the *Prince of Wales*, 74, carrying Barrington's flag, and the *Boyne*, 68. At the same time three more of Byron's ships under Rowley had been detached to his rear to cover the convoy. Byron, whose ships were by no means in order, signalled that they should engage 'and form as soon as they could get up.'[29]

As a result, the three ships with Barrington were somewhat isolated, and suffered severely. Three more of the British fleet, which had been to leeward, now, in the words of Byron's report, 'sustained the fire of the enemy's whole line as it passed on the starboard tack.'[30] These ships were so crippled that they dropped astern of the rest of the British fleet. Meanwhile Rowley, with the *Monmouth* and the *Suffolk*, which Byron ordered to rejoin the fleet, cut across to the head of the British line and engaged the French van, which was still led by Suffren in the *Fantasque*. This had been heavily engaged, losing 22 men killed and 45 wounded in the action. Rowley's two ships also suffered severely.

By 3:00 p.m. the fleets were sailing north-west in parallel lines, but four British ships – the *Grafton*, *Cornwall*, *Lion*, and *Fame* – far behind the line, were dropping to leeward and hence towards the enemy. William Cornwallis, the captain of the *Lion*, could see that if he continued to follow the British fleet on his present course he would find himself in the middle of the French fleet, so he put up his helm and stood across the French line, escaping to Jamaica. The other three sustained further damage as they headed past the French fleet, but they too managed to escape. Suffren was shocked that d'Estaing who could, if he had so chosen, have fallen on these British stragglers, had not captured or attempted to destroy them. He did, though grudgingly, give d'Estaing some credit, writing to Mme de Seillans: 'The general conducted himself both on land and at sea with great courage. The victory cannot be disputed, but if he had been as much of a sailor as he was brave, we would have prevented the escape of four dismasted vessels.'[31]

Although observing that the escape of the *Lion* and the other crippled vessels 'was due simply to the strained and inept caution of the French admiral', Mahan expressed the view that 'Byron's action off Grenada, viewed as an isolated event, was the most disastrous in results that the British had fought since Beachy Head, in 1690.'[32] It could have been worse; if Byron had been obliged to bear down to renew the action in an effort to save the stragglers, the disaster might, in Mahan's words, 'have been a catastrophe.' Byron, he considered, was the author of his own misfortune, by attacking with unnecessary precipitation and in a state of disorder.

On 14 July Suffren and d'Albert were sent, with the *Fantasque* and *Sagittaire* and two frigates, to take possession of the Union and Grenadine Islands, a task which

---

29 Mahan, *Major Operations*, p.107.
30 Mahan, *Major Operations*, p.108.
31 Lacour-Gayet, *marine militaire*, p.208.
32 Mahan, *Major Operations*, p.110.

they accomplished without difficulty. D'Estaing was generous in his praise of Suffren, writing to Sartine in the following month: 'The zeal, the talents and the courage which characterised M le Commandeur de Suffren had decided the outcome of this operation. He regrets that this has been the only chance he has had to show his thoroughness and promptness, and his ability to prevent the slightest disorder in these islands which surrendered to him.'[33]

While d'Estaing could certainly have achieved more, he could at least point to the fact that the French now controlled the whole chain of islands from Guadalupe to Grenada, with the solitary exception of Saint Lucia. In France the bells were rung to celebrate the victory.

D'Estaing followed Byron to his anchorage in the roadstead of Saint Kitts but, not surprisingly, could not tempt his opponent to accept the challenge. D'Estaing sailed next to Santo Domingo; there, he received an appeal from the American governor of South Carolina to join in a combined operation to take the British held city of Savannah. He agreed to do so, but with the condition that he must leave America by mid-September. He arrived off Savannah on 1 September with 20 ships of the line and seven frigates escorting a convoy carrying 5,000 troops. On arrival, Suffren was sent in command of a force of three ships of the line and three frigates to blockade a number of British warships that had taken refuge up the Savannah River. During this operation he was able to capture a number of British vessels. However, the subsequent land operations, in the course of which d'Estaing himself was seriously wounded, did not go well. On 26 October, fearing the onset of winter storms, d'Estaing set sail for France, detaching a squadron to take the troops back to the West Indies, and sending another to the Chesapeake.

Suffren was back in Toulon early in the New Year. He looked back at what he regarded as d'Estaing's record of failure in the Americas; so much more, he felt, could have been achieved. His experiences there had, though, enabled him to develop further his own conclusions about sea warfare. He was confirmed in his belief that the French navy must set aside its cautious tactical principles and seek instead to win decisive victories. He returned to France with the particular commendation of d'Estaing, who recommended that both Suffren and d'Albert should be promoted to *chef d'escadre*: 'M. le Commandeur de Suffren has given ... Outstanding proof of zeal and activity in every mission he has been given, and of courage and ability and battle. He is one of His Majesty's finest officers and if he cannot be promoted at once, he deserves some mark of His Majesty's satisfaction.'[34]

He was not promoted at once. He was, though, awarded a pension of 1,500 livres. Sartine told d'Estaing that Suffren would perhaps be the best *chef d'escadre* in the King's service, but pointed out that Suffren was fortieth, and d'Albert fiftieth in the list of captains. Acknowledging this, d'Estaing wrote to Sartine to say that 'M. de Suffren unites in himself all military and nautical talents. He is an excellent and resourceful tactician, full of audacity and lust for action.'[35] D'Estaing could see all too clearly just how much the French navy suffered from the importance attached to

---

33 Lacour-Gayet, *marine militaire*, p.211.
34 Cavaliero, *Admiral Satan*, p 45
35 Cavaliero, *Admiral Satan*, p.45.

seniority rather than merit; he believed that Suffren's promotion would serve as an incentive to younger officers.

For the moment Suffren was preparing for his next mission, fitting out the *Zélé* in Toulon to join the Spanish fleet in Cadiz with d'Albert in the *Marseille*. A continuing problem was the difficulty of manning their ships; Suffren wrote mournfully: 'I am armed passably well for a fight, badly for navigation and very badly for a long campaign. I have so few really good sailors that if I lose any of those I have I shall be in real difficulties.'[36] When they joined the Spanish fleet, Suffren and d'Albert were sent out to search for a small British squadron under Commodore George Johnstone that had been preying on shipping passing down the Iberian coast from Ferrol to Cadiz. They did not find him, but it would not be long before Suffren was to cross swords with Johnstone in very different circumstances.

At Cadiz, the Spanish naval commander-in-chief, *Teniente General* Luis de Córdova y Córdova, was principally concerned with blockading Gibraltar. However, in August the whole of the Combined Fleet there put to sea in the hope of intercepting British convoys bound for the West Indies, and on 9 August, 200 miles west of Cape Saint Vincent, a convoy of 64 store ships, troopships and merchantmen was sighted. The escort, which was commanded by Commodore John Moutray, consisted of the *Ramillies*, 74, and two frigates. The convoy stood no chance, and only eight escaped. The escort, having ordered the convoy to scatter, sailed westwards pursued by Suffren and d'Albert together with a number of other French ships of the line but the British ships were coppered, and soon outdistanced their pursuers. Suffren took 16 vessels of the convoy. Moutray was court-martialled and dismissed his ship. The decision to prosecute him was grossly unfair; it was the Admiralty's decision to send so weak an escort with so valuable a convoy proceeding in dangerous waters that had led to the disaster. As Mahan observed it was the greatest single blow that British commerce had received during war in living memory, and 'a general inclination prevailed to lay the blame on some individual, who might be punished according to the magnitude of the object, rather than in proportion to his demerit.'[37]

Suffren drew the obvious conclusion from the easy escape of the *Ramillies*, writing to Sartine to urge that the whole of the French fleet be coppered without delay. Sir John Knox Laughton summarised Suffren's eloquent paper on the subject:

> In this paper he pointed out that, as the English had already coppered several of their ships, and were engaged in coppering others as fast as possible, it must be considered not merely advantageous, but absolutely necessary, for the French to do the same; otherwise the enemy would always have the option of battle, or of retreat; would be able to keep the sea longer, and, even with inferior forces, to prey on the French commerce. He then proceeded, in illustration of his views, to give instances where ships had been manifestly at a disadvantage through not being coppered; he entered into the minute details of how and where a sufficient supply of copper was to be obtained;

---

36 Cavaliero, *Admiral Satan*, p.46.
37 Mahan, *Major Operations*, p.158.

and concluded with again strongly urging the necessity of coppering their own ships, and inducing their allies to copper theirs.[38]

In the autumn of 1780, under the overall command of d'Estaing, the French fleet returned to Cadiz, and reunited with the squadrons that had been left in America under de Grasse and de la Motte. Meanwhile, the affairs of the French navy had passed into new hands; Sartine, who had heavily overspent the navy's budget, was succeeded in October by the Marquis de Castries. Jonathan Dull observed that he was selected for his acceptability to a diverse group of factions:

> Certainly Castries possessed real merits – dedication, intelligence, decisiveness, a gift for organisation, and like Sartine a concern for the individual French sailor. As a member of the council, however, Castries was less impressive than as a naval minister. His dedication to his work was accompanied by an inability to see beyond the needs of the service, his intelligence by arrogance, and his gift for organisation by inflexibility. Above all, Castries lacked the gift of compromise, the suppleness, the sense of subordinating means to a larger end needed for the conducting of diplomacy.[39]

The change of naval minister had an immediate effect on Suffren's career, as he wrote in February 1781: 'I left Versailles on Tuesday; not having seen M. de Castries, I wrote to him, and he sent me an invitation to dinner. There, we talked for a long time. He told me of his great desire to employ me in an agreeable post, and I have no doubt that he will, when he is able.'[40] Castries was greatly impressed by their discussion, in the course of which he mentioned India. Importantly he felt that he had been able to get to know Suffren both as a man and as a sailor. He resolved that he would see to it that he was given the command of a squadron.

Suffren, though, was not immediately optimistic. On 26 February he wrote gloomily to Mme de Seillans to tell her that two new *chefs d'escadres* had been appointed; 'One a poor sort of fellow, and the other has only held post command twice and then only to commit such acts of folly that he has had to be kicked upstairs. I would never ask for promotion at this price, but it is a strange irony that you can be promoted more easily if you are good for nothing.'[41]

He was not, however, to wait long for his meeting with Castries to bear fruit. On 4 March he was offered the command of a squadron of four ships of the line and a force of troops. He was to go first to strengthen the Dutch garrison at the Cape of Good Hope, and then go on to join the squadron at Mauritius. He would not, however, assume the rank of *chef d'escadre* until he reached the Cape. A fortnight later he wrote to tell Mme de Seillans his news. He was conscious that once in the Indian Ocean he would come under the orders of the existing commander-in-chief

---

38 Laughton, *Naval Studies*, p.102.
39 Jonathan Dahl, *The French Navy and American Independence* (Princeton: Princeton University Press, 1975), p.202.
40 Lacour-Gayet, *marine militaire*, p.473.
41 Cavaliere, *Admiral Satan*, p.49.

The Marquis de Castries. (Public Domain)

at Mauritius, Comte d'Orves but as he remarked, 'the least happy circumstance would put one at the head of a splendid squadron, and there to win glory, that for which one would do anything.'[42] He added that in the Indian Ocean he would at last enjoy the honour and privilege of a *chef d'escadre*. For the moment though he said that his appointment was a secret and that he had not even told his parents.

---

42 Lacour-Gayet, *marine militaire*, p.474.

2

Hughes

Rather less is known about the early life of Edward Hughes than about his great opponent Pierre André de Suffren, with whom his battles in the Indian Ocean would, in due course, effectively define his career. He was born in 1720, into the well-off family of Alderman Hughes, at one time mayor of Hertford. From early in his life, he was intended for a career in the navy, which he joined at the age of 15, aboard the newly commissioned *Dunkirk*, 60. This bore the broad pennant of Commodore Digby Dent, and was part of the British fleet based at Jamaica. In 1736 Hughes transferred to the *Kinsale*, 40, (Captain John Forrester), and two years later joined the *Diamond*, 40, (Captain Charles Knowles). The connection with Knowles was to prove particularly valuable to Hughes in his later career. Aboard the *Diamond* he took part in the capture of Portobello in November 1739. Three months later he transferred to the flagship of Vice Admiral Edward Vernon, the *Burford*, 70, (Captain Thomas Watson). His service had evidently been well regarded, as in August 1740 he was commissioned lieutenant aboard the fire ship *Cumberland*. In the following year he left her to serve aboard the *Suffolk*, 70, (Captain Thomas Danvers) which took part in the bombardment of Cartagena.[1]

After spending five years in the West Indies Hughes returned to England and rejoined the *Dunkirk*, serving under Captain Thomas Cooper, and was aboard her in the indecisive battle fought off Toulon on 11 February 1744. In July he followed Captain Cooper to the *Stirling Castle*, 70, but soon after this Cooper was cashiered as a result of his conduct during the Battle of Toulon, and Captain John Fawler took command. Hughes was not, however, destined to remain long aboard the *Stirling Castle*, and in October 1745 he transferred to the *Marlborough*, 90, (Captain Richard Watkins). The *Marlborough* returned to England in 1746, and Hughes went on shore.

He did not remain ashore for long, however, choosing to travel as a passenger aboard the *Warwick*, 60 (Captain Robert Erskine). The *Warwick* was destined for Louisbourg, where Hughes had some hope that his career might prosper under the sympathetic gaze of his former commanding officer, Charles Knowles, now a commodore serving on that station.

For the voyage across the Atlantic the *Warwick* was sailing in company with the *Lark*, 44, commanded by Captain John Cruickshank. En route they encountered the Spanish *Glorioso*, 74, which had just delivered £3 million worth of treasure to

---

[1] John Charnock, *Biographia Navalis* (London: Faulder, 1798), vol.VI, pp.65–68.

Vice Admiral Sir Edward Hughes, 1786, mezzotint by Jones after Reynolds. (Anne S.K. Brown Collection)

Ferrol and was on her way to Cadiz. In the action that ensued, the *Warwick* was, in her captain's opinion, inadequately supported by the *Lark*, and the Spanish vessel was able to escape. This led to bitter recriminations on the part of Erskine who, it was alleged by Cruickshank, sent Lieutenant Hughes to Commodore Knowles when they arrived at Louisbourg with a strong complaint about Cruickshank's conduct. Not surprisingly, the latter deeply resented this, and he contended that Hughes had misrepresented the events of the action against the *Glorioso* and had poisoned the mind of Commodore Knowles against him. In the event, Cruickshank was suspended from command of the *Lark*, and Hughes was appointed temporarily to take his place. At his subsequent court martial, Cruickshank was found guilty of neglect of duty, and Knowles then officially appointed Hughes on 6 February 1748 to the command of the *Lark*. The appointment was in due course confirmed by the Admiralty, and Hughes was ranked as post captain with effect from that date.

Hughes remained in command of the *Lark*, serving on the Jamaica station, before in July 1748 returning to England, where he began a lengthy period ashore on half pay. It was not until January 1756 that he next went to sea, in command of the newly commissioned *Deal Castle*, 24, aboard which he served in the Channel Islands until July 1757. There followed a considerable career advance when he was posted to the 70-gun *Somerset*, which he commanded during the operations conducted by Boscawen which led to the capture of Louisburg in 1758. After this he sailed in company with Boscawen when the latter returned to England with a small part of his original squadron. As they approached the Channel on 27 October, they sighted a French squadron under *Capitaine de Vaisseau* du Chaffault at the entrance to the Soundings. Boscawen had only his flagship, the *Namur*, 90, and three other ships of the line, the *Royal William*, 84, the *Bienfaisant*, 64 and the *Somerset*, together with several frigates. The French commander had with him five ships of the line, a frigate, and a captured British East Indiaman. Passing the British squadron on the opposite tack he delivered a broadside which the British returned with difficulty, as they could not open their lower ports in the high winds. Boscawen then stood after the French and on the following day succeeded in retaking the Indiaman.

In 1759 the *Somerset* formed part of the fleet of Vice Admiral Sir Charles Saunders assembled to attack Québec. After the well conducted operation which culminated in the taking of the place, the *Somerset* returned to England as part of a small squadron, by now bearing Saunders' flag. As they entered the Channel the admiral learned that the French fleet under Conflans was out, and that Hawke had gone in pursuit of him. He at once steered for Quiberon Bay, but, too late to take part in the battle, and subsequently hearing of its successful outcome, set course again for England.

In the following year, with Hughes still serving as flag captain to Saunders, the *Somerset* sailed for the Mediterranean. When, in 1762, Saunders transferred his flag to the *Blenheim*, Hughes again accompanied him. In April 1763 the *Blenheim* returned home, and Hughes began another lengthy period on half pay.

When he went ashore at the conclusion of the Seven Years War, Hughes could look back on a reasonably successful career as a post captain, but which could not however be described as in any way outstanding. With the coming of peace, there were a large number of post captains on half pay, and he may well have doubted whether he would get an opportunity to advance his career further. And although he had no doubt picked up a certain amount of prize-money, he had not yet got very far towards amassing the considerable fortune that he would in due course succeed in acquiring in the later stages of his career.

As it turned out, it was the Falklands crisis with Spain in 1770 which gave him his chance to resume active service, when he was appointed again to the *Somerset*, which was to serve as a guard ship at Portsmouth. The *Somerset* remained in commission after the crisis was resolved, and Hughes was in command until in October 1773, when he was appointed a commodore.

Aware that the post of commander-in-chief in the East Indies was about to become vacant, Hughes expressed his interest to Rear Admiral Sir Hugh Palliser, the influential member of the Board of Admiralty who worked particularly closely with Lord Sandwich, the First Lord. Palliser strongly recommended that Hughes be given the position, writing to Sandwich on 11 August 1773:

> I think your Lordship cannot bestow the favour upon one who is either more deserving or who will take more pains to acquit himself to your Lordship's satisfaction. One thing which I think an essential quality your Lordship will be sure to find in him, that is, that he will not wander out of the path that may be prescribed to him to follow any schemes or whims of his own, nor never will study to find fault with his orders, but always how he may best execute them for His Majesty's service.[2]

Historian Sir Herbert Richmond explained the considerations which led, in due course, to the Admiralty making the appointment:

> Besides being an officer with a considerable experience of combined operations, he was looked on as a 'safe' man: one who could be trusted to carry out his orders, for whom orders were sufficient, and who would indulge in none of those inconvenient departures from precedent or the liberal interpretations of instructions – 'schemes or whims'– that are so distressing to certain types of the official mind.[3]

Edward Hughes could be depended on in particular to comply with the principles of the fighting instructions currently in force, not least in maintaining a close line of battle. In due course, therefore, the appointment was duly made, in succession to Sir Robert Harland, and Hughes sailed in November with his broad pennant aboard the *Salisbury*, 50.

His career thus far had already shown that he was a calm and reliable commander:

> A sea officer with an impeccable sense of public duty, cool in his bearing, generous in his sentiments, impartial in his behaviour, his phlegmatic calm

---

2   Admiral Sir Herbert Richmond, *The Navy in India 1763-1783* (London: Ernest Benn, 1930) pp.88–89.
3   Richmond, *Navy in India*, p.89.

and serene confidence inspired a genial trust in everyone who met him ... Everyone knew that he was not a man to get easily excited. His so far rather undistinguished career had emphasised the qualities of attention to detail, tenacity and courage. He was a stickler for the right forms and would not allow himself to be betrayed into making a mistake through haste. He was, moreover, a man in whom the milk of human kindness was not easily curdled – though it was certainly to be soured in the months ahead – and the care he took of his men, while it did credit to his heart, also incurred him the reputation of mollycoddling ... If Hughes never shirked action and never wavered before the ferocity and unexpectedness of an attack, he was never able to gain an advantage which subsequent hesitation did not lose. Unlike his approaching rival, he was not prepared to stake all on an intuition or hazard all on a bold stroke. Time and time again Hughes was to miss chances from a fractional caution and, in the improbable war upon which he was soon to find himself engaged, he was always slower, by a critically small but vital margin, than his rival.[4]

At this point relations between France and Britain were relatively calm, following an alarm in April when the French appeared to be mobilising a fleet with a view to possible action against Russia. This quickly subsided, and in the Indian Ocean it was apparent that there was no immediate threat from the French there, so Harland was ordered home with the whole of his squadron, and Hughes went out with a much-reduced force, consisting of the *Salisbury*, the frigates *Seahorse*, 24, and *Dolphin*, 24, and the sloop *Swallow*, 14.[5]

Before departing for England, Harland had been asked by the Bombay Presidency to take his squadron to that city to assist in garrisoning it while the Bombay Marine conducted some operations against the fleet of the Mahrattas, a request which Harland point blank refused, regarding it as his duty to keep his squadron on the east coast of India, and he remained in Trincomali until Hughes arrived to take up his post.

Hughes sailed into Madras Roads on 16 May 1774 to take up his post. He brought with him instructions similar to those given to his predecessors although, unlike them, he was not given plenipotentiary powers, since these were no longer seen as necessary. He was told that, in the present situation, it had been thought appropriate to reduce the strength of the East Indies Squadron. He was ordered to give all such assistance to the East India Company as he could, 'consistent with our engagements expressed in the 11th Article of the Treaty of Paris ... At the same time cautiously avoiding whatever might be construed an act of hostility against the settlements, possessions or subjects of any European Prince or potentate. And you shall assist at all councils of war wherein any service, in which our naval forces do cooperate, shall be taken into consideration.'[6]

---

4   Cavaliero, *Admiral Satan*, pp.93–95.
5   Richmond, *Navy in India*, p.67.
6   Richmond, *Navy in India*, p.74.

His formal instructions were accompanied by an explanatory letter from Lord Weymouth, the Secretary of State. In this, Hughes was told that the best intelligence suggested that the French naval and land forces in India had been diminished. Weymouth added however that in his opinion any schemes which they might have had been only 'laid aside for a more suitable occasion.'[7] In consequence, Hughes was told to keep a watchful eye on the French at all times, in particular assessing their strength in India itself and also, importantly, at Mauritius.

The British government had a lasting and well justified suspicion of France and her possible intentions in India, for reasons which Sir Herbert Richmond summarised:

> Proposals for an attack upon Bengal made by the governor of Chandernagore had fallen into the hands of the British; military stores were being supplied by the French to Bazalet Jung through a port on the Coromandel coast; and the attachment of Hyder to the French, and of them to him, confirmed the probability that the outbreak of an Anglo-French war would be quickly followed by an alliance against the English. Although, therefore, the French naval and military forces had been so drastically reduced watchfulness could not be relaxed.[8]

However, the period that Hughes was in command in the East Indies proved largely without incident at sea. The East India Company did, though, become embroiled in what became known as the First Mahratta War, when they supported Ragonath Rao, the uncle of the Peshwa of the Mahratta Confederacy, who had seized power on the death of his nephew in November 1772, but who subsequently faced an internal rebellion against his rule. The Bombay Presidency saw it as an opportunity to gain control of Bassein and Salsette and the other islands surrounding the harbour of Bombay. In Calcutta, the Governor General and the Council thoroughly disapproved of this venture, writing that the treaty with Ragonath Rao was invalid, and that the war was 'impolitic, dangerous, unauthorised and unjust.'[9] In the course of the subsequent operations, the fortress of Tannah and the island of Salsette were seized, while at sea the Bombay Marine succeeded in destroying the Mahratta navy. The war finally ended in March 1776. The terms of the peace were disappointing; the territory which had been gained was lost and the question of the Mahratta succession remained unsettled.

Events on the other side of the world had now begun to have their effect on India. The likelihood that the French would intervene on the side of the American insurgents increased substantially in 1776. Very great activity was reported in Brest in particular. The possibility had now to be considered that a French squadron would be fitted out to go to the East Indies. This would, though, not be something for Hughes to consider. He had by October 1776 completed three years in his appointment as commander-in-chief, and Commodore Sir Edward Vernon was now named to relieve him, arriving in mid-1777. Hughes returned to England, and on 23

---

7   Richmond, *Navy in India*, p.75.
8   Richmond, *Navy in India*, pp.75–76.
9   John Keay, *The Honourable Company* (London: Harper Collins, 1991), p.403.

January 1778 was promoted to rear admiral. By the time he returned home from India, Hughes appears to have put on weight to such an extent that in appearance he might almost be said to match that of Suffren. At any rate, a writer in the *Bengal Gazette* felt able to describe him as 'a short, thick-set, fat man; his skin fits remarkably tight about him; has very rosy gills, and drivels a little at the mouth from the constant use of quids.'[10] The painter Sir Joshua Reynolds depicted him as a very corpulent individual. Like Suffren, but unlike very many Europeans, he appears to have been perfectly at ease in the Indian climate.

Hughes shared with his great opponent a very considerable appetite. William Hickey, who provided such a memorable recollection of Pierre André Suffren, was also able to leave an account of Edward Hughes, with whom he dined aboard the *Superb* in 1783. It was a time when those on shore were limited only to a little mutton and claret. Hickey was told that 'our gallant admiral took great care to provide himself with a professed cook, and usually employed both a French and an English one.' On this occasion it was the French chef who cooked the dinner, his English colleague having been killed in action. Hickey recorded very favourably the quality of the beefsteak with which he was served.[11]

Once war had broken out with France in 1778, it appeared to the directors of the East India Company that although, as proved to be the case, the French settlements in India might be captured without undue difficulty, a French expedition would very probably be sent from Europe to launch an attack on British possessions there. In December 1778, intelligence was received of the fitting out of a squadron under *Chef d'Escadre* Charles-Henri-Louis d'Arsac de Ternay at Brest which was intended for the East Indies. In fact its objective was ultimately changed and it was sent to North America, but the project had concentrated the mind of the British government, and it was ordered that a squadron of seven ships of the line should be prepared to meet the French squadron.

The East India Company had evidently been impressed with Hughes during his previous tenure of the command in the East Indies and asked that he be appointed once more to the post in order that full advantage could be taken of the experience he had gained there, and this was agreed. Before, however, sailing to take up this position, Hughes was appointed as temporary commander-in-chief at Portsmouth while Admiral Sir Thomas Pye was engaged in presiding over the court martial of Admiral Keppel. This concluded in early 1779, and in March Hughes sailed once again for India.

---

10 Richmond, *Navy in India*, pp.90–91.
11 Cavaliero, *Admiral Satan*, p.95.

3

India in 1780

The French came late to India, some six decades after the British, Dutch and Portuguese had begun to establish trading outposts. However, they were in advance of these rivals in conceiving the project of acquiring a large territorial empire. This was the brainchild of the ambitious Joseph-François Dupleix, who had arrived as a young man in the employment of the French Compagnie des Indes. On 5 January 1739 he wrote that 'we are on the eve of a great revolution in this Empire', going on to point out that in the current political conditions a *grand derangement* to trade was to be expected, but that it could 'only be advantageous to Europeans.'[1] In 1742 Dupleix moved south from Chandernagore, the French base in Bengal, to become Governor of Pondicherry and director-general of the Compagnie des Indes. One of his first steps was to build up the Compagnie's military strength, appointing the able Marquis Bussy as its commander.

The Indian historian S.P. Sen has pointed out that opinions have been divided about Dupleix's political ideas. On the one hand, he wrote, 'the admirers of Dupleix hold him up as a pioneer among empire builders and credit him with a mature and well thought out political plan, which failed only because of the apathy and negligence of the French Government and the Company.'[2] On the other hand, Sen quotes the French historian Alfred Martineau who believed that Dupleix was only gradually driven to the concept of empire building by unforeseen circumstances, and that the project failed due 'at least as much to his own wrong moves and miscalculations as to the indifference of the home government.'[3] However, what Dupleix did succeed in doing was pointing the way which led in due course to the establishment of European dominance in India and ultimately to the British Indian Empire. Dupleix was dismissed in 1754 following a period in which French defeats at the hands of Robert Clive had saved Madras for Britain. During his years in office Dupleix had been at first remarkably successful in extending French power; at its peak, it has been estimated that about 100 million people were subject to French rule or influence. Apart from the failed attempt to conquer the Carnatic, France's position remained strong at the time of the outbreak of the Seven Years War in 1756.

---

1 William Dalrymple, *The Anarchy* (London: Bloomsbury, 2019) p.44.
2 S.P. Sen, *The French in India 1763-1816* (New Delhi: Munshiram Manoharlal, 1971), p.27.
3 Sen, *French in India*. p 28

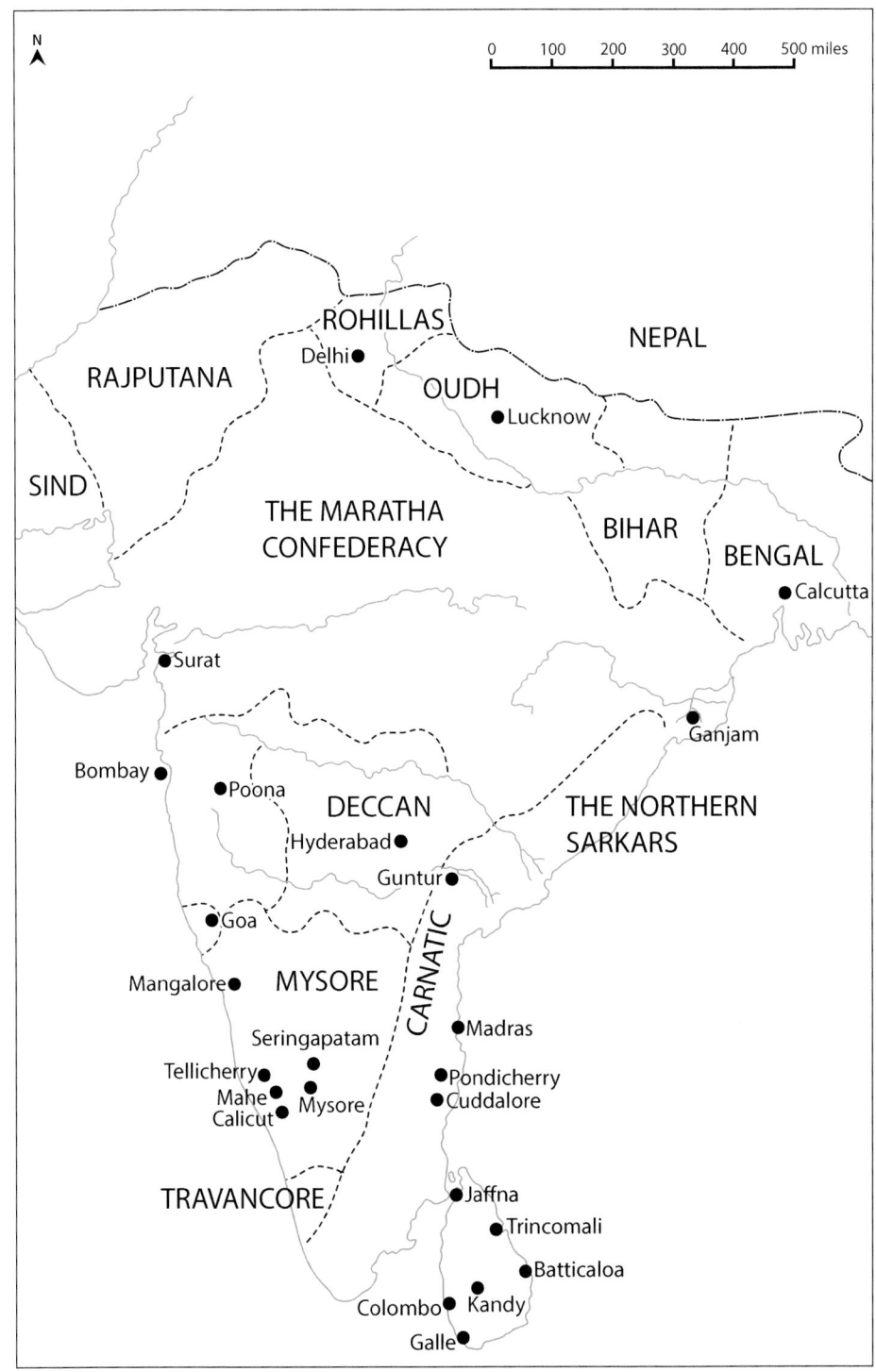

India in 1780, based on a map in Cavaliero, *Admiral Satan*.

That autumn Louis XV and his Council of Ministers took the decision to bolster the French position in India by the despatch of substantial military and naval forces to the region. In command of this force would be the 58-year-old Comte de Lally-Tollendal, who had impressed the Compagnie des Indes by the production of a paper endorsing the policy of the Compagnie in the situation following the recall of Dupleix. Lally was in many ways a surprising choice. The French Minister of War, Comte d'Argenson, described him as an intemperate, cross-grained man who did not suffer fools gladly; 'imperious, short tempered and despotic, he bullied subordinates and rowed with equals.'[4] Although he was not given as large a force as first intended, he would have some 2,000 seasoned French troops in addition to the 1,000 European troops of the Compagnie. The first detachment left France at the end of December 1756, although not arriving until August 1757, and the rest, including Lally, sailed in a convoy commanded by *Chef d'Escadre* Comte d'Aché in May 1757.

The French objective in thus committing significant forces to the Indian theatre at the start of the Seven Years War was intended to create a diversion which would weaken Britain elsewhere. The campaign did not, however, go well. Before Lally arrived in India, Clive had succeeded in retaking Calcutta, which had been occupied by the Nawab of Bengal. He had followed this up with an advance on Chandernagore, which he took in March, and had then won a brilliant victory at Plassey on 23 June 1757.

Lally's operations were largely unsuccessful, due not least to a series of wrong decisions. He also fell out with Bussy, who was a far more capable commander, and finally, after having embarked on a siege of Madras he was obliged to abandon it after defeat by Lieutenant General Sir Eyre Coote at Wandewash. The French cause was crucially compromised when d'Aché, after a series of engagements with a British squadron under Vice Admiral George Pocock in which he had generally come off worst, insisted on leaving the Coromandel coast and returning to Mauritius. As a result, Pondicherry, together with the other French settlements, ultimately fell into the hands of the British. The unfortunate Lally, who was taken prisoner, subsequently returned to France where he was made a scapegoat for the French failures and subjected to a monstrously unjust show trial on a charge of treason. He was convicted, sentenced to death, and executed in 1766.

Voltaire wrote scathingly of the net effect of the Seven Years War on the French possessions in India:

> At last there was left to the French in this part of the world only regret for having spent immense sums for over forty years for maintaining a company which never made the least profit, which never paid to its shareholders and creditors from the profits of its commerce, which in its Indian administration lived only on secret brigandage and which had been sustained only by a part of the farming of tobacco granted to it by the King; a memorable and perhaps useless example of the little knowledge which the French have had so far about the grand and ruinous commerce of India.[5]

---

4   Frank McLynn, *1759* (London: Pimlico, 2004), p.167.
5   Sen, *French in India*, p.51.

Unlike the war of 1744–1748, which was essentially a struggle between the British and French trading companies with the aim of weakening a commercial competitor, the Seven Years War was fought with a national objective. This was to decide whether Britain or France should be the dominant European power in India, with the possibility of succeeding to the possessions of the Mughal Empire. It was a contest which Britain had won decisively; the terms of the Treaty of Paris of 1763 restored France only to the position she had occupied before Dupleix embarked on his programme of expansion. By Article 11 of the treaty France recovered all settlements and factories which it possessed in 1749. However, with an eye to future possible conflict, France was prohibited from fortifying Chandernagore or maintaining troops in the settlement beyond the necessity for law and order.[6]

In 1764 Jean Law de Lauriston was appointed governor of the French settlements. He arrived at Madras on 29 January 1765, and in the course of that year formally retook possession of each of the French settlements. Bruised by the outcome of the Seven Years War, the policy of the French in India was aimed at retrieving, to some extent, their previous status:

> Their first thought was to rebuild their position on the same footing of equality with the English which had existed before the war. The very humiliating terms of the Treaty of Paris made them determined to work for a revival of their lost political influence. It was no doubt too late to attempt a restoration of the old balance of power. But Frenchmen in India, whether officials or adventurers in the service of the Indian princes, were full of hopes and believed that they could still retrieve the position of their nation by building up alliances with important country powers.[7]

In the aftermath of the Seven Years War, the Compagnie des Indes was in a parlous state. It faced the huge expense of rebuilding the settlements restored to France by the Treaty of Paris, and it was only the relaxation of the control previously exercised by the French government that enabled it to start afresh. Nevertheless, although its level of trading activity was quickly revived, it was crippled by mounting debts and the ruin of its credit in India. It soon became necessary for the government to intervene, and by a decree of August 1769 the Compagnie's privileges were suspended. There followed its liquidation, and the acquisition by the French government of its property, buildings, and warehouses both in France and India, its ships, naval and military stores, and some 2,450 slaves which it then owned.

The acquisition of the property of the company as a national asset did not immediately strengthen the hands of those who sought to rebuild the French position in India. Under Law's direction, though, the work of rebuilding Pondicherry did proceed rapidly. Some 200 European and 2,000 Indian houses were erected in the space of five months. Within a year a powder magazine had been built on the site of the old fort, as well as several warehouses and government offices. The town was now laid out on a grid system; careful attention was paid to the design of the buildings,

---

6   Sen, *French in India*, p.34.
7   Sen, *French in India*, p.36.

and a great number of trees were planted. At the same time there was a rapid growth in population. By 1768 it was estimated that including the garrison there were some 1,000 Europeans there, and the Indian population was of the order of 60,000.[8]

Jean Law had the services of an engineer named Bourcet, who produced a plan to enclose the whole of the newly rebuilt town within a line of fortifications which would principally be earthworks. After some dispute with the local *Conseil*, work began on these in 1769, but the hostility of the *Conseil* continued and Bourcet was recalled and replaced by another engineer, named Desclaisons. He preferred to construct the fortifications with brick and lime, and pulled down the bastions which had been erected in order to replace them with those of his own design. Ultimately, he was himself recalled and Bourcet returned in 1775, embarking on the construction of three bastions with a battery to guard the eastern side of the town. He died in 1776. All of this seriously delayed the completion of fortifications. which were still incomplete by the time war with Britain broke out in 1778.[9] Law, with a good deal of justification, complained of the inadequacy of the garrison. This was, however strengthened after the takeover of the company. By 1772 there would be two battalions of infantry and two companies of artillery, together with a battalion of sepoys.

The administration of French India by the government in Paris did not immediately lead to any significant developments in French policy in India; but the coming to power of Choiseul, with his determination to avenge the defeat of the Seven Years War, steadily brought about, for a while at any rate, a reassessment of the options available. Choiseul, mindful of the superior naval power of Great Britain in European waters, was in no doubt that for any invasion of Britain to succeed, that power must be diluted by diversions in other theatres of war, one of which must be India. This of course had been attempted in the Seven Years War with a pronounced lack of success. As before, Mauritius, or the Ile de France as it was named by the French, would serve as a naval and military base for a surprise attack on India. Between 1768 and 1770 a large number of troops, and a substantial squadron, were sent to the island. However, with Choiseul's fall from power, and the destruction of part of the squadron in a disastrous hurricane, the scheme for an attack on India was, for the moment, abandoned.

The death of Louis XV in May 1774 brought about a considerable change in the effectiveness and the policies of the French government. Louis XVI was an inexperienced ruler, but he had a sincere desire to restore French power and influence, and he had a number of able ministers who looked anew at the prospects of reversing the outcome of the Seven Years War. Vergennes, his Foreign Minister, was the most significant member of the new government, and his policy was in effect that of Choiseul. The new Navy Minister, Sartine, was an able administrator whose strengthening of the French navy was a decisive factor in enabling France to consider itself in a position to challenge the power of Great Britain.

Richmond, analysing the strategical object which would in due course pit a British squadron of a dozen warships in battle against a French squadron of approximately similar strength, observed that the connecting link which united a struggle in India

---

8   Sen, *French in India*, pp.57–58.
9   Sen, *French in India*, pp.61–62.

with the main object of a war against France was, quite simply, trade. In 1742 a suggestion had been made that in the event of war, the respective trading companies in India should agree to preserve neutrality. This had appealed to the board of the East India Company as well as to the Compagnie des Indes, but not at all to the British government. It saw no reason, with its maritime superiority, to put out of bounds an area in which advantages might be gained. In 1753 the idea of neutrality was again floated, but again was not taken up.[10] After the end of the Seven Years War, and the effective nationalisation of the Compagnie des Indes, the idea of a neutral zone was not revived. French policy was now to be a concern of the Crown and its military advisers. This meant that the attainment of a position of advantage in India would not only benefit trade, but also, importantly, have considerable strategic value; the launch of an attack on British possessions in India was once again seen as a potentially effective diversion which would weaken Britain's military and naval power in Europe.

This approach to the strategic situation meant that unlike the position in previous wars, during which the attacks on British possessions had not formed part of any overall plan, these would now be an essential element of a complete strategy. At the same time, British policy in India itself lacked any clear direction, which substantially increased the scope of the opportunity presented to the French; as Richmond put it, the dangers to British possessions and interests were due to many causes: 'But of these far from the least was the failure to distinguish the keystone of the situation and to direct the efforts of the Navy and the Army in full cooperation towards the attainment of an object common to both.'[11]

However, although the probability of war with Britain steadily increased, so that the strategic value of creating a diversion in India never left the mind of French planners, the French government, oddly, did nothing to strengthen its possessions in India. It was obvious that if war did break out, Britain and the East India Company would move at once on the poorly defended French possessions, and that these would be extremely vulnerable, yet no action was taken.

Only at Pondicherry was there any possibility of putting up a serious resistance to British assault. After an exchange of correspondence with the Madras government, Bellecombe, the governor of the town, drew the conclusion that war would indeed break out, and he set about doing what he could to strengthen the town's defences. Some 5,000 workmen were employed in the task of filling up the gaps in the lines of fortification under the direction of Dulac, the newly appointed chief engineer, and by strenuous exertions these were more or less completed. Small bodies of troops were raised from the European population, as well as a sepoy force, and these brought the garrison up to a total strength of 988 European troops and 1,153 sepoys, and sufficient provisions were stockpiled to enable the town to stand a siege of several months.[12]

It was well understood, by French and British alike, that sea power was crucial in any struggle between them in India. All the experience of previous conflicts,

---

10 Richmond, *Navy in India*, pp.18–26.
11 Richmond, *Navy in India*, p.31.
12 Sen, *French in India*, p.75.

and in particular d'Aché's feeble abandonment of the Coromandel coast in 1759, had demonstrated that this was the case. Now, in 1778, as the French prepared for the inevitable attack on Pondicherry, they were fortunate to have in Indian waters a squadron under *Chef d'Escadre* Jean-Baptiste-François Lollivier de Tronjoly, which consisted of the *Brillant*, 64, *Pourvoyeuse*, 38, *Sartine*, 26, *Lauriston*, 24 and *Brisson*, 26. At this time, the British squadron under Vernon comprised the *Ripon*, 60, *Coventry*, 28, *Seahorse* 24, and *Cormorant*, 14. Since Tronjoly, on the face of it, enjoyed a slight numerical superiority, Bellecombe was entitled to feel hopeful of his prospects of defending Pondicherry.

The only way of transporting munitions and provisions for a close and prolonged investment of the town available to the British was by sea. If Tronjoly could defeat Vernon, or at least be able to remain before Pondicherry, he could effectively interdict this crucial supply route, at least for long enough for reinforcements to arrive from the Ile de France. Bellecombe transferred 800 men from his garrison to Tronjoly's squadron, together with a large quantity of munitions, and asked him to launch an all-out attack on Vernon. He also reminded him of the disastrous consequences of d'Aché's withdrawal from the coast in 1759.[13] Ominously, though, Tronjoly's orders from Paris were, as had those of d'Aché been on the previous occasion, to the effect that the defence of the Ile de France and the Ile de Bourbon (Réunion) must be his principal object.[14]

Vernon had been in correspondence with the Council at Bombay, which had urged him in a letter which he received on 8 July to bring his squadron round to the east coast to defend the city. He asked the Council at Madras if they had any objection to his doing so. Their view, bearing in mind that Tronjoly was at Pondicherry, was that it would be better to remain on the Coromandel coast, both with a view to destroying Tronjoly's squadron and for the protection of British shipping. On 22 July Vernon, who entirely agreed with this opinion, received a letter at Madras announcing the outbreak of war in Europe. Lord Weymouth wrote to him: 'In case the military and naval force in India should be so far superior to that of France as to give reasonable expectation of success in any important measure, it is His Majesty's pleasure that it should be attempted, and proper authority has been given for that purpose to the Company.'[15] In discussions with the Madras Council, Vernon agreed to support the attack on Pondicherry which was now being planned. He was given the two 24-gun Indiamen *Glatton* and *Valentine* to strengthen his force, with which he sailed on 29 July.

It seems that Vernon assumed that, with his squadron thus strengthened, Tronjoly would not fight, but would withdraw under the guns of Pondicherry, and he wrote: 'My chief attention, therefore, must be to prevent any reinforcement being thrown in, which it is said they expect, as they lately dispatched the *Subtile*, a frigate of 24 guns, to Mauritius.'[16]

---

13 Sen, *French in India*, p.76.
14 Richmond, *Navy in India*, pp.82–83.
15 Richmond, *Navy in India*, p.80.
16 Richmond, *Navy in India*, p.81.

In very light winds, Vernon made his way slowly towards Pondicherry. His progress was further hampered by the poor sailing qualities of the *Glatton*, and he sent her back to Madras. It was not until 8 August that he was in sight of Pondicherry, and two further days elapsed before he was able, on the morning of 10 August, to identify Tronjoly's squadron as consisting of five warships.

No doubt to Vernon's surprise, the French squadron at once put to sea with the benefit of an offshore breeze. This, however, changed soon after midday to a sea breeze, giving Vernon the weather gauge. He recorded that with so little wind, and the uncertainty of its continuance, he thought it necessary to bring the French to action. As soon as the ships were in range, a close engagement began, which lasted some two hours. In the course of this, Vernon suffered much greater damage to his masts and rigging, and he chose to retire to the north-east to keep the wind so that on the following day he would still have the weather gauge.

This, in Sen's opinion, gave Tronjoly an opportunity; with the slight advantage he had gained, he could follow Vernon, and renew the attack, with the possibility of turning an indecisive action into a positive victory. A bolder commander would have taken this course, but Tronjoly retired under the guns of Pondicherry and landed his killed and wounded. To Bellecombe's consternation, he then announced his intention of leaving the Coromandel coast and sailing to the Ile de France. The governor begged him to remain. It was not necessary, he said, for Tronjoly to fight again; it would be sufficient if he remained at Pondicherry. But Tronjoly would not be moved, and on the morning of 21 August he suddenly put to sea.[17]

On that day Vernon sighted Tronjoly under sail, apparently steering north-east, but he was unable to get in touch with the French squadron. On the following day, the French were sighted a long distance to the southward. Vernon found that he could not overhaul them, so he returned to Pondicherry and anchored as close in as possible to blockade the place. He was able to capture the *Sartine*, which had become detached from the rest of the squadron. Returning to Pondicherry to look for it, she was chased by the *Coventry* and *Seahorse* which, putting to sea at once, took her after a long chase. There is some dispute about the casualties suffered in the action between the two squadrons. Sen thought that the British had suffered greater casualties, but according to Vernon's report, quoted by Richmond, the French lost 71 killed and 98 wounded, and the British 11 killed and 50 wounded.[18]

For the French defenders of Pondicherry, the departure of the squadron was disastrous:

> The action of Tronjoly was, in fact, still more criminal than that of d'Aché, since he even took away with him the huge quantities of munitions and the 800 men given him by Bellecombe. If he had returned the munitions and the men, it would have considerably strengthened the defence of Pondicherry. In his official report to the Minister about the incident, Bellecombe vehemently complained against the conduct of Tronjoly, and bitterly regretted

---

17 Sen, *French in India*, p.76.
18 Richmond, *Navy in India*, p.84n.

INDIA IN 1780 41

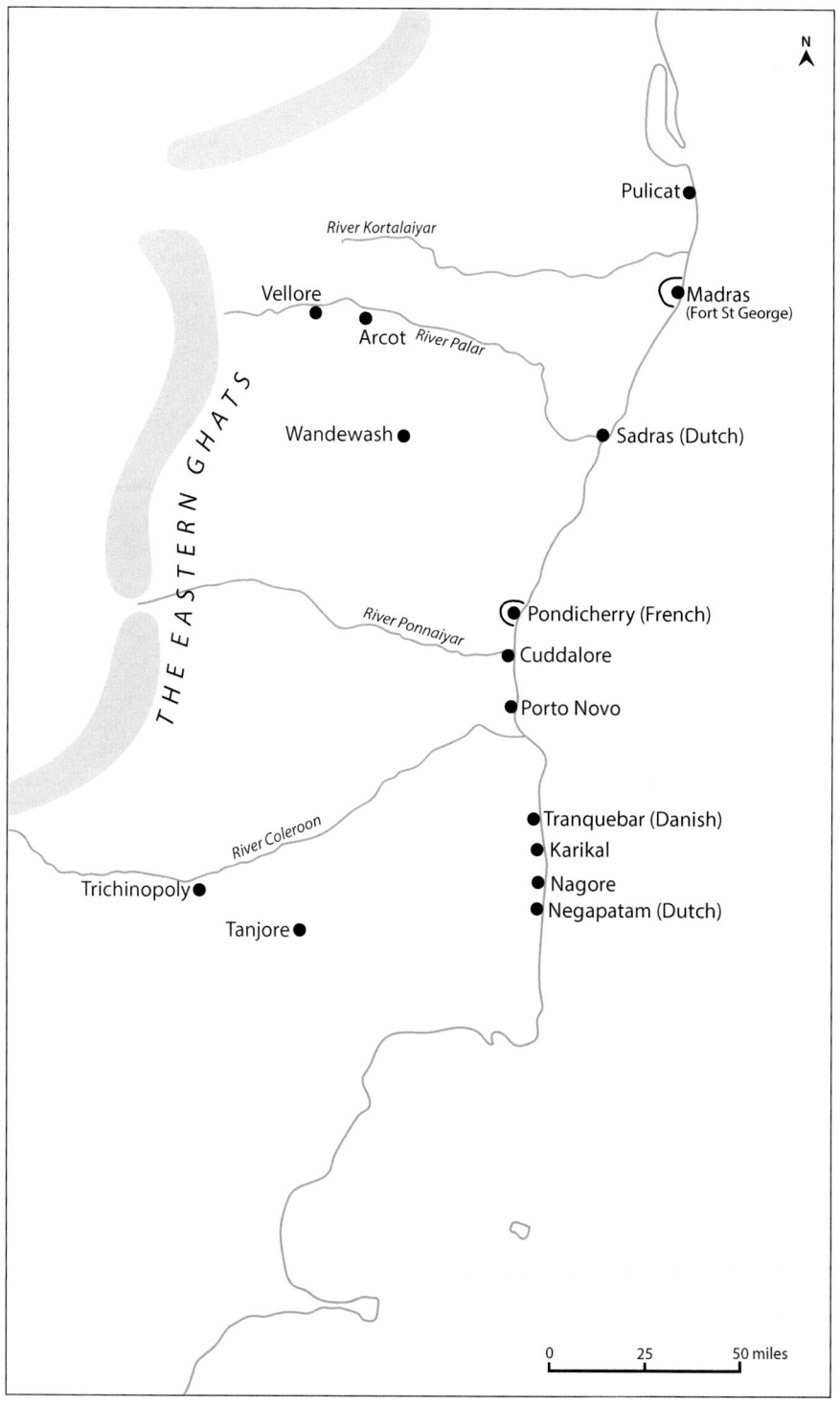

The Carnatic, based on a map in Cavaliero, *Admiral Satan*.

having given him, in full faith, munitions and men which weakened the defence of the town.[19]

Tronjoly, in his explanation to Bellecombe of his reasons for leaving, pointed to a shortage of victuals and ammunition, and his concern that while his enemy would receive reinforcements, he could expect none. This being the case, he would find himself blockaded in Pondicherry and forced to surrender when it fell. Tronjoly was evidently someone for whom his glass was always half empty, and he appears not to have attached any weight to Bellecombe's arguments that he should remain. The result of his departure was that, as must inevitably have been the case, Pondicherry was obliged to capitulate on 18 October, but not before it had put up a surprisingly stout defence, inflicting heavy losses on the attackers, who outnumbered the garrison by more than five to one. British losses were 224 killed and 693 wounded; the French lost 200 killed and 480 wounded. Vernon, his squadron now reinforced by three more Indiamen from Madras, and two from Bengal (each of which carried 40 guns), had maintained a close and largely effective blockade during the siege.

The remaining French possessions were in no state to resist their occupation by British forces, with the exception of Mahé, and all of those on the east coast were taken within weeks of the outbreak of war becoming known. Vernon retained the two Bengal Indiamen, but released those from Madras, and prepared to support the expedition against Mahé. This, however, was delayed because the troops that it was intended should carry out the operation were obliged to march across southern India. Meanwhile a serious problem arose; the Bombay Council had sent a force under Goddard to capture Poona, but he was defeated and obliged to surrender. This raised the question of whether it was in these circumstances wise to attack Mahé, but after anxious thought it was decided to proceed.

There then followed a further serious complication; Hyder Ali, the Nawab of Mysore, announced that Mahé, and all the settlements on the Malabar coast were under his protection, warning that he would oppose any attack, and would also invade the Carnatic. For the British, this was a threat to be taken very seriously, but they were already committed. Their troops under Colonel Braithwaite had reached Anjengo on the Malabar coast, and Vernon arrived there on 1 February 1779. To prevent any reinforcements arriving at Mahé he sailed at once to blockade the place. He did not expect any interference from Tronjoly, and in this he was proved correct; although the latter had received two additions to his squadron, he remained at Port Louis on the Ile de France. Braithwaite's force quickly overcame French resistance at Mahé, which capitulated on 19 March.

Hyder Ali was predictably furious that the British should have defied the announcement of his protection of Mahé and the other small French settlements on the Malabar coast and determined on revenge. He detested the British and in particular the East India Company. He now began to plan to execute the invasion of the Carnatic, which he had warned would be carried out if an attack was launched against Mahé. To Warren Hastings, the Governor General in Calcutta, the conduct

---

19 Sen, *French in India*, p.77.

Hyder Ali, 1762.
(Anne S.K. Brown Collection)

of the Madras Presidency had been wrongheaded in the extreme. By going out of its way to annoy Hyder Ali, it had brought on itself a threat which, had the French had a substantial body of European troops available could have threatened the very existence of the East India Company. Hastings was conscious that such was a real possibility, as Keay states:

> Should the French also choose this moment to unleash one of their troop carrying armadas into Indian waters, the company must be done for. To Hastings, as to posterity, it beggared understanding that the subsidiary presidencies could have behaved so blindly, so selfishly, and so incompetently in this hour of crisis. What was the use of the governor general's supervisory powers if they could be so blatantly flaunted?[20]

In the event, in 1779–1780, the French did not seek to take advantage of the situation by following through at once on the strategy of causing a diversion in the Indian theatre of war. Nevertheless, they remained in close touch with Hyder Ali, to whom they supplied arms, ammunition, and advisers. The possibility that a French force might suddenly appear on the coast of India was constantly in the mind of those endeavouring to pursue a coherent British strategy.

---

20 Keay, *Honourable Company*, p.411.

4

Hyder Ali

When Hughes finally sailed for India on 7 March 1779, he took with him a squadron consisting of the *Superb* (flag), 74, five 64s – *Exeter, Eagle, Burford, Worcester,* and *Belleisle* – and the sloop *Nymph*, 14. The squadron escorted a convoy of 13 East Indiamen, carrying the first battalion of the 71st (Highland) Regiment of Foot as a reinforcement for the British troops in India. He carried orders which had originally been drafted on 28 December. These explained that it was now considered necessary that the situation in India be supported by the Crown. His relationship with the local authorities of the East India Company was to be the same as that of his predecessors; it was carefully defined so that he should not find himself in a false position:

> He was to be a member of all Councils in which operations involving the use of the squadron should be discussed, and to cooperate in the operations decided upon; with the provision, designed to safeguard the squadron against misuse, 'consulting nevertheless what may be practicable and fit for our ships and most advisable for the general service'– a very necessary provision. The usual covering letter from the Secretary of State informed him that 'the attempts the French have lately made to gain an establishment on the coast of Bombay is an object of very material importance, and requires also your particular attention.'[1]

Before Hughes had sailed, however, another objective had been identified, which required action on the part of his squadron as it made its way eastwards. The French Council of Ministers, on hearing that d'Estaing had, in the course of his campaign in North America, been obliged to retreat to Boston, and also having received intelligence of a British plan to send an expedition to the West Indies, took a number of decisions involving detachments from *Lieutenant-général* Comte d'Orvilliers' fleet in Brest. One of these was to send the Marquis de Vaudreuil with two ships of the line, the *Fendant*, 74, and the *Sphinx*, 64, and five frigates to the coast of West Africa to attack the British slaving stations there. *Capitaine de Vaisseau* de Vaudreuil sailed on 15 December 1778.[2]

When Vaudreuil arrived in West Africa, he faced little opposition, because the West African Squadron had first been called away to cover a number of returning

---
1 Richmond, *Navy in India*, p.91.
2 Dull, *French Navy*, p.125.

East Indiamen, who were believed to be threatened by an American squadron which was preparing to intercept them. Subsequently the squadron had been transferred to the North American coast. Since Hughes would be sailing down the West African coast en route to the Indian Ocean, he was ordered to recapture Gorée – an island slave-trading centre off the coast of what is now Senegal. A temporary addition to his force was made, which consisted of the *Vengeance*, 74, the frigates *Actaeon* and *Hyaena*, and the bomb vessels *Vesuvius* and *Etna*.[3]

Three weeks later news was received that the French had abandoned their plan to send a force of five ships of the line to the Indian Ocean, and a sloop, the *Delight*, was sent after Hughes with orders to send back three ships. It had been hoped that these orders would reach him at Gorée, but the operations there had been completed so swiftly that Hughes had sailed for India by the time the *Delight* arrived, so his orders were sent overland to Bombay, which was to be his next port of call. From there Hughes made his way around the Indian coast to Madras, arriving in January 1780.

Since the occupation of Mahé, Vernon and his squadron had had little to do, other than to take action against the privateers which were a constant threat to trade, so that when Hughes arrived, he found that the situation was relatively quiet. The French squadron at the Ile de France had shown no disposition to visit the coast of India. As the year went by, however, there were frequent suggestions of possible reinforcements arriving from France which might lead to an expedition being mounted.

The French had so far done little to prepare for any significant endeavours in the Indian Ocean. The only reinforcements which had been sent out from France in the run up to the outbreak of war were the *Flamand*, 56, and a frigate, which arrived in the Ile de France in early 1778. Nevertheless, concerns on the part of the British government and the East India Company that France would at any time despatch substantial forces to the region were entirely understandable. In early 1779 intelligence had been received that the French were planning to send out a powerful squadron under de Ternay including five ships of the line. However, as time went by, and the squadron was still not ready, opinions in the French government as to its proper strategic employment began to change.

During 1779 the Council of Ministers reached the conclusion that it was not practicable to take the offensive in the Indian Ocean, and that a smaller force would suffice. As previously noted, the plan to send de Ternay and his squadron was accordingly abandoned, and following the long delays in completing its preparation the decision was taken to send him to North America. Three ships of the line, it was considered, were all that would be required to maintain parity in the Indian Ocean.[4]

In place of de Ternay's squadron, a force under *Capitaine de Vaisseau* Jean-Baptiste Thomas, comte d'Orves, had been sent out, arriving at the Ile de France in September 1779. Its effectiveness had been seriously damaged by the outbreak of a major epidemic of scurvy, which affected a large part of its crews. In the event, having reached the Indian Ocean, d'Orves remained in harbour at Port Louis for more than a year.[5] His arrival brought the total force there under Tronjoly to a

---

3 Richmond, *Navy in India*, p.92.
4 Dull, *French Navy*, p.169.
5 Lacour-Gayet, *marine militaire*, p.477.

not inconsiderable strength; but that particularly ineffective commander made no attempt to use it, contenting himself with a number of fruitless cruises in which his object was merely to prey upon British merchantmen.

D'Orves took over the command towards the end of 1780. As with previous commanders, his instructions made the defence of the islands his first priority, but he perfectly understood that they were not at risk, and he resolved to take action. He had, however, been ordered to await the arrival of a further reinforcement before commencing offensive operations.

This reinforcement was to consist of the *Protée*, 64, *Ajax*, 64 and the frigate *Charmante*, under the Comte du Chilleau. It was assembled, together with a convoy of 18 merchantmen carrying two battalions of troops, at Lorient, from where it sailed at the beginning of February 1780. It was, however, unlucky enough to run into Digby's squadron of the Channel Fleet, which was on its way back to England after having taken part in the relief of Gibraltar. Digby had with him 15 ships of the line, escorting a large convoy of empty store ships, transports and victuallers. West of Brittany, on 23 February, he sighted Chilleau's convoy and escort. It was at once apparent to Chilleau that he was hopelessly outnumbered. Determined to save his convoy, he ordered it to scatter, and made sail towards the British squadron in his flagship, the *Protée*. In the ensuing engagement, the *Protée* put up a determined resistance before, inevitably, being obliged to strike her colours. But Chilleau's sacrifice was not in vain; only three French snows were taken and the rest of the convoy, together with the *Ajax* and *Charmante*, succeeded in escaping.[6]

Thus Hughes found on his arrival that the situation insofar as the French were concerned was in no way threatening, and he had at once complied with the Admiralty's order to send back three ships of the line; the *Belleisle*, *Asia* and *Ripon* departed on 6 April.[7] Subsequently, though, the Secretary of State sent an order to Hughes to suspend the instruction to recall the ships if it was found that there was the possibility of striking an important blow at the French, or if the Company's interests required their retention. Hughes did not receive this letter until 30 May, by which time it was probably too late to catch the ships at the Cape, but in any case it was of no consequence, since the Company was firm that there was no action which could be taken at that time. This was an opinion that Hughes shared.

In June, however, the position changed abruptly. Hyder Ali was now ready to take the step that he had threatened, and he marched into the Carnatic with an army of 90,000 men. At the same time there came news that the French squadron at the Ile de France had been reinforced by a ship of the line, the *Sévère*, 64. This made the possibility of a French intervention on the Coromandel coast somewhat more likely, and Hughes took up a position off Negapatam, where he would be well placed to intercept any French squadron. He was, however, handicapped by a lack of scouting vessels, as he later wrote to Lord Hillsborough: 'I beg that you will be pleased to inform their Lordships that His Majesty's service in this country being in the highest degree distressed from want of frigates and sloops of war, I have directed

---

6   David Syrett, *The Royal Navy in European Waters during the American Revolutionary War* (Columbia: University of South Carolina, 1998), p.93.
7   Richmond, *Navy in India*, p.93.

the Naval Storekeeper to purchase a ship at this port which will make an excellent sloop of war of 18 guns.'[8] The shortage of frigates was, of course a serious and perpetual problem for many British commanders during the wars of the eighteenth and nineteenth centuries.

In August there came news from Bombay of the arrival at the Ile de France of the *Ajax*, 64, *Elephant*, 36, and *Argus*, 12. These arrivals brought the French squadron close to parity with the British. Information from the Cape suggested that the French were certainly up to something, and the Bombay Presidency became alarmed, sending a letter to Hughes urging him to sail there at once. Hughes, though, took the view that any French move would be on the Coromandel coast, and he remained in position off Negapatam for the time being. His intention was that he should remain there until mid-September, after which the short time remaining before the monsoon would mean that it would then become more likely that the French would aim at Bombay.

Events in the Carnatic, however, now intervened to make it necessary that in any case Hughes should remain on the Coromandel coast. A force of some 3,720 men under Lieutenant Colonel William Baillie had been defeated and captured by Hyder Ali on 10 September at Pollilur, 30 miles west of Madras, and the main body of the British army, after losing 500 men and most of its baggage, had been obliged to retreat to Madras. Hyder Ali went on to capture Arcot, and to lay siege to a number of British forts.[9]

The threat to Madras, which was extremely poorly defended, caused an immediate panic. Souillac, the governor of the Ile de France, had meanwhile begun negotiations with Hyder Ali, who sought French military assistance. These negotiations were conducted by Piveron de Morlat, who following the fall of Pondicherry had been acting as a French diplomatic agent. Souillac believed that the opportunity for effective operations against the British had now arrived; in addition to Hyder Ali's invasion of the Carnatic, the Mahrattas were also active.[10] In these circumstances it was to be expected that there would now be greater activity on the part of the French squadron, especially since the ineffective Tronjoly had been replaced by d'Orves. It was clearly essential that Madras be reinforced as soon as possible and two ships were despatched to Masulipatam to bring 800 sepoys, and another to Vizagapatam to collect 300 more. For Hughes, the immediate necessity was to refit his squadron before the French arrived, for which he must proceed to Bombay. At the same time, it was vital that he nevertheless remain on the Coromandel coast as long as possible. He calculated that by mid-October the danger of a landing would have receded, and he could then safely sail to Bombay. Hughes wrote on 14 September to Warren Hastings and the Council at Calcutta to remind them of the necessity to remove one threat by making peace with the Mahrattas:

---

8   Richmond, *Navy in India*, p.95.
9   Colonel G.B. Malleson, *Final French Struggles in India and on the Indian Seas* (London: W.H. Allen & Co, 1878), p.5.
10 Sen, *French in India*, p.221.

I have no doubt that a regular plan of operations is settled between him [Hyder Ali] and the French, and that a very large body of regular troops will by some means or other be sent to Hyder's assistance. Strongly impressed as I am with this certainty, and the possibility and even probability that the French may bring a superior naval force into these seas, I think it my indisputable duty to warn you, Sir and Gentlemen, of the evident necessity there now exists to guard not only the company's territories on this coast, but even Fort St George itself from the arms of France and Hyder Ali at this time when the whole national strength is required to make head against the combined force of France, Spain and our rebellious colonies.[11]

Hyder Ali, he pointed out, was at present the most dangerous enemy, and all dissipation of strength elsewhere must be avoided. There was now the prospect of making a favourable peace with the Mahrattas, who had been driven out from the country of the Rana following the capture of Gwalior, while Bombay and its territory were secure.

The reply from Hastings was reassuring. It had indeed been decided to make peace with the Mahrattas, while substantial reinforcements, led by the redoubtable Sir Eyre Coote, would be sent to Madras. Meanwhile, since Hughes was now en route to Bombay, it was suggested that he should attack Hyder's bases along the Malabar coast, and relieve the Company's settlement at Tellicherry, which was under siege. Hughes sailed for this place, and succeeded in supplying the garrison with provisions, stores, and ammunition before sailing on to seek out Hyder Ali's fleet.

He first arrived at Calicut on 8 December, where he found that Hyder's force there at anchor in the roadstead included two grabs, with two ketches, a snow, and a number of gallivants. Hughes at once decided to launch an attack with the boats of his squadron. He succeeded in cutting out and capturing one grab and forced another on shore. 'Grabs' were large, highly manoeuvrable warships, frequently used by corsairs, with a low and sharply

Sir Eyre Coote. (Public Domain)

---

11 Richmond, *Navy in India*, pp.97–98.

projecting prow, carrying triangular and lateen sails.[12] The attack was carried out by 22 boats from the *Exeter*, *Burford*, *Eagle* and *Sartine* (which had been captured in August 1778). Unfortunately, the *Sartine* was lost, having been warped into shoals in order to fire on the enemy ships and striking rocks in low water. Within a very short time the two grabs had been taken, the ketches were burned and 10 of the gallivants were also captured. The effect of this was to entirely neutralise Hyder's fleet for the time being.

After this success Hughes went on to Bombay, arriving on 20 December. In discussion with the authorities there, he learned that the latest intelligence indicated that the French squadron at the Ile de France now had six ships of the line and 11 frigates, plus there were also a number of powerful privateers. It was said that there were 8,000 troops on the island. Hughes had five ships of the line and three frigates with which to oppose an invasion, which might be directed at either the Malabar or Coromandel coasts and could be launched at any time after mid-January. It had been apparent to Hughes, before he left Madras, that the situation was becoming extremely grave, as he warned Lord Hillsborough: 'I think I may venture to say that unless we preserve a clear superiority at sea in India and a speedy period is put to the ruinous war with the Mahrattas, the affairs of the Company in this part of the world will be in great danger in a very short space of time.'[13]

Coote was of much the same mind as Hughes, sharing his dismay at the wrong-headed policies which the Company had been pursuing, and agreeing with him that it was necessary to pursue a vigorous campaign against Hyder Ali. To beat him decisively was essential, and this required both the concentration of all the available forces and the prevention of any help reaching Hyder from the French. It was also necessary to conclude peace with the Mahrattas. He proposed to cooperate with Goddard and the army of the Bombay Presidency, which he believed could provide an effective diversion. For his part, it would be for Hughes also to cooperate with Goddard so long as the season allowed, and provided that there was no certain information of a French squadron on the Coromandel coast. If there was, Hughes had told the Madras authorities: 'I shall immediately push at the enemy there. But if no such force arrives on your coast and a peace is happily concluded with the Mahrattas, I am of the opinion that General Goddard's army, aided by his Majesty's squadron under my command, might render signal services against Hyder and relieve the Carnatic.'[14]

In January 1781 Coote had begun operations against Hyder Ali's army in the Carnatic, marching south from Madras. When Hyder Ali heard of this, he raised his various sieges and concentrated his forces with the intention of cutting off communication between Coote and Madras. Coote moved slowly, strengthening the garrisons of the principal forts as he went, and suppressing an insurrection which had broken out in Pondicherry. From there, he headed to Cuddalore. Hyder marched

---

12 Philip McDougall, 'British Seapower and the Mysore Wars of the Eighteenth Century', *The Mariner's Mirror* (2011) 97:4, pp.299–314.
13 Richmond, *Navy in India*, p.101.
14 Richmond, *Navy in India*, pp.102–103.

parallel to him to the west, cutting him off from obtaining supplies from the interior. As a result of this, the only way in which Coote could now be supplied was by sea.[15]

Meanwhile, in Bombay the Council, while accepting that peace with the Mahrattas was a necessity, considered that the best way to achieve it was to strike a decisive blow at the Mahratta capital at Poona. Before doing so, it was proposed that Goddard should take action to capture Arnaul, a small fort on an island on the northern boundary of Bassein, that would secure this territory, which had been taken in December. Thereafter the army would then march on Poona. Hughes was asked to cooperate in the capture of Arnaul, which he did by sending the *Worcester* and *Coventry* to support the army. He was, though, suspicious that the Bombay authorities saw the expansion of their territory as their first priority rather than securing peace. He wrote himself to the Peshwa in Poona, in his capacity as the King's representative, to urge the need for peace; the response, however, was to the effect that the Company was not to be trusted, and with this before him Hughes was convinced that peace terms were not likely to be readily agreed, at least until Hyder Ali was driven from the Carnatic.[16] Arnaul was taken without difficulty, but the army under Goddard was not strong enough to make progress towards Poona in the face of heavy odds, and he was obliged to retreat after suffering serious losses. Peace, in consequence, was not immediately attainable.

In the Carnatic, Coote had captured Carangooly on 21 January and next marched on Wandewash, which he relieved two days later before moving on to Pernacol. It was while manoeuvring for position against Hyder Ali's army, that Coote's situation suddenly and unexpectedly became extremely threatened. D'Orves had appeared off Pulicat, with a squadron of five ships of the line, a 50-gun ship, two frigates and a sloop.

---

15 Sen, *French in India*, pp.222–223.
16 Richmond, *Navy in India*, p 105

5

D'Orves

It was at once clear to Coote that the arrival of the French squadron was a critical development which could have disastrous consequences for British interests in southern India. The decision to send the squadron had arisen from a discussion between d'Orves, after he had taken command of the squadron in succession to the inept Tronjoly, and François de Souillac, the governor of the Ile de France, in the course of which they reviewed their situation in the autumn of 1780. It is unclear which of the two was the moving spirit behind the decision to send the squadron to the Coromandel coast. Richmond gives the credit for this to d'Orves, whom he describes as 'not content to remain idly at Port Louis. His instructions made the security of the islands his principal object, but he recognised that, strongly garrisoned, they were in no danger.' Richmond points out that d'Orves was subordinate to, and under the direct orders of Souillac, whose permission he needed to leave the island: 'He pressed for this permission and for freedom to act, and eventually persuaded the governor of the islands to permit him to proceed, but only under the most stringent qualifications.' These were that he must not undertake any operation which would risk damage to his ships or prevent them from joining with the reinforcements expected in May, and he was not to land any of his men.[1]

On the other hand, Sen is inclined to suggest that it was Souillac who decided to send out the squadron with a regiment of troops in order 'to come to a definite understanding with Hyder and to prepare the ground for large scale military operations against the English in South India.'[2] Whoever was responsible for deciding the plan, d'Orves sailed from the Ile de France on 14 October. This was too late for operations on the Coromandel coast, and he proceeded in the first instance to Achin in northern Sumatra. In January 1781, when the season made it practicable to operate off the Indian coast, he put to sea, and arrived on the Coromandel coast at the end of the month. At the moment of his arrival, Coote had started to march towards Madras, but then headed for Pondicherry, where he had, incorrectly, been informed that supplies of food could be obtained. While there, he destroyed the surf boats which would be essential if the French sought to land troops, guns, or military stores. Finding no supplies at Pondicherry, and unable to provoke Hyder Ali into an engagement, Coote headed south to Cuddalore. D'Orves anchored off the place on

---

1 Richmond, *Navy in India*, pp.108–109.
2 Sen, *French in India*, p.222.

29 January. He had with him the *Orient*, 74, four 64s, the *Brillant*, *Sévére*, *Bizarre* and *Ajax*, the *Flamand*, 50, *Consolante*, 40, *Subtile*, 24 and *Expédition*, 12.[3]

Hyder Ali, closing on Coote's army, overtook him on 8 February, and immediately grasped the superb opportunity which now presented itself, with d'Orves able to prevent Coote from receiving any supplies by sea: 'At last, he thought, he had them. Coote possessed only the ground on which his army marched. He was between the sea guarded by d'Orves, and the grain producing country shut out from him by Hyder.'[4]

Coote was under no illusions about his situation. The only way out, it seemed to him, was to induce Hyder to fight, but the latter was far too smart to fall for this; he knew that, placed as he was, Coote must surrender without firing a shot.

Hyder Ali now asked d'Orves, to whom he explained the situation, to land the troops he had with him, and to remain in position off the coast until Coote should surrender. To his amazement, d'Orves refused to do either of these things, thereby foregoing the prospect of inflicting a decisive, and crucial defeat on the British. Malleson observed that 'never had France such an opportunity. It was an absolute certainty. There was neither risk nor chance about it. The English fleet under Sir Edward Hughes was off the western coast. D'Orves had but to remain quietly where he was for a few days and the English must be starved into surrender.'[5]

For Sen, 'the action of d'Orves amounted to a criminal neglect of national interests in a much greater degree than that of d'Aché (1759) or of Tronjoly (1778) … By this one step, betraying timidity and selfishness, d'Orves at once cut off the negotiations which Souillac had entered into with Hyder.'[6] Souillac later set down his emphatic opinion on the lost opportunity:

> By this surprising obstinacy of M. d'Orves, about which I sent a report to the minister at the time, we lost the occasion, never to come again, of becoming the absolute masters of the Coromandel coast. This army of Cuddalore, consisting of 14,000 men of whom 3–4,000 were Europeans, composed the entire English force in that part. Madras could not have defended itself, and the junction of our troops with those of Hyder Ali would have enabled us to conquer Tanjore and Masulipatam with all its dependencies.[7]

While Souillac's disappointment is entirely understandable, it must be borne in mind that it was he who imposed the conditions attached to the orders which seemed to d'Orves to tie his hands.

Coote, reporting to the East India company, commented on what would have been his situation if d'Orves had acted with common spirit, remarking that 'we are entirely indebted to his irresolute behaviour for the little security we now enjoy on this coast.'[8]

---

3   Richmond, *Navy in India*, p.106n.
4   Malleson, *Final French Struggles*, p.7.
5   Malleson, *Final French Struggles*, p.8.
6   Sen, *French in India*, p.223.
7   J.S. Roux, *Le Bailli de Suffren dans l'Inde* (Marseille: Barlatier-Feissant, 1862), p.68.
8   Sen, *French in India*, p.224n.

The reasons which d'Orves gave for his abrupt departure from the coast were a lack of provisions and water, and the fact that his crews were worn out. Given the scale of the opportunity which lay before him, and the fact that only a brief extension of his stay on the coast would have been required, the ringing denunciations of his conduct are understandable. Richmond, however, looks beyond d'Orves's character and personality for the explanation of his conduct:

> D'Orves's orders were precise, and the system under which he had been brought up did not encourage the growth of the spirit which acts independently ... d'Orves may have had the inclination to act, as he had the inclination not to remain passively at Mauritius. His spirit, such as it was – weakly, possibly – could receive no nourishment from a system which exacts a rigid observance of orders. The probability appears to be that he was an ordinary man, possibly – though not certainly – below the average. A system of command which does not make allowance for the mentality of the ordinary man, which tends to deter him from taking responsibility instead of encouraging him to take independent action, which leaves to him the minimum of liberty of judgment and action, is a bad system.[9]

All the same, in the particular circumstances of the squadron, it would not have taken an outstanding commander to seize the moment; many contemporary admirals would have been capable of doing so.

As it was, d'Orves sailed away on 15 February, leaving Hyder to continue his operations in the Carnatic unsupported. He fought a number of pitched battles, suffering several defeats, but his mobile forces roamed across the province, inflicting in their turn defeats on the British, whose resources were stretched almost to breaking point.

The first definite news that d'Orves had arrived on the Coromandel coast had not reached Hughes at Bombay until the second week in March. Learning that the French had landed no troops, he felt little concern about the position, since he was unaware of the dangerously exposed situation of Coote's army. In any case, his squadron was not yet ready to put to sea when the information of d'Orves's arrival reached him. Since there was now no immediate crisis in the Carnatic, he felt that he could complete his refit, and make preparations for a further relief of Tellicherry, and also for an attempt to capture Mangalore, before he himself returned to the Coromandel coast.

However, the failure of Goddard's stroke at Poona led the Bombay Council to feel that they must continue operations against the Mahrattas in an effort to recover their lost prestige, and this put paid to the projected expedition to Mangalore. Thus, since he could be of no assistance to the army inland, Hughes embarked the forces for the relief and reinforcement of Tellicherry and sailed there at the end of April. That task completed, he went on his way to the east coast, arriving at Cuddalore on 15 May. Going ashore to confer with Coote, he found that, as before, they were of the same mind as to the failure to make peace with the Mahrattas. Coote had written to

---

9   Richmond, *Navy in India*, p.110.

Hughes on 21 April on the subject, to say that he shuddered for the consequence; if a settlement had been reached with the Mahrattas, the critical situation in which he found himself would not have arisen: 'As it is, and if no steps are taken for a speedy accommodation I think with you that the total ruin of the British interests in India must ensue.'[10]

Coote's principal problem remained the lack of supplies. His inadequate transport meant that his movements were greatly limited because the country was devastated, there were no supplies at Cuddalore and Hyder held all the approaches by land, the Tanjore district had been thoroughly plundered, and he had no money. All of this was bad enough, but the possibility of the return of the French squadron had been even more serious. For Coote, therefore, the arrival of Hughes and his squadron provided security against French interference and protection for the supplies sent to him by sea.

But Hughes, too, had his own supply problems since he was running short of water. He had left Bombay with no more than six weeks' water on board, and he had already been at sea for four weeks. This was the fault of the badly organised supply system at Bombay, about which Hughes had forcefully complained before he put to sea. It was therefore necessary for him to leave Cuddalore for Madras on 1 June. There he took on water, as well as a large quantity of guns, stores, and ammunition which he took back to Cuddalore. He was unable, however, to take in addition a considerable number of bullocks, which had been collected at Madras for the use of Coote's army, since he could not risk encumbering his ships in case of an encounter with the French squadron. Taking on water at Madras, however, was not itself easy, due to the surf on the coast, which meant that it must be carried out to the ships of the squadron by boats of which there were not nearly enough. Here was a problem which affected Hughes throughout his campaigns for the rest of the war.[11]

On 1 July, Coote moved out from his position at Cuddalore to attack Hyder Ali's army in a strongly entrenched position near Porto Novo. He had with him only 8,500 men to attack a force of 180,000, but nonetheless won a victory, which would have been more decisive if his lack of cavalry and transport had not made it impossible to follow up the retreating enemy. It was a considerable achievement, but it did not bring to an end the setbacks faced by the British in southern India.

In August, the Madras Presidency resolved to take action to relieve Arcot, and a force of some 4,000 men under Sir Hector Munro marched inland, pausing at Kanchipuram to await a junction with another force, about 3,000 strong, under Baillie. This led to the disastrous defeat of Baillie's force at Pollilur on 10 September.[12]

Meanwhile the overall strategic situation had significantly changed with the outbreak of war between Britain and the Dutch Republic at the end of 1780. In the West Indies, the occasion to capture weakly defended Dutch possessions was quickly seized; similar opportunities were to be found in the Far East. In both London and Paris plans were prepared to take account of the changed situation.

---

10 Richmond, *Navy in India*, p.113.
11 Richmond, *Navy in India*, p.115.
12 Keay, *Honourable Company*, p.418.

Hughes learned of the outbreak of war with the Dutch when the sloop *Nymph* arrived on 22 June with a letter announcing the formal declaration of war, together with a further letter from Lord Hillsborough. This told Hughes that the Secret Committee of the East India Company in London was sending orders to India that consultations should be held with him to determine the best means of acting against the Dutch, 'by taking and destroying their men of war and other vessels, and for the invasion and conquest of their settlements, islands and possessions in India.' Among these, there were two key objectives in particular: the ports of Negapatam, on the Coromandel coast; and Trincomali in Ceylon. Explaining the decision to go to war, Hillsborough wrote:

> The utmost endeavours were used to dissuade the States General from the very unfriendly resolution of appointing convoys for their trade to France and Spain, which, when licit wanted no protection and would suffer no interruption from us, but when illicit could not be protected by convoy … These principles, so just in themselves, apply with double force to the Republic of Holland, who by every tie of gratitude, every motive of interest, and by the clearest stipulation of positive treaty, is bound to stand forth in our defence.[13]

The decision to issue the declaration of war, which was made on 20 December, reflected not only the real concerns about the way which the Dutch were aiding France and Spain but also the considerable opportunities that the new situation provided. Lord Hillsborough's letter to Hughes gave news of the decision to mount an expedition to the Dutch held Cape of Good Hope; 3,000 troops were to be sent there, with a powerful naval escort. If the attack succeeded, the troops were to remain there as a garrison, but if not, 2,000 would go on to India to reinforce the British forces there.

This was a plan which had had as its origins a series of proposals for action against Spain in the Pacific Ocean, dating back from a time well before the question of war with the Dutch arose, and which had been much discussed by the British Cabinet since the middle of 1780.

Richmond reviewed these proposals in the context of their relevance to Britain's principal objects in the war following the government's acceptance that the war in North America had become a secondary consideration:

> If there be one principle in war which stands out, pre-eminent among others, the violation of which infallibly calls down retribution, it is the employment of force upon enterprises which did not contribute to the attainment of the principal object of the war. What, if any, relation had an expedition to capture Dutch possessions at the Cape of Good Hope to the object of the war? Would the loss of the colony by the Dutch, or the gain of the colony by the British, affect the struggle with the powers engaged?[14]

---

13 Richmond, *Navy in India*, pp.117–118.
14 Richmond, *Navy in India*, pp.119–120.

The answer, he concluded, lay in the answers to the questions of what the object of the war was, and how it was to be attained. The principal object, he found, was to distress France and defend British possessions, and the means to achieve this was to establish maritime superiority in the vital areas. Applying these principles, he concluded that the action against the Cape was indeed a valid means of obtaining the necessary maritime superiority, since it was vital to the maintenance of the French base at Mauritius, which was, in its turn, absolutely essential to French sea power in the Indian Ocean.

Mauritius was in fact barely self-supporting in respect of its local inhabitants. It did not have the resources to support large military or naval garrisons. Accordingly, the French relied heavily on large quantities of provisions from the Cape as well as, to a lesser extent, Madagascar. It was clear to Hughes that here was a weakness in the French position that could be exploited, and he had suggested to Lord Weymouth in 1779 that a squadron should be stationed at False Bay to prevent supplies passing from the Cape to the Ile de France and the Ile de Bourbon. A squadron there would also be well placed to protect homeward bound East Indiamen.[15] The occupation of the Cape was thus a proper strategic object. Ironically, the same could not possibly have been said for the previous proposals from which the scheme had originated.

---

15 Richmond, *Navy in India*, pp.120–124.

6

Johnstone

The genesis of the scheme which was transformed into the expedition to the Cape was an entirely different project. It began with a proposal from Sir John Dalrymple for a squadron of privateers to be assembled to proceed to the Pacific, which would, it was hoped, catch the Spanish entirely unprepared. Its objective would be to prey upon the Spanish commerce on the coast of South America. It would sail via the Cape of Good Hope and New Zealand to the coast of Chile and then, taking advantage of the prevailing southerly winds, it would work its way northwards as far as Panama. From there, the force would then proceed to India or China to sell the prizes taken, after which it could return to its hunting ground and repeat the process.[1]

When the scheme was put to him, Lord George Germain approved the proposal, but in the late summer of 1780 it became a government project, based on a different scheme put forward by William Fullarton and Thomas Humberstone. They proposed to raise two regiments and to fit out warships to cruise in the Pacific with the objective of capturing the Acapulco treasure fleet. Not only the British government but also the East India Company were interested in the plan. The Company had in mind to support it with ships and troops. Its plan was that the expedition would in the first place go via India and, if as anticipated war broke out, capture Dutch possessions there before going on to attack Spanish colonies in the Western hemisphere.[2]

As First Lord of the Admiralty, Lord Sandwich had been giving particular consideration to the projected expedition, writing a lengthy memorandum setting out his views on how it should be conducted. From this paper, it is clear that he was among those who considered the scheme practicable. It was his view that not less than four ships of the line should be employed, either under Hughes or another suitable officer. He noted that the timing would depend on whenever the season would permit the force to go to the South Seas, and that its orders would be to distress the enemy wherever Hughes judged them to be most vulnerable. He also addressed with some care the question of whether the squadron should be equipped in India, and sail to Chile from there, or alternatively should sail round Cape Horn from England. He much preferred the latter alternative. The only disadvantage that occurred to him was that 'the destination of such a squadron will be liable to be discovered, and the enemy will thereby be enabled to defeat it.' He suggested ways in which false

---

1   Piers Mackesy, *The War for America 1775-1783* (London: Longmans, 1964), p.373.
2   R.F.A. Fabel, *Bombast and Broadsides* (Birmingham: University of Alabama Press, 1987), p.144.

information might be circulated to guard against the French finding out its true destination. He concluded his memorandum with the thought that 'if the squadron sails from home, perhaps it may be so contrived that after passing the South Sea it may meet a detachment from India at an appointed rendezvous in order to attack Manila, as was first intended in Lord Anson's expedition.'[3]

On 1 August the Cabinet approved in principle the plan for a joint expedition to the Pacific. It was to include a ship of the line, the 98th and 100th Regiments of Foot, each of 1,000 men, and 2,000 Company sepoys. The Company, indifferent to the diplomatic consequences, remained keen that the expedition's first objective should be the Dutch Spice Islands, followed by the capture of bases in the Spanish Philippines. This suggestion of action against Dutch possessions was emphatically ruled out by Lord Hillsborough. Although relations with the Dutch were continuing to deteriorate, it was still hoped that war might be avoided, so it was agreed that the first objective should be the Spanish islands. The planned sailing date for the expedition was fixed for December 1780.[4]

However, a further variation was considered as a result of a proposal put forward by the egregious Commodore George Johnstone, which came before the Cabinet on 2 November.[5] This proposal, involving a 'small' expeditionary force, which was described in the Cabinet minute as Johnstone's second project, received approval on 25 November. It was based on information which had been received concerning a rebellion in Spanish America, and also on accounts of the sailing of a treasure fleet from the River Plate, due to leave in December. Unfortunately, early in that month the East India Company announced that as a result of the outbreak of war with the Dutch, it could no longer spare any forces for actions in the Western hemisphere. As a result, the plan was changed again, and it was decided to combine the two forces, and first to conduct the operations in the River Plate, and then to proceed to the South Seas via the Cape of Good Hope.[6]

These plans had originally come into existence at a time of Dutch neutrality, though relations with the Dutch were steadily deteriorating. Most members of the Cabinet supported the Admiralty in believing that it was going to be necessary to take action rather than to allow the Dutch to continue to carry essential naval stores for the French. In particular, Sir Charles Middleton, the Comptroller of the Navy Board, was pressing for measures to prevent the Dutch supplying copper to the French dockyards. At the same time, the opportunity to snap up Dutch possessions was a tempting benefit of going to war. On the other hand, adding the Dutch Republic to Britain's enemies would increase the cost of conducting the war, while the Dutch navy, with some 20 ships of the line, was a potentially significant factor in the naval war.

Thus, it was soon after the breach with the Dutch finally came in December that the South Seas expedition and its River Plate addition were abandoned. The

---

3 The memorandum was found among his papers, undated and in Sandwich's handwriting. Richmond, *Navy in India*, pp.420–423.
4 Mackesy, *War for America*, p.374.
5 Fabel, *Bombast*, p.144.
6 Mackesy, *War for America*, pp.374–375.

Company had withdrawn its support, because all its forces would now be required to secure its possessions against possible attacks from the Dutch. Instead, the British government revised its plan in order to take account of the military and naval situation in the Indian Ocean as it now stood in the changed situation. Having regard to the ongoing campaign against Hyder Ali, the prospect of the French being able to take advantage of the Dutch possession of Ceylon as a base for operations on either coast of India was an extremely serious consideration. And the Dutch possession of the Cape of Good Hope was another crucially important factor, since it afforded another base from which privateers could operate against naval and commercial navigation from Britain to India. In addition, another significant factor was that the Cape was an essential source of provisions for the Ile de France. Piers Mackesy quoted the standing contention of the East India Company to the effect that 'whichever of these powers [Britain and France] shall possess the Cape, the same may govern India.' He went on to observe:

> From this time a new principle appears in British strategy: to ensure that France did not become the successor in the Indian Ocean to the decaying power of Holland. Twice in the next twenty five years Ceylon was occupied; three times expeditions were sent to seize the Cape of Good Hope. And the first of these expeditions was launched at once. The 3,000 troops who had been gathered for the River Plate and the South Sea were switched to this new objective: a mission tactically offensive but strategically defensive.[7]

It seems to have been settled relatively early in the course of the evolution of these plans that Johnstone would be in command. At all events he had come ashore from his previous posting of Portugal in September 1780, and was not officially reassigned. He soon had what may have been a significant audience with the King on 6 October, when it is entirely possible that his next posting, to command the projected expedition, was already under consideration.

George Johnstone was an ambitious and arrogant individual with a highly developed sense of his own ability and importance, who in the course of a turbulent life and career succeeded, on occasion, in persuading others, for a time at any rate, to share that view. Born in 1730, he had joined the navy in 1746 after a spell in the merchant service. He was soon in trouble. As a midshipman in the *Lark*, he is said to have challenged his captain to a duel after the latter refused him a certificate testifying to his competence and diligence.[8] In due course he passed his lieutenant's examination in 1749, but with no naval employment immediately available he then returned to the merchant service, captaining a vessel trading to the Caribbean. When, in 1756, war with France again broke out, he returned to the navy, serving aboard first the *Sutherland*, and then the *Bideford*. An incident in the latter vessel led to his court martial on a charge of insubordination. Though found guilty, his previous record of bravery in combat was taken into account, and he merely suffered a reprimand. He was aboard the *Dreadnought* in an action off Cape François in

---

7   Mackesy, *War for America*, p.380.
8   Fabel, *Bombast*, p.2.

October 1757, and was next posted to the *Augusta*, in which he was serving when the ship successfully attacked a French convoy off the island of Gonave. His captain, Arthur Forrest, described Johnstone as a 'brave, active, diligent and capable officer.'[9] This was not an opinion shared by Rear Admiral Thomas Cotes, commanding on the Jamaica station, with whom Johnstone had a violent dispute over prize-money. This led to his suspension for a while before he was sent as a lieutenant aboard the sloop *Trial*. This posting led to another serious conflict with authority, when he demanded the court martial of her captain, Thomas Cookson, for what he alleged was incompetence. Nothing came of this, but Johnstone found himself briefly serving as acting captain of the *Essex*, 70, in June 1759.

Following this, after a period of ill-health, he was given command of the sloop *Hornet*, 14, in which he served in the North Sea (where he faced a mutiny, which he duly put down) and then on the Lisbon station. There, he took several prizes, while it fell to him to convey to Rodney in 1762 the news of the declaration of war against Spain. Later that year, promoted to post captain, he commanded the *Hind*, 24.

With the end of the war, Johnstone's career took a new turn. One of the terms of the peace settlement was the cession by Spain to Britain of the province of West Florida, and Johnstone, in a memorandum which was presented anonymously, put himself forward for consideration as colonial governor. His campaign for the post was successful, the Earl of Bute, the Prime Minister and a fellow Scot, appointing him in November 1763. Johnstone arrived in Pensacola to take up his duties on 21 October 1764. During his term of office he was reasonably successful in establishing, and working with, a provincial legislative assembly, but he was not so successful in his relationship with the military authorities. Their reports before he arrived had not been very optimistic. The early immigration into the province largely consisted of soldiers, while the forts, whether put up by the French or Spanish, or by the British, were effectively the most important buildings.[10]

Johnstone, though, was buoyant about the economic prospects of West Florida, which he grandiosely described as the 'Emporium of the New World.' At first, he had been able to establish a good relationship with the Creek Indians, but this did not last; by 1766 he was contemplating war against them. During the same period his hopes of building up commercial prosperity encountered various setbacks and engendered considerable controversy, and he found himself at odds with Lord Shelburne, the newly appointed Secretary of State for the Southern Department. Nevertheless, he was active in promoting various schemes within the colony. His biographer noted that in his despatches 'invariably he minimised West Florida's defects and inflated his own achievements. In some ways the spring of 1766 was the zenith of his governorship.'[11] However, thereafter his situation almost at once began to deteriorate; there were fierce internal quarrels, especially with the military, and Shelburne decided on 13 February 1767 that he must be dismissed. At this moment Johnstone was on his way back to England for a leave of absence.

---

9   Fabel, *Bombast*, p.5.
10 Fabel, *Bombast*, p.30.
11 Fabel, *Bombast*, p.31.

Back home, he became involved with the internal politics of the East India Company, and at the same time sought to enter Parliament. Having gained the patronage of Sir James Lowther, he was elected as member for Cockermouth in 1768. Subsequently, in 1774, he was elected to represent Appleby. He was a vigorous supporter of the Rockingham-led opposition, and consistently opposed the ministry of Lord North. He favoured conciliation with the American colonists, and this was a factor in his being appointed in 1778 as a member of the peace commission sent to America. However, although at first he got on well with the other peace commissioners, his relationship with the Americans rapidly deteriorated, and he was accused of attempting to bribe prominent American citizens.[12] As a result, the Continental Congress declined to have any dealings with him, and he returned to England in October 1778.

By the end of that year Johnstone was beginning to change his attitude to the North administration, and by early 1779 was actively discussing with ministers the possibility of his crossing the floor of the House. This he finally did in February and was rewarded with the command of the squadron operating off the coast of Portugal. He did not, however, lose interest in politics, and actively argued for the cession of Gibraltar to Spain. It seems that he did have authority to put out feelers to the Spanish government on the subject, but nothing came of it. His tenure of office in command of the Lisbon squadron was broadly successful, and a number of prizes were taken. Once back in England, he resumed his active career in the House of Commons. He had previously been especially critical of both Howe and Keppel, and generally spoke in support of the administration.

It was, therefore, as an officer who had shown reasonable competence on his return to duty, and as a member of the House who had become a firm supporter of Lord North's ministry, that he was appointed to command the projected expedition, the objective of which was changed with the outbreak of war with the United Provinces. His appointment was, as his biographer remarks, a reward for political services rendered; it is clear 'that without his political support for the North administration, particularly in attacking Howe and Keppel, Johnstone would not have been appointed to its command… It was a misjudgement. At no point in his conduct of the expedition did Johnstone seem to realise the magnificent strategic coup possible if only he would concentrate his time and efforts on the important tasks.'[13] It is not at all clear whether Johnstone, and also Medows, the military commander, were involved with Fullarton and Humberston in the original scheme which they put forward. Johnstone was certainly active in the discussions with regard to the scheme in the autumn of 1780. G. Rutherford, in his essays on the subject of Johnstone's expedition to the Cape, regarded it as 'not proved, but it would be easy to argue that they had.'[14] Certainly, the prospect of making money from the venture was something that would have keenly interested Johnstone. His predilection for taking prizes at the expense of correct naval decisions remained constant, even when the

---

12 Fabel, *Bombast*, p.103.
13 Fabel, *Bombast*, p.147.
14 G. Rutherford, 'Sidelights on Commodore's Johnstone's Expedition to the Cape, part II', *The Mariner's Mirror* (1942) 28:4, pp.290–408.

objective was revised to an attack on the Cape. Rutherford shared Fabel's view: 'He still seems to have regarded his task from a privateering point of view and to have been obsessed by the thought of prizes to a degree remarkable even in an admiral of the period when important issues were at stake. Unfortunately for him he came up against a man who was ahead of his contemporaries in his conception of naval warfare and was willing to give up his prizes and even sacrifice his convoy in order to get to the Cape first.'[15]

The expedition's objective was to be in two parts. First, it was to attempt the conquest of the Dutch settlement at the Cape of Good Hope. Thereafter, depending on the outcome of this operation, 2,000 troops were to be conveyed to strengthen the British forces operating in India. Conducting this expedition, Johnstone was not under the orders of the Admiralty, but of Lord Hillsborough, the Secretary of State for the Southern Department.

His force consisted of five ships of the line: the *Hero*, 74, *Monmouth*, 64, the *Isis*, *Jupiter*, and *Romney*, all 50s; four frigates (*Apollo*, 38, *Jason*, 36, *Active*, 36 and *Diana*, 28); and the fireship *Infernal* and bomb vessel *Terror*. Importantly, all of these vessels had been coppered. Johnstone chose to fly his flag not in the *Hero*, the largest vessel in his squadron, but in the *Romney*, which had been his flagship in his previous assignment. There were also seven armed vessels, two cutters and a sloop. This squadron was to escort a convoy of transports, store ships and East Indiamen; all told, the expedition comprised 47 vessels. The military component, 3,000 strong, was under the command of Major General William Medows, who had performed extremely creditably in St Lucia.

The need for urgent action against the Cape was not merely to take advantage of an opportunity which would seriously hamper the French use of their base at the Ile de France. It was also calculated to prevent the French using the Cape as a base from which they might transport ships and troops to seize the island of St Helena. This island was not self-supporting and depended on the Cape for supplies. These supplies could now be expected to cease at once, and St Helena would be unable to support the increased garrison called for by the threat of a strong force established by the French at the Cape. Nor would it be able to supply ships calling there en route to Britain from India and China.[16]

---

15 Rutherford, 'Sidelights', p.408.
16 Richmond, *Navy in India*, p.126.

7

Preparations in France

The concerns which Sandwich had expressed about the difficulty of preserving secrecy were entirely justified. Knowledge of the projected expedition soon reached Paris and Amsterdam, and it came as no surprise in either place. Vergennes had in fact already guessed, before the end of 1780, that the force being assembled in England would have its objective switched to an attack on the Cape.[1] In any case, the overall situation in the Indian Ocean had been the subject of continuous review in France, and as has been seen, reinforcements had been sent out to the Ile de France, both in respect of ships and troops. By the end of October Castries had made an enquiry as to which four coppered ships of the line would be quickly available, and what officers there were with knowledge of the eastern theatre.

Given that there was no expectation of an early end to the war, operations in the Far East offered an attractive means of scoring an important victory, since the prospect of inflicting a decisive defeat on Britain in the West Indies had now receded. The current hostilities between the Company's forces and those of the Mahrattas and Hyder Ali suggested that this might be an opportune moment to intervene. This would, though, depend on ensuring the security of the Ile de France and guaranteeing a reliable flow of provisions. Once the Cape ceased to be neutral territory, it was plainly vulnerable to attack by the British.

Thus it was that steps were immediately taken to notify Souillac and the authorities at the Cape of the declaration of war between Britain and the Dutch Republic. The frigate *Sylphide* was despatched with the news; she reached the Cape on 31 March. There, the governor took steps to detain all homeward bound Dutch vessels, landing their cargoes, and removing their guns in order to strengthen his defences. Ships were sent off to Batavia in the East Indies and to Colombo with the news of war. The ship sailing to Colombo arrived on 6 June, two weeks before Hughes had the information.

The news of Johnstone's squadron and the convoy which accompanied it was hardly a well-kept secret. In March, the *Scots Magazine* published a more or less accurate report:

> On the 13th sailed … from Portsmouth, under the command of Com. Johnstone, a fleet, consisting of one ship of 74 guns, one of 64, three of

---
1 Dahl, *French Navy*, p.219.

50, three of 32, one of 28, two of 16, one of 14, one bomb vessel, one fire ship, and seven armed ships, having under their convoy the *Hastings, Queen, Chapman, Valentine, Osterley, Lord North, Latham, Essex, Asia, Hinchenbrook, Locke, Fortitude* and *Southampton*, East Indiamen, and a fleet of transports.[2]

The plan to despatch a substantial squadron to the Indian Ocean formed part of the overall campaign strategy for 1781 on which Castries and Fleury in the Ministry of Marine had been working. The return to Brest in February of d'Estaing and his very considerable fleet meant that the French now had 47 ships of the line in Atlantic ports available for allocation to the various theatres of war. The process of developing the campaign plan took Castries and his staff some six weeks. One of the imponderables was the continuing uncertainty about what the Spanish, when it came to it, would actually sign up to, while the diplomatic situation, following Britain's declaration of war against the Dutch Republic, remained extremely complex.[3]

In terms of numbers, the most significant component of the campaign plan was the intention to send a large fleet to the West Indies, with the secondary objective that it should also operate off the coast of America. In producing this plan, Castries suggested that, rather than increasing it by half a dozen more ships of the line, a more useful destination could be found for them following the Dutch involvement. The proposal that the French should despatch a squadron to the Indian Ocean was welcomed by the Dutch Estates General, since it was already known that the British planned to send Johnstone's force there.

When the Spanish response to the French campaign plan finally arrived at Versailles, it was focused particularly on the operations that would be undertaken by the French fleet in the West Indies, which of course was Spain's principal transatlantic area of interest. In Europe, Spanish attention was concerned especially with Gibraltar, where they were awaiting the outcome of the expected British attempt to relieve the fortress.[4]

In making his preparations for the fleet to go to the West Indies, Castries had encountered a command problem. A number of possible individuals had been considered, who had either declined the post or who were ultimately thought to be unsuitable. In the end the position went to de Grasse, apparently at the insistence of the King. However, on the other hand, when it came to consideration of the appointment of a commander for the squadron for the Indian Ocean, Castries had little hesitation in appointing Pierre André de Suffren. After his first meeting with him, he was in no doubt that he was the man for the job. Unlike Johnstone's appointment, which had been made early in the British planning process, and was accordingly soon widely known, it was not until 4 March that Suffren was formally offered the command of the squadron now being prepared for the Cape.

Castries had been obliged to remain in Versailles until the Spanish reply had been received. This arrived on 8 March, and Castries then set off to Brest to oversee the

---

2 Fabel, *Bombast*, pp.147–148.
3 Dull, *French Navy*, p.216.
4 Dull, *French Navy*, pp.220–221.

final preparations for de Grasse's fleet and Suffren's squadron, which were to sail together. In Brest, he found the process of readying the fleet had taken much longer than the six weeks previously estimated. The last ship of the line had only been moved into the roadstead on 8 March.

Soon after his arrival, Castries received news from Vergennes, who had further intelligence about Johnstone's expedition. This was based on an entirely false report planted by a British secret agent to the effect that Johnstone's force was to proceed directly to India. This followed the suggestion put forward by Sandwich in his memorandum previously quoted. It purported to be based on a set of instructions, entirely false, directed to Darby, Johnstone and Medows, and named the objective of the expedition as being the Dutch possessions in the East Indies to the east of the Cape of Good Hope, beginning with those immediately to the west of Malacca, and then going on to Java and Batavia. If these possessions could be taken, they were to be held, but if this proved to be impossible all the works, defences and stores there were to be completely destroyed.[5] It was stated that the squadron was to consist of six ships of the line, and it was falsely suggested that it was first to accompany the Channel Fleet in its bid to relieve Gibraltar, and then go on to Madeira to pick up a convoy, before then proceeding to St Helena.

This deception, however, had a rather different effect to that intended. In the face of this information, Castries considered it prudent to add a further ship of the line to Suffren's squadron.[6] When it reached the Ile de France, it would bring the French fleet in the Indian Ocean to a total of 11 ships of the line, making it marginally superior to Hughes' fleet, which had 10. The intention was that after accompanying de Grasse as far as Madeira, Suffren should part company and proceed directly to the Cape but was to remain only long enough to disembark the troops he carried; he was then to proceed to the Ile de France.

Preparations for sailing were completed by 19 March. Three days later the wind shifted to the east, enabling the huge fleet to put to sea. Its departure was a hugely impressive sight: 'On all sides of the harbour and the roadstead an enormous crowd gathered to watch this great spectacle. It was for them the occasion for an outburst of patriotic sentiment.'[7] Castries, returning to Versailles to report to the King, might justly feel proud of the fleets which his navy was sending out to deliver America and to win victory in India.

The fleet which now put to sea consisted of 25 ships of the line, with three frigates and a corvette. It escorted a convoy comprising over a hundred transports and store ships. Of this fleet, Suffren's squadron comprised five ships of the line: there were two 74 s (*Héros* and *Annibal*); three 64s (*Artésien*, *Vengeur* and *Sphinx*); and there was the corvette *Fortune*, 18.

François Caron, in his relentlessly critical review of Suffren's career, has given an account of each of the vessels that comprised this squadron. His flagship *Héros*, constructed at Toulon as recently as 1778, had already gained a reputation as a poor sailer. However, its performance during the ensuing campaign did not confirm its

---
5 Richmond, *Navy in India*, pp.133–134.
6 Francois Caron, *Le Mythe de Suffren* (Vincennes: Service historique de la marine, 1996), p.91.
7 Lacour-Gayet, *Marine militaire*, p.479.

poor qualities, though Caron believes that it did not prove to be the exceptional sailer suggested by Raoul Castex. The latter pointed to the fact that it was always at the head of the line; Caron suggests that this was no more than was due to it taking the best position to lead the attack. The *Annibal* was also practically new, but for some inexplicable reason it had not been coppered. It was, however, an excellent sailer, and had previously carried the flag of La Motte Piquet. The *Artésien* was an older vessel, built at Lorient some 25 years previously; it was much travelled, and had taken part in all the battles in North America. Twice coppered, it was an excellent sailer in spite of its age. The *Vengeur* was very old; its hull had been rebuilt with an additional skin of planking, as well as being coppered, and it was in consequence a poor sailer. The *Sphinx* was the oldest of all, having been built in 1753; it had taken part in the battle of Quiberon Bay. Finally, the *Fortune*, which had been captured from the British in 1780, 'presented none of the qualities required in this type of light warship; extremely slow, she manoeuvred badly, making the task of her commander extremely difficult.'[8]

In view of some of the difficulties that were later to arise, it is also useful to note Caron's observations on the commanders of the ships at the outset of the expedition. Barthélémy Tremigon, captain of the *Annibal*, he describes as 'a brilliant, energetic officer, brave and honest, celebrated for his skill in manoeuvre, who knew the Indian Ocean well', having previously served the Compagnie des Indes. Cardaillac, of the *Artésien*, who had served as flag captain to Latouche-Treville, had a good reputation but without any outstanding qualities. The captain of the *Vengeur*, Suffren's 40-year-old cousin, Chevalier de Forbin, was relatively inexperienced, and had never served outside the Mediterranean. He maintained a stream of complaints about the condition of the *Vengeur*. Charles Louis du Chilleau de la Roche, the commander of the *Sphinx*, had experience of the Far East, and had earned the good opinion of d'Estaing in America. Finally, the *Fortune's* commander was *Lieutenant de vaisseau* Bernard de Lusignan, who brought to his difficult task both tenacity and pugnacity.[9]

In most respects Suffren could not complain of the personal attention which Castries gave to the preparation of his squadron. The minister did, however, deny Suffren's request that his friend and colleague with whom he served in North America, d'Albert de Rioms, should sail with him. D'Albert would have made an excellent second in command in whom Suffren would have had complete trust. The fact that the only light vessel selected for the squadron was the regrettable *Fortune* meant that Suffren had only a limited capability for reconnaissance.[10]

Suffren was also somewhat handicapped by the number of troops which he must take with him. With these, he was originally intended first to recapture Gorée, leaving a garrison, and then go on to reinforce the garrison at the Cape before taking the remaining troops to the Ile de France. He carried 600 men of the Regiment d'Austrasie, 500 of the Regiment de Pondicherry, who had been repatriated when the place was captured, and a company of artillery from the Regiment de Metz.

---

8   Caron, *Mythe de Suffren*, p.98.
9   Caron, *Mythe de Suffren*, p.98.
10 Cavaliere, *Admiral Satan*, p.61.

Many of these soldiers had been newly recruited. Only a few had been to sea, and before long many of them would be suffering severely from seasickness.

Suffren's squadron was accompanied by seven vessels armed en flûte; though carrying 22 guns these were de-mounted so that they were effectively without armament. These were the *Grand Bourg, Saint Anne, Maurepass, Brisson, Union, Esperance,* and *Les-Trois-Amis.* There was also a Swedish vessel, *La-Paix-et-l'Abondance.* Just before sailing Castries notified Suffren that, according to the latest information, Johnstone had sailed only a few days previously, and he was able to give him a more or less accurate estimate of Johnstone's strength.[11] Also, at the last minute, it had been decided that Suffren should not delay his progress to the Cape by the projected stop at Gorée.

The overriding intention of the French plan was for Suffren to make his way to the Cape as quickly as possible, arriving there before Johnstone. Raoul Castex, in his *La manoeuvre de La Praya*, pointed out the advantages of an alternative strategy, that of tackling Johnstone's force in Europe. He quoted a letter to Castries of 9 January from Bouvet de Lozier, a veteran of struggles in the Indian Ocean under Louis XV, and a former governor of the Ile de Bourbon:.

> Prevent, Monseigneur, these English vessels from reaching India. Send forces equal or a little superior to fight them in European waters. The English vessels that are headed for India ordinarily pause at Madeira to take on wine and provisions for their crews. Our squadron should wait for them and attack them on leaving port. They will be at least crippled in the action, and in no state to continue their voyage.[12]

In the context of the naval war, and the traditional British policy in relation to French fleets based in Brest and other Atlantic ports, it was remarkable that de Grasse and Suffren were able to leave port and make their way towards their intended destinations unimpeded. Richmond examined the circumstances in which this had been allowed to occur:

> The question naturally arises, how came it about that a fleet of this size should be able to sail, after several days of light easterly winds in which a close watch upon Brest was practicable without any difficulty, unhindered by the British fleet? In the preceding wars it had been a cardinal principle of British strategy to maintain a strong squadron to the westward which should intercept and give battle to the enemy if he put to sea. In that position, and by that military predominance in a vital area, this force gave direct protection to the kingdom, and to the main mass of trade in its approaches, and cover to the many scattered positions and squadrons abroad against any descent by a greatly superior force.[13]

---

11 Caron, *Le mythe de Suffren*, p.100.
12 Raoul Castex, *La manoeuvre de La Praya* (Paris: L. Fournier, 1912), p.132.
13 Richmond, *Navy in India*, p.136.

While it was true that the balance of naval forces was less favourable than in previous wars, the numbers were not so unequal as to make it impracticable to maintain an effective watch on Brest. The fact of the preparations being made there was known in London, and it was obvious where most of this large fleet would be heading. Yet, as Richmond points out, Darby, with the Channel Fleet, which consisted of 30 ships of the line, was sent to Cork a bare week before de Grasse put to sea.

This move was part of the preparation for the relief of Gibraltar; Cork was the port from which provisions for the convoy were to be supplied. The whole question would be debated angrily in Parliament a year later. The defence put forward on behalf of the government was that the relief of Gibraltar 'was looked for by the whole nation' and that it was expected that the relief expedition would be opposed by the Spanish fleet in the Straits. It was argued, therefore, that it would not have been prudent to risk losing Gibraltar for the chance of meeting de Grasse. Richmond would have none of this. The relief was not, he wrote, 'the pressing necessity it was represented to be.' It was not merely 'a bare chance of meeting the French;' previous experience had shown that the fleet could hold the station even in winter weather. And the French had sailed in very light winds with its mass of transports: 'The opportunity for an unencumbered and superior fleet like Darby's to act against the expedition was almost unlimited.'[14] Nothing should have deflected the fleet from its purpose of giving battle to the main French fleet: 'This deflection was the main cause for the failure of the attempt to capture the Cape, and, in all probability, for the hard fought struggle which took place in the Indian Seas under the direction of one of the finest fighting sea commanders in history, and that so gravely threatened British dominion in India.'[15]

Castex noted the curious fact that neither the British Admiralty, nor the French Ministry of Marine, nor de Grasse, nor Johnstone, nor Darby, sought in any way a confrontation with the enemy at the point in time when the French fleet left Brest. Each of the admirals concerned had been given a clear objective, and none of them were at all disposed to consider what might be the benefits of meeting the enemy other than in accordance with that objective. As Castex points out, such a confrontation, whatever its outcome, would have had enormous consequences.[16]

Castries certainly had some anxiety about it. After his return to Versailles, he wrote to Hector, the Port Commandant at Brest:

> I learn on arriving here that the English fleet, composed of 32 or 33 ships of the line, left Portsmouth on the 13th … If so, it is quite possible that our fleet might find itself in contact with the enemy at the point at which their courses cross. I am very impatient to have news of the passage of our fleet.

He asked Hector to let him know as soon as possible when de Grasse had safely arrived.[17] As Castex noted, the British Admiralty was equally anxious to avoid such

---

14 Richmond, *Navy in India*, p.138.
15 Richmond, *Navy in India*, p.139.
16 Castex, *Manoeuvre de La Praya*, pp.204–205.
17 Castex, *Manoeuvre de La Praya*, pp.204–205.

an encounter, apparently calculating that Darby was strong enough to deal with the Spanish, but not with the French.

On 15 March Castries had despatched the frigate *Fine* to the Ile de France with orders for Souillac and d'Orves. After reviewing what was known of British intentions, they were informed of the composition of Suffren's squadron and the accompanying troops. The orders left it to Souillac and d'Orves to decide what would be the most useful operations to undertake: to go to the Cape; or to order Suffren to join them after its safety was assured; or to leave for India without waiting for him to attack British trade and possessions there. They could, it was calculated, withdraw about 1,800 men from the islands for such an attack. At 4,000 miles distance it was recognised that attempting to select the positions to be attacked would be imprudent. The orders went on to add that the King confined himself 'to informing the Comte d'Orves that what he expressly forbids is inactivity; unfortunate events and inaction will be equally contrary to his views.' D'Orves was to profit by the superiority, or at least equality with the enemy 'to ruin their commerce and destroy those of their settlements that he can attack with success.' He would be blamed only if he did not 'employ all the resources which his will and courage can inspire to render the campaign equally profitable and glorious to his army.'[18]

---

18 Richmond, *Navy in India*, pp.406–409.

8

Porto Praya

Preparations for the departure of Johnstone's squadron had not gone particularly well. On 17 February a collision in the Downs between the *Raikes* and the *Resolution* meant that both had to be sent to Sheerness for repairs. On 19 February trouble aboard the *San Carlos*, a vessel which was seriously undermanned, resulted in two soldiers being put in irons. The troopship *Pondicherry* was also so seriously undermanned that it had not joined the convoy assembling in the Downs by 23 February; Johnstone suggested that the troops she carried should be employed to work the ship. On 12 March the crew of the *Porpoise* refused to weigh anchor, and on the following day, as the convoy prepared to sail, the crews of the *Raikes* and the *Resolution* also refused to come to their duty, complaining that they were five years in arrears of pay. However, by 3:00 p.m. on that day Johnstone was finally able to put to sea.

When he did so, he had been preceded by one day by the Channel Fleet under Darby, which had been directly followed by another convoy bound for the West Indies. Johnstone was anxious to keep his force separated from either of these, since it reduced the likelihood of his being observed, and he reckoned that his speed would be greater if he moved independently. Progress at first, though was slow; Johnstone took three days to reach a point off the Lizard.[1] He gave both Ushant and Cape Finisterre a wide berth as he made his way southwards and was 200 miles to the west when he passed Cape St Vincent. By the time that de Grasse and Suffren sailed from Brest, Johnstone was already approaching the Azores. He faced a short delay on 6 April when the *San Carlos* collided with the *Hero*, but overall he had managed to keep up a good pace, considering that a number of the ships of his convoy were poor sailers. Apparently, the ordnance ship *Prudence* and the victualler *Jupiter*, both of which were rotten, were particularly slow.

Sensibly enough, Johnstone exercised his squadron from time to time in sea manoeuvres. His captains found him extremely difficult to please. On 27 March, for instance, he ordered the squadron to sail in line abreast. The manoeuvre did not go well. Thomas Pasley, the captain of the Royal Navy's *Jupiter*, 50, who was generally very well disposed to Johnstone, wrote: 'Such conduct I never saw – constant signals thrown out that such and such ships were out of line with the *Romney*. I can only say that in my opinion he acted throughout this day both unlike a seaman and an officer.' Pasley went on to add that Johnstone appeared to be 'dissatisfied with every

---

1   Fabel, *Bombast*, p.148.

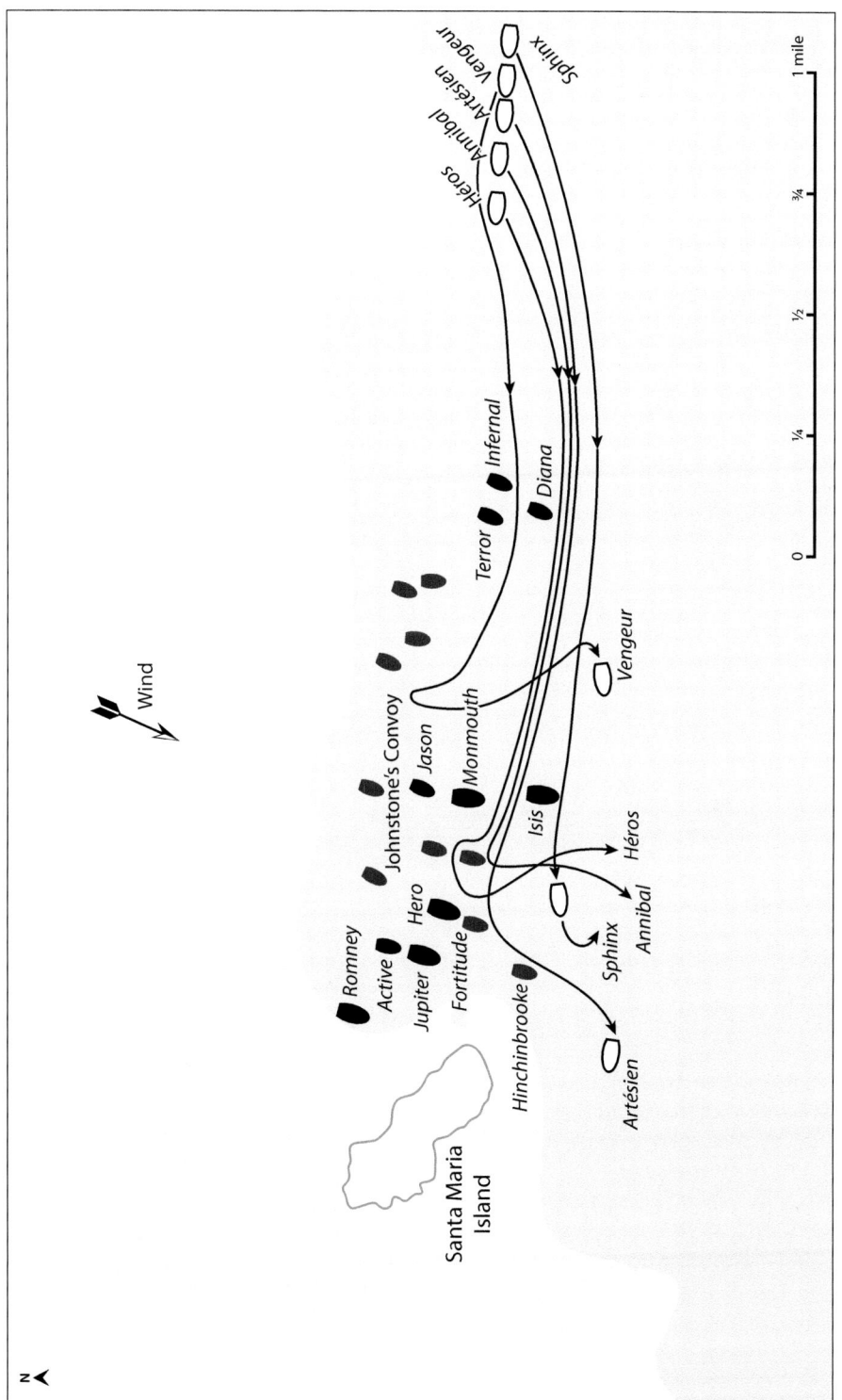

The Battle of Porto Praya, based partly on a map in Cavaliero, *Admiral Satan*.

officer under his command', except with himself.[2] Not only was Johnstone dissatisfied with the captains of his squadron, his relationships with the captains of the convoy were no better.

As he made his way southwards, Johnstone had very much in his mind the possibility of picking up a few prizes. On 29 March he sent the sloop *Porto* and the cutter *Lark* to Madeira to collect wine. Three days later, Pasley, in the *Jupiter*, with the frigate *Active*, was detached with the specific objective of looking for prizes (though Johnstone later claimed, somewhat unconvincingly, that he had sent them ahead to prepare for the reception of the main body) and on 4 April the sloop *Shark* was sent to Brazil.

It is not entirely clear just how far Johnstone was at this point aware that Suffren's squadron was already following in his footsteps, but it was in any case obviously unwise of him to detach any part of his squadron while any possibility existed of encountering an enemy force.

Drafting Suffren's final orders, dated 17 March, Castries had firmly ruled out any idea of seeking out Johnstone and fighting him before he reached the Cape. The urgent priority, as he saw it, was for Suffren to get the Cape first. Thereafter, he was not to remain at the Cape to await orders from the Ile de France. He was to disembark his troops, take on as much in the way of supplies as he could, and then press on direct to join d'Orves at the Ile de France. Castries assured him that he need be in no fear of meeting superior forces.[3]

On 28 March, at dawn, the combined fleet encountered a Swedish vessel, with which the *Fortune* spoke, learning that Rodney had taken, and looted, the Dutch island of St Eustatius; this provided a clear indication of the vigour with which the British were acting following the outbreak of war with the Dutch, and which accordingly reinforced concerns about the action being taken against the Cape. This news was subsequently confirmed by another Swedish vessel.

Suffren parted company from de Grasse off Cape Roca on 29 March and in accordance with his instructions thereafter did his best to reduce Johnstone's lead. However, he too was not without problems; a delay was imposed on him when two of his transports, the *Esperance* and *Saint Anne*, collided, both suffering damage. As he approached Madeira, on 3 April, he did not pause to take any precautions against encountering an enemy, no doubt because the information which he had been given made it certain that Johnstone's lead was such that there was no chance of meeting him so soon. In fact, at this point, only about 300 miles separated the two squadrons.

On 9 April Suffren detached the cutter *Clairvoyant*, together with five merchant vessels carrying troops to relieve the garrison of Senegal. He entrusted to her captain a letter to Castries, reporting on his progress to date, and the delays caused by the problems of the *Esperance* and *Saint Anne*. Suffren also reported on a disturbing shortage of water, particularly aboard the *Artésien*, which had only a supply for 65 days. Before leaving Brest the vessel had taken on sufficient water only for the Atlantic crossing, since it had originally been intended to form part of de Grasse's fleet before being at the last minute transferred to Suffren's squadron. Bearing in

---

2 Fabel, *Bombast*, p.149.
3 Castex, *Manoeuvre*, pp.185–186.

mind the time taken thus far, he told Castries that he would be forced to call at the Cape Verde Islands to take on water and supplies. He also reported a higher level of sickness in the squadron than might have been expected; nevertheless, he reassured him that it was nothing about which to be concerned. In the course of this letter, he made no reference to Johnstone, whom he believed would be himself intending not to stop until he reached St Helena.[4] By 10 April he was some 60 miles from Hierro in the Canaries and had still some 1,000 odd miles to cover before he reached the Cape Verde Islands. On that day Suffren learned from two Portuguese fishermen that Johnstone was still well ahead. In fact, thanks to several days of calm encountered by the French squadron, the British had been able substantially to increase their lead. Suffren suffered a further delay on this day when it became necessary for the hapless *Sainte Anne* to be taken in tow by the *Sphinx*.[5]

The Cape Verde Islands belonged to Portugal, neutral in the present war, though generally better disposed towards Britain than to her enemies. Porto Praya was an anchorage on the southern coast of the largest of the islands, Sao Tiago. Johnstone arrived at this port on 10 April with the intention of taking on water, but in case it was found that there were insufficient resources to meet his requirements, he took the precaution of sending the *Monmouth*, *Diana*, *Infernal*, and *Terror*, with two East Indiamen and 10 transports, to the neighbouring island of Maio. Pasley, of the *Jupiter*, had told Johnstone that there was plenty of water to be had at Maio, and dividing the force in this way might save time by making use of both facilities. That is, if it was actually necessary to do so at all, as Metcalfe, the captain of an East Indiaman, later wrote that all the ships of the expedition had sufficient water to reach the Cape without stopping.[6] As it was, Porto Praya was found to have plenty of water, and so Johnstone called back his ships from Maio, which rejoined him on 14 April.

Johnstone seems to have been entirely relaxed about the extent of his lead over Suffren in the race to the Cape. At all events, he gave a dinner party on 14 April, and a dance aboard the *Southampton* on the following evening, while he allowed 1,500 men to go ashore for recreation.[7] This was in spite of the information which he had gained from letters left in the port by a French privateer, the *Serapis*, which he bribed the authorities to release to him. From these he learned that Suffren, heading south in his wake, might himself call at Porto Praya to take on water. Johnstone seems not to have taken the possible threat very seriously, telling only Pasley about it.[8] He did not even take the precaution of posting a frigate outside the harbour to give early warning of an approaching enemy.

Nor had Johnstone taken any particular care about where his ships had anchored within the bay, and when those arrived from Maio he allowed them to anchor where they chose. As a result, his squadron, and the ships of his convoy, were extremely badly placed, and anchored in an entirely higgledy-piggledy manner across the

---

4 Castex, *Manoeuvre*, p.227.
5 Castex, *Manoeuvre*, p.228.
6 Fabel, *Bombast*, p.157.
7 Cavaliero, *Admiral Satan*, p.64.
8 Fabel, *Bombast*, p.150.

bay. Nearest in to the land lay the *Romney*, and then came the mass of victuallers and transports. The frigate *Jason* was on their port side, and the *Hero* behind the centre, while the *Jupiter* and the *Active* were to starboard. Next came the transports which had come in from Maio, with the *Monmouth* to port and then three Indiamen beyond her. About a mile towards the easternmost point of the bay lay the *Isis*, and beyond her the *Diana*, the *Infernal* and the *Terror*. It was a deployment that was quite unfitted to receive any attack.[9]

As he approached Porto Praya from the north-east on the morning of 16 April, Suffren sent Cardaillac in the *Artésien*, at the latter's request, on ahead. He could have sent the *Fortune*, but the *Artésien* was the fastest ship in the squadron and, in any case, it was its need to take on water which was the most pressing. He had no suspicion that Johnstone's force was there, supposing that due to his most recent delays he had now dropped well behind his rival in the race to the Cape. However, as it was, at 8:30 a.m. on that day the *Artésien* approached Point Bicuda and almost at once sighted the masts of the nearest British ships. He tacked to clear the point, and signalled to the *Héros* that he had sighted four unidentified ships. A few minutes later, they could be seen from the *Héros*, and at 8:57 a.m. Cardaillac signalled that they were British. Suffren realised at once that this was Johnstone's squadron and wasted little time in reflection. At 9:00 a.m. he made the signal for the line of battle, and according to his log:

> … and at the same time to close the line of which we took the head. The *Annibal* was with us, the *Artésien* a little to windward, the *Vengeur* and *Sphinx* were still far astern. We then made the signal to crowd sail. As we came closer inshore to windward of the anchoring ground the point hid the ships from us, but we soon discovered them as we approached and we recognised five battleships with the jack with a red field at the poop and one of them with the red broad pendant at the masthead, three frigates and about thirty-five to forty convoy ships which left us in no doubt but that this was Commodore Johnstone's division, destined for India, and which we knew by the neutrals we had examined, had left Plymouth [sic] ahead of us.[10]

In thus deciding to launch an immediate attack, Suffren ignored both his orders, which expressly stated that he was to sail direct to the Cape, as well as the provisions of international law requiring the observation of the sovereignty of neutral waters. He had to make up his mind quickly, but he did not hesitate for a moment. So far as his orders were concerned, he calculated at once that the negligent way in which the enemy squadron was deployed gave him the chance of achieving a decisive victory, which he saw as the best means of ensuring that he reached the Cape first. Johnstone's biographer reflected that his decision was one which no other French commander would have taken:

---

9   Cavaliero, *Admiral Satan*, p.64.
10 Rutherford, *Sidelights*, pp.290–291.

The orthodox tactical and strategic doctrine of the eighteenth century French navy was defensive; the underlying principle was 'preserve your ships!' In action the French line always sought to get to leeward, because it was easier to disengage thus than from the windward position. In gunnery the French always aimed high, firing on the upward roll, destroying the masts and rigging of the enemy to hinder him from pursuit. The orthodox French commander, in Suffren's position, would have left Johnstone alone and incurred no blame for doing so.[11]

Later, after he had reached the Cape of Good Hope, Suffren took the opportunity to explain himself. Responding to a letter from Castries of 1 July, which not unreasonably asked why he had turned aside from his principal object, Suffren wrote on 10 August a letter offering a justification of his disregard of neutrality and of his orders. He wrote that he took the decision to attack Johnstone at La Praya in the real hope of destroying him, taking advantage of the opportunity which the disorder of the enemy's anchorage, and the surprise which he achieved, had given him:

> The destruction of the English squadron would cut off the root of all the plans and projects of that expedition, gain for us a long time the superiority in India, a superiority whence might result a glorious peace, and hinder the English from reaching the Cape before me, – an object which has been fulfilled and was the principal aim of my mission.[12]

He acknowledged that he might possibly be criticised by the council of state for his violation of neutral territory. He candidly, and not without humour, wrote that he might defend his conduct in several ways: he might suggest that the English opened fire first; or that La Praya was not a port at all, but merely an open beach; or he might recall the battle of Lagos, when he was himself captured by Boscawen under the muzzles of neutral Portuguese guns; or he might refer to his orders directing him to attack the English everywhere:

> But I will admit to you, Monseigneur, that I went in to attack them of deliberate intention, hoping that in favour of surprise and of the disorder in which they were anchored, I should destroy them; that I should bring M. d'Orves a reinforcement upon which he had not counted; and that finally, with superiority established in India, peace would result.[13]

Caron, who regards the attitude of Castex to Suffren as being sycophantic, suggests that, rather than stopping with his whole force at the Cape Verde Islands, an entirely different course of action might have been adopted. Suffren could have chosen to leave behind the two slow sailers under the protection of the *Artésien*, which were

---

11 Fabel, *Bombast*, p.151.
12 Captain A.T. Mahan, *The Influence of Sea Power upon History 1660-1783* (Boston: Little, Brown, and Co, 1894), p.424.
13 Richmond, *Navy in India*, p.143.

not indispensable for the purpose of saving the Cape, and with the rest of his force sail on as quickly as possible to his crucially important destination. Caron goes on to describe the stop at La Praya as 'incomprehensible.'[14] This, with the greatest respect to the distinguished admiral, is surely an overstatement of the position. Suffren's squadron was not overly large for the significant responsibilities that it was to undertake, and to reduce its strength by leaving one of its most important units behind was something that any prudent commander would hesitate to do. With the limited information available to him, Suffren knew that it was entirely possible that Johnstone might reach the Cape first, or that the two squadrons might arrive at more or less the same time. In the engagement that must follow, the *Artésien* would be an important part of Suffren's squadron. To adopt Caron's prescription, of course, Suffren would have had to take the decision well before his squadron reached the latitude of the Cape Verde Islands. Certainly, if Suffren had indeed acted in this way, he would doubtless have reached the Cape first, thanks to Johnstone's extended stop at Porto Praya; but that is all a matter of hindsight, and Suffren had no reason to believe that Johnstone would in fact surrender the lead that he had established in this way. In all these circumstances, it is difficult to accept his decision to keep the *Artésien* with him as one that can reasonably be described as 'incomprehensible.'

Suffren could see at a glance that the enemy was hopelessly unprepared, but he had to make a choice between attacking with only three of his ships of the line to take best advantage of this or wait until the *Vengeur* and the *Sphinx* could take their position in the line. His log recorded his decision:

> We should have liked to wait for them; but we feared by lying-to to fall to leeward of the anchoring ground and of the enemy and be obliged to ply to windward to regain our position. Besides, this manoeuvre would have given the enemy time to recover and make ready for an engagement, which was what M. de Suffren wished to avoid. He decided to begin the attack, hoping to be imitated by the others.[15]

Suffren had taken a snap decision, and as a consequence, there having been no time to prepare the attack, it was not properly coordinated. Suffren's ships were strung out; two of them, neither of which were fast sailers, were well behind the other three. He gave no specific instructions as to the form of the attack, reckoning, as his log explained, that he must act fast if he were to obtain the benefit of the surprise he had achieved. Unwisely, he left it to his captains to act as effectively as they could. The result was that they themselves were also taken by surprise and were quite unprepared. The *Annibal*'s captain, Barthélémy de Trémignon, had not realised that Suffren intended to launch an attack in a neutral port, and as his ship rounded the point his decks were not cleared of livestock and water butts, nor his guns cast loose. The remaining captains, used to clear cut instructions as to the targets at which they were to aim, did not know which to select. Suffren's flag officer was so surprised that, at first, he hoisted the wrong order of battle and was obliged immediately to change

---

14 Caron, *Mythe de Suffren*, p.105.
15 Rutherford, 'Sidelights', p.292.

it. The *Héros* now took the lead, followed by the *Annibal*, and the *Artésien* was ordered into third place. Well behind came the *Vengeur* and the *Sphinx*, the latter hastily casting off her tow; they were ordered to make up the distance as quickly as they could.

Passing the *Diana* and the smaller vessels moored around the western end of the bay, the *Héros*, as it sailed in on the starboard tack, made for the principal warships of Johnstone's squadron. As the *Héros* came abreast of the *Isis*, it fired a few shots, steering a course to pass inside the *Isis*. This took the *Héros* towards the *Monmouth*, which it was Suffren's intention to engage at close range by dropping anchor, but the spring on its cable did not hold, and it carried on towards the *Hero*. As it did so it then fouled one of the transports. Suffren's log records that he 'drove aboard a merchant man, eight of whose men boarded us through the gun ports of the lower battery, but by veering out cable we sheered off.'[16] The *Héros* then came abreast of the *Hero*, where it succeeded in anchoring under a heavy fire. It was now about 11:00 a.m.

Behind her, Trémignon, aboard the *Annibal*, whose crew was still hastily clearing the decks and running out its guns, executed a brilliant manoeuvre by steering his ship between the *Hero* and the *Héros*. He then succeeded in anchoring ahead of and to windward of the French flagship; for the moment, and for about a quarter of an hour, his ship was unable to reply to the fire endured by the *Annibal* from the *Monmouth* and the *Jupiter*, and also the musketry from the nearest transports. The *Héros*, too, was coming under heavy fire from the *Hero* to port and the *Isis* on her starboard quarter, as well as the *Fortitude* East Indiaman.[17]

Firing was now intense. The *Héros*, and the *Annibal* when it was able to do so, were firing both broadsides. As the battle continued, after about half an hour, Trémignon was fatally wounded and carried below. His second in command, Morard de Galles, was soon after himself injured but continued in command. On both sides, casualties, and damage, steadily increased, and the *Annibal*'s mizzen mast went over the side.

Following the first two French ships came the *Artésien*. Cardaillac endeavoured to bring his ship into a position from which it was possible to take the *Hero* on both sides. He tried to anchor, but it would not hold, and the *Artésien* drifted on to close with the *Fortitude*, which he took to be a warship. The two ships came together, and a French boarding party was sent over when the *Fortitude*'s bowsprit became entangled with the *Artésien*'s back stays. Both ships now began to drift away from the *Hero*. Cardaillac made another attempt to anchor, but as he did so he was struck in the head by a stray bullet and killed outright. His second in command, de la Boixiere, hurried to the quarterdeck, but 'could not be warned soon enough to repair the confusion caused by his chief's death. Besides he could not be sure of the captain's intentions.'[18] The *Artésien*'s stays snapped, and the *Fortitude* drifted clear. The *Artésien* next ran aboard the transport *Hinchinbrook* which it carried out to sea.

---

16 Rutherford, 'Sidelights', p.293.
17 Cavaliero, *Admiral Satan*, p.67.
18 Rutherford, 'Sidelights', p.293.

Meanwhile eight of the *Artésien*'s men, who had boarded the *Fortitude*, remained there as prisoners.

From well behind, the *Vengeur* and the *Sphinx* now entered the bay. As the *Vengeur* rounded the point, it engaged the *Diana* and the smaller vessels around it, seriously damaging the *Terror* and the *Infernal*. The latter cut its cable and drifted out to sea and was boarded and taken. As the *Vengeur* sailed on towards the closely engaged ships ahead of it, its captain, Forbin, apparently gave the order to anchor, but in the heat of battle his voice was not heard. The *Vengeur* now bore away, narrowly avoiding the rocks at the end of the harbour. Apparently, the reason it did not anchor there was because Forbin believed the water was too deep. By 11:30 a.m. its part in the action was concluded.[19]

The *Sphinx*, after it had cast off its tow, only succeeded in rounding Point Bicuda by 11:15 a.m. As Castex points out, even then it would have been well placed to tackle the *Isis* but, in the event, it failed to anchor, and merely carried on behind the *Vengeur*, ultimately following it out of the bay, and accordingly gave no support at all to the hard pressed *Héros* and *Annibal*. It had however, on its way in, cannonaded the ships at anchor that it passed. The *Fortune*, meanwhile, never entered the bay at all.

By noon it was clear to Suffren that the situation of the *Héros* and the *Annibal* had become critical. The *Héros* had suffered severe damage to its masts, sails and rigging. For a while he was not even able to make a signal to the *Annibal*, but he turned and made his way out of the action and could only hope that Trémignon, whom he assumed still to be in command, would follow. His log recorded his decision:

> At midday, M. de Suffren, not thinking he could continue the fight in a manner so much to his disadvantage, wished to make the signal to cut cables; but all our cut halyards did not allow of his hoisting the flag. He gave the order to cut, hoping the *Annibal* would imitate us. We bore away to starboard and put to sea. The *Annibal* soon followed us, and we were already preparing to take possession of ten or twelve English vessels which had put to sea during the fight when we had the grief of seeing the said ship, when only just out of range of the enemy's fire, lose her main mast and soon afterwards her foremast. Our convoy had been lying-to to windward since the beginning of the fight. We had signalled to it to crowd sail and to continue on its course while we should be busy fighting the enemy, and to the *Sphinx* to take the *Annibal* in tow.[20]

The *Annibal* was in a fearful state; at one point her ensign had been shot away. Aboard the *Monmouth* it was thought that she had struck, but Morard de Galles called for a napkin and nailed it to the mast. When he saw the *Héros* come around, he cut his cable and, still firing both broadsides, followed the flagship out of the battle. Just as soon as he was safely out of range his mainmast came down and had

---

19 Castex, *Manoeuvre*, p.296.
20 Rutherford, 'Sidelights', p.294.

to be cut away, followed a little later by the upper section of its foremast. Thereafter, the *Sphinx*, in accordance with Suffren's signal, took it in tow.[21]

From the start of the battle Johnstone had been able to exercise little effect on its outcome. When at 9:30 a.m. the *Isis* signalled the arrival of unidentified ships to the north east, the commodore was aboard a rowing boat, ordering the relocation of some of the ships of his convoy. He returned to the *Romney*, and signalled to all ships to prepare for battle, ordering those men on shore to return to their ships. As the enemy drew nearer, he realised that the *Romney*'s position meant that her guns were partly masked. As he later recorded, it could only 'fire into openings, and that under a precision which was cautiously observed; neither could she veer away cable to open a larger space, as the *Jason* lay right astern of her.'[22] Accordingly, Johnstone, accompanied by Major General Medows, went aboard the *Hero*. It was not practicable in the time available to redispose his squadron, which fought from where it was anchored.[23]

Once the French had disengaged, Johnstone returned to the *Romney* and convened a council of war on her quarterdeck. Pasley recorded his recollection of the discussion:

> The action was over by Twelve O'clock and the signal made for all Captains. I in consequence waited on my Commodore – our Council on this occasion was public on the Quarterdeck. 'Shall we, Gentlemen, Cutt and follow our Blow by giving them Battle again before they recover from their drubbing?' Most heartily did I give my asssent, but (sorry am I to say it) numerous difficulties was started by some against this Gallant Resolution; they were, however, obviated by his declaring it to be his fixed intention, and ordering all on board again to execute the Signal to cut or Slip which he intended immediately to display.[24]

The question which Johnstone posed was obviously the right one and the answer should have been equally obvious to all concerned, but it seems that among those present the captains of the *Isis* and the *Monmouth* were firmly opposed, and Medows was apparently of the same view. Johnstone himself recorded that he brought the debate to an end by saying the ships of the squadron should slip their cables and put to sea as soon as possible. That may have been what he said, but there was in fact little sense of urgency. The *Romney* did not slip her cable until 2:40 p.m. The *Jupiter* followed at once, and then the *Hero*, but the *Monmouth* did not move for half an hour and the *Isis* after about an hour.[25]

The *Isis* had been at one time or another a target for each of the French ships as they moved through the bay and had accordingly suffered more damage than any other of the squadron. Johnstone, though, was unimpressed by the report which

---

21 Cavaliere, *Admiral Satan*, pp.69–70.
22 Rutherford, 'Sidelights', p.294.
23 Fabel, *Bombast*, p.154.
24 Rutherford, 'Sidelights', p.295.
25 Fabel, *Bombast*, p.156.

Evelyn Sutton, the captain of the *Isis*, made requesting time to make further repairs to his mast and rigging; he dismissed it, saying that the damage was 'nothing at all.' When Johnstone signalled for his ships to form line of battle, the foretopmast of the *Isis* came down, causing further delay. In his subsequent report of the battle, Johnstone wrote that he 'immediately shortened sail to give time to the *Isis* to clear the wreck, which was done in half an hour or forty minutes. This increased our distance from the enemy. As soon as I saw the *Isis* could make sail, I bore up and set the foresail, and made the signal for the line abreast.'[26]

From the quarterdeck of the *Héros* about two miles away, Suffren could see the British evidently preparing to follow him. He had sent the *Fortune* to direct his convoy 'to continue their course for their destination and that we could convoy them no longer.' The *Fortune* also had orders to take possession of the *Infernal*, which was lying derelict and from which the *Fortune* removed her captain, Henry Darby, five sailors and nine soldiers of the 98th Regiment. Suffren then 'made the signal for line of battle sailing on the larboard tack and to prepare to renew the fight, which was very promptly executed. The *Sphinx* led, towing the *Annibal*, then the *Héros*, *Vengeur* and *Artésien*. The enemy was no more than a cannon shot and a half away, but they kept the wind and their movements appeared undecided.'[27]

It was however not until about 5:30 p.m. before Johnstone signalled his squadron to form line of battle, but soon after this he began to have second thoughts. His own account of his consideration was contained in his report:

> When we came near the enemy, I found the *Isis* and *Monmouth* had dropped astern between two and three miles, though both sail much better than the *Romney*. Their signals were therefore made to call up to their station, the *Monmouth* immediately answered and made sail accordingly but the *Isis* still kept behind. By these various instructions and delays, added to a strong current, the enemy had drawn far to leeward of St Jago. The sun was set; the sea had increased; I could not propose a decisive action that night.[28]

The subject was subsequently explored in some detail as a result of the court martial of Captain Sutton, Johnstone having decided, quite unfairly to make him a scapegoat for the delays which he used to justify his failure to pursue the enemy. Sutton's account of Johnstone's proceedings is somewhat different:

> At 6 o'clock or half past five he made the signal for the line ahead, by which means, as he had run past the enemy, we soon got into line, the French about two miles from us. When in a line ahead, the Commodore put up his helm as if he meant to engage, but never stood by towards them; but at last he got so near that had he steered for them a quarter of an hour the French

---

26 Rutherford, 'Sidelights', p.297.
27 Rutherford, 'Sidelights', p.297.
28 Rutherford, 'Sidelights', p.297.

would have begun firing … About six the sun set, the enemy very near, for we now and then went slanting down to them for a little while.[29]

Suffren was watching closely. It seemed to him that the enemy's movements were undecided because they approached no nearer, and by 6:00 p.m. his convoy was three leagues to leeward and consequently beyond molestation. The French squadron lit their lights at nightfall on the tops and poop but the British did not. Suffren lost sight of the enemy at 8:30 p.m.

Johnstone's biographer wrote that the decision caused him, or so he alleged, 'an anguish such as he had never before experienced.' According to the commodore he took the decision 'after maturely weighing the subject in all its consequences with those persons on whose judgement I have most confidence.' Fabel went on to examine Johnstone's thinking in more detail. He was concerned that if he pursued Suffren through the night he would expose his convoy to danger and would find himself so far to leeward of the Cape Verde Islands as to be in the grip of the prevailing north-east winds and south-west currents:

> He discounted Suffren's chances of getting to the Cape swiftly, because he thought he would go first to Brazil for food and water. If the Frenchman did head for the Cape in spite of thirst and hunger, Johnstone calculated that he would have to detach two of his disabled ships to the West Indies for repairs, which would enable him to attack Suffren in Table Bay with a great numerical advantage.[30]

Accordingly, Johnstone returned to La Praya and stayed there for two weeks, making repairs and completing the provisioning of his squadron. He finally sailed for the Cape on 2 May.

Richmond dismisses Johnstone's excuses out of hand:

> His reasoning is pitiful to read. It is the reasoning of an undecided man. If he supposed the Cape to be the destination of the French squadron, no opportunity more favourable for frustrating its designs than that offered could be hoped for. While his own squadron was little injured, one French ship was reduced to an unmanageable hulk, and he had reason to believe the *Héros* had suffered severely. To postpone action was to give the enemy time to restore the superiority of their squadron, and if he should subsequently meet the French at sea, he must then fight them under the disadvantage of having a convoy to defend, whereas now his convoy was in harbour, well to windward, and, for the time, absolutely secure from attack.[31]

By his decision Johnstone turned what had been a tactically successful engagement into a strategic defeat. Caron points out that, in the hands of a bolder commander,

---

29 Rutherford, 'Sidelights', p.298.
30 Fabel, *Bombast*, p.157.
31 Richmond, *Navy in India*, p.147.

the British squadron could have left the bay much sooner and closed on Suffren's squadron. Hampered as he was by the gravely damaged *Annibal*, Suffren would in the ensuing engagement at the very least have suffered further damage, and would have been by no means certain to escape and press on to reach the Cape first.[32] Certainly, it would seem that Johnstone could have left his smaller ships to escort his convoy to sea and follow in his wake while he pressed on southwards, with an excellent chance of winning the race. As it was, the French had suffered heavier casualties, having 105 men killed and 223 wounded, while the British losses were 36 killed and 130 wounded.[33]

Naturally, in his report of the battle, Johnstone put as good a face as he could on its outcome:

> The action bordered upon a surprise and the service in which we were engaged rendered it liable to much confusion; yet upon the whole until the enemy were beat off I saw nothing on our part but steady, cool and determined valour. As soon as the *Jason* was out of the way the *Romney* was cast by a spring on her cable and went to sea under the acclamations of the whole fleet.'[34]

Suffren was fortunate that he was opposed by a commander as incompetent as Johnstone, whose nerve had failed him at the critical moment. To be allowed to make his way unhindered to the Cape, and to arrive there comfortably ahead of his adversary, was something that Suffren had no right to expect. His admirers justly point to the importance of the strategic victory which he had achieved by his bold attack at Porto Praya, but it has to be conceded that it was a stroke that was rash in the extreme and that it had exposed him to the serious risk of his mission falling at its first hurdle. As Richmond says, 'the lack of order, the omission to have prepared his subordinates to act, cannot be defended. For the omission, it may well be allowed that Suffren and had no opportunity of consulting his Captains and instructing them in what he wished to do; and that the meeting was unexpected.'[35]

---

32 Caron, *Mythe de Suffren*, p.159.
33 Richmond, *Navy in India*, p.146.
34 Cavaliero, *Admiral Satan*, p.71.
35 Richmond, *Navy in India*, pp.148–149.

9

The Cape of Good Hope

Suffren adopted neither of the courses of action which Johnstone had hopefully suggested that he might, neither sending the *Annibal* to the West Indies for repair nor steering for Brazil for water and repairs. Instead, he was firmly resolved to proceed south at the best speed he could manage, with the *Sphinx* towing the *Annibal*. On the morning of 17 April, he learned that both Trémignon and Cardaillac were dead, as well as the full extent of his not inconsiderable casualties. He bemoaned the fact that he had no frigates. If he had, he later reported to Castries, he could have taken and manned seven or eight of the ships of Johnstone's convoy. As it was, the *Jupiter* recaptured the *Hinchinbrook* on 17 April, while the French abandoned the *Infernal* when it appeared that Johnstone was planning to pursue them.[1]

Suffren, meanwhile, had lost touch both with his convoy and the *Fortune*. He was optimistic that he could arrive at the Cape before Johnstone's squadron and convoy. His ship's log expressed his doubt whether 'the damage which we have inflicted on the warships and especially on the convoy allows them to put to sea within ten or twelve days.'[2]

By 19 April the north east trade wind was gradually abating, as the squadron approached the region of the equator. Suffren sent carpenters and others aboard the *Annibal*, and the work of making good the damage sustained during the course of the battle went on apace. Aboard the *Héros*, the main mast and the mizzen mast were fished. On 20 April, the maintopmast of the *Annibal* was hoisted into position to serve as a jury mainmast, which meant that she was now able to contribute to her own progress, although in the coming weeks she was mostly under tow by one or other of the ships of the squadron.[3]

Suffren always looked back on the encounter at Porto Praya as a battle that might have had hugely important results. Writing to Mme de Seillans at the end of 1781, he was bitterly regretful: 'La Praya should have immortalised me. But I missed, or was made to miss, a unique opportunity. With my five ships I could have made the peace – and a glorious peace at that!'[4] This was a considerable overstatement, but Suffren always believed it. Much later he gave William Hickey an account of the action: 'Had all my captains done their duty with the same ardour that the

---

1 Fabel, *Bombast*, p.159.
2 Rutherford, 'Sidelights', pp.299–300.
3 Castex, *Manoeuvre*, pp.363–364.
4 Cavaliero, *Admiral Satan*, p.74.

Annibal and *Héros* did, it would have proved a woeful day for England. Three of the commanders forever disgraced themselves, involving therein the noble families to which they were allied. These poltroons hung back and never brought their ships within gunshot of the enemy.'[5]

In this, he was scarcely being fair to his captains; but by then he had fought several battles in the Indian Ocean about which he had rather more reason to complain, and hindsight no doubt sharpened his complaints.

In the same conversation with William Hickey, he told the Englishman that in the days after the battle of Porto Praya two of his captains had said that to go directly to the Cape was 'impracticable and unjustifiably wild and chimerical', bearing in mind first, that they had water for only 20 days, and secondly the seriously damaged condition of the *Annibal*. Suffren would have none of this, decreeing that if there was not enough water for each man to have a quart a day, then they must content themselves with a pint. Suffren and his squadron arrived in Simon's Bay at the Cape on 21 June, where he was subsequently rejoined by the *Fortune* and the ships of the convoy at intervals between 23 June and 14 July.

Johnstone meanwhile remained at Porto Praya until 2 May, making necessary repairs, and also composing his despatch to Lord Hillsborough to report on the battle. This, having regard to the events of 16 April, was a document which needed drafting with some care. He showed it to Pasley, who thought it 'by no means the most Masterly production of his Pen', but when it reached London on 8 June it evidently did the trick, for Porto Praya was hailed in the Press as a great victory. The opposition, of course, attacked Johnstone in the Commons, but Lord North and others defended him, and for the moment Johnstone's reputation remained intact. After he had set off on 2 May for the Cape, however, he reached for his pen again and produced a document on the subject of the measures to be taken as a result of Porto Praya. As usual he sent a copy to Pasley, who was duly impressed:

> It seems wrote with great judgement and shows his abilities in digesting matters of the highest moment. I confess I think he has in his present situation the choice of difficulties to encounter ... And it is next to an impossibility to extricate himself without the interposition of Providence. Some unlooked-for, some unexpected/stroke in our favour alone can clear away the cloud that hangs over us.[6]

There was a good deal of uncertainty among the leaders of the expedition as to how next to proceed, so much so that the suggestion of diverting its course to Buenos Aires and thus reviving the original objective was seriously discussed, though it is uncertain how far Johnstone considered it as a practicable alternative. He had still not abandoned the attack on the Cape as his objective, sending the frigates *Jason* and *Active*, with the *Lark* and the *Rattlesnake*, on ahead to see what the situation was there, and whether a French force had landed. Pasley, who all along had feared

---

5 Cavaliero, *Admiral Satan*, p.75.
6 Rutherford, 'Sidelights', p.300.

that Suffren might beat them to it, had nevertheless still not given up hope, writing in his diary on 27 June:

> We are within about four Hundred leagues of the Cape of Good Hope, to which place we are now advancing with all possible Expedition, full of anxious wishes, doubts and fears. The Dutch must long have known of the intention of this expedition and consequently must be well prepared, as we can trace two different expresses besides M. Suffren's. He too, if only stopped to water and refresh, may be so close at our heels as to make his appearance two or three days afterwards ... If we should (which is not impossible) gain possession of Seamen's [sic] Bay ere Suffren makes his appearance, I have no doubt but that we should be able to give him the second part of the same tune we complimented him with at St Iago.[7]

These hopes were dashed when on 9 July the *Jason* and the other ships sent forward rejoined the squadron with the news that Suffren had arrived at the Cape on 21 June.

If this came as a sad disappointment, it was nevertheless accompanied by a tempting consolation. From passengers in a Dutch East Indiaman which the *Active* had taken as a prize, it was learned that there were five more Dutch East Indiamen in Saldanha Bay, about 65 miles north west of the Cape. Reporting to Lord Hillsborough the news that the race to the Cape had been lost, Johnstone told him that he was now resolved to enter Saldanha Bay.

This, and the whole subject of the expedition's immediate action, had continued to be the subject of prolonged discussion between Johnstone and his senior commanders. With their eyes on personal gain, many of them, including Pasley, had been advocating the switch of their objective to the River Plate. The latter recorded his own view of what should be done:

> If I durst advise, I would say: enter Saldanha Bay, take or destroy the five India ships – that done proceed to Table and False Bays, bully Monsieur Suffren and his squadron, dispatch the India ships (eight already trusted without convoy surely three may be), proceed to St Helena, Water and Refresh, and with your whole force of ships and troops attack Buenos Ayres, My Life you gain a conquest – glory, honour, Yea and Riches too. But I am only a passenger.[8]

When Suffren arrived at Simonstown on 21 June he was met with a mysterious silence on shore, although the Dutch flag was still flying. It was only at 4:00 p.m. on the following day that the prearranged signal was seen which confirmed that the Cape was still in Dutch hands. The commandant of Simonstown came on board the *Héros* to tell Suffren that when the squadron was first sighted, it was taken to be British, and many of the inhabitants had packed up their houses and withdrawn into the countryside or hidden behind closed shutters. Joachim van Plattenberg,

---

7   Rutherford, 'Sidelights', pp.301–302.
8   Rutherford, 'Sidelights', p.302.

the Dutch governor of the Cape had, as soon as it had been learned that Johnstone's expedition was on its way, sent the richly laden Dutch East Indiamen that were en route to Europe to hide in Saldanha Bay. When he learned of this move, Suffren was far from impressed, and told the governor so, but there was nothing that he could do about it.

Having learned of the ships in Saldanha Bay, Johnstone now had an extremely attractive target at which to aim, but he had also to consider the possibility of launching an attack on the Cape, even though the French had arrived to strengthen the garrison. But first, though, he proceeded to the attack on the Dutch East Indiamen. This took place on 21 July. The intention on the part of the Dutch had been that if attacked, all of the vessels should be set on fire; and this was done, but so swiftly did the British attackers board them that in all cases but one the fires were put out before much damage was done. The exception was the *Middelburg*; still blazing she was towed to the lee shore of the bay but blew up 10 minutes later.[9]

As for the attack on the Cape itself, Johnstone went through the motions of offering to land Medows and his troops, but he was at pains to point out to the general that he 'could not promise to keep up an uninterrupted communication with you if Monsieur Suffren should make a movement with his Squadron to attack me.' To this, Medows was emphatic in his reply, saying that with the troops he had he would as well think of attacking Paris as the Cape under those circumstances, and he asked Johnstone to despatch himself and his troops to India as soon as possible.[10]

When Suffren learned that Johnstone had attacked the Dutch East Indiamen in Saldanha Bay, the *Fortune* and one ship of his convoy were at that time in Table Bay, while the rest of the French ships were in False Bay, the *Annibal* still not yet remasted. In Hout Bay there were four more East Indiamen. Suffren could see that his situation was not without risk, and he convened, unusually, a council of war to discuss it. The decision arrived at was to remain at anchor until the *Annibal* was fit to sail; she would be given for the time being the masts of one of the convoy. Meanwhile, Suffren took steps to fill the vacancies in the command of the *Annibal* and the *Artésien*. To the former he appointed her lieutenant, Morard de Galles, and to the latter the second officer of the *Sphinx*, Pas de Beaulieu.[11]

On 23 July Johnstone's convoy appeared off Table Bay, to the consternation of the inhabitants. Suffren, however, learning that the ships that had been sighted were merely transports, declined to put to sea. Another council of war was convened, and it was decided that 'not knowing the strength or number of the enemy to await more decisive news; if it was learned that they were attacking Table Bay the four ships would put to sea.'[12] In the following days, however, reports were received suggesting that the British had departed, and this was authoritatively confirmed on 28 July.

Suffren wrote to Castries to report:

---

9   Fabel, *Bombast*, p.161.
10 Rutherford, 'Sidelights', p.304.
11 Cavaliero, *Admiral Satan*, p.78.
12 Rutherford, 'Sidelights', p.305.

From July 22 to 27, the most anxious period, I assured the governor that if the English squadron came to the Cape I would go out and attack them with my four ships, and that as soon as the *Annibal* could follow I would sail to blockade them at Saldanha, that if the wind prevented me from putting to sea I would send the Count de Conway 200 sea troops.[13]

In this despatch, Suffren went on to assess his situation vis á vis Johnstone's squadron, which was, as he explained, not without difficulty:

Although I am inwardly sure that Johnstone's five ships together with three frigates are infinitely stronger than the force I can take out, I would have gone to look for them in spite of the fear that if I was dispersed either being worsted in a fight or by storm (frequent in these waters) the enemy might have come to False Bay and destroyed the *Annibal* and the convoy for Ile de France. If I had tried to find them, I should not have been able to double the Cape in the strong North North West winds that were blowing on the 24th and 25th, and the north-west gale which prevailed during the 27th, 28th and 29th.

He need not have been concerned. The threat from Johnstone was beginning rapidly to evaporate. On 25 July the commodore sent to St Helena his Dutch prizes, with four store ships, escorted by the *Diana, Jason, Infernal, Terror* and *Rattlesnake*. Two days later, having transferred Medows and his staff to the *Monmouth*, he sent it on its way to India accompanied by the *Hero, Isis*, and the rest of his original convoy. Separately, the *Active* also left for India. Aboard the *Romney*, with the *Jupiter* and the *Lark*, Johnstone cruised about the Cape until 6 August, in the hope of encountering Suffren's convoy. Then, having found nothing in the way of prizes, he went off to St Helena to rejoin the rest of his ships. There he also found the *Hannibal*, 50, which had been sent down from England to escort home-bound trade in case Johnstone had not arrived in time. Johnstone allowed the *Hannibal* to cruise for a fortnight off the Cape and a further fortnight off the Ile de France, where it picked up two prizes from a French convoy before returning with them to St Helena. Captain Anthony Parrey's original orders had been to join Hughes in India if he met Johnstone, so Johnstone sent the *Hannibal* on its way. Unfortunately, en route, it met the French fleet under d'Orves, and was taken, entering the French service as the *Petit Annibal*. Aboard her the French found despatches which disclosed the whole of the current situation in India.[14]

Johnstone meanwhile sent his convoy to England with the *Romney* and the *Jason*, and himself sailed in the *Diana* for the tiny island of Trinidada. He had conceived the notion of establishing a British colony there, a venture which proved wholly unsuccessful. He finally returned to England in February 1782, having paused at Lisbon where he married a Miss Charlotte Dee. Back home, he found that the North

---

13 Rutherford, 'Sidelights', p.305.
14 Rutherford, 'Sidelights', p.307.

ministry had fallen, and this effectively ended his naval career; he went on half pay, never to serve again.

Before leaving the Cape, Suffren sent a despatch to Castries outlining his views as to what might be done in India:

> I have as yet done no more than study the war in India at a distance: not being in command I have only to obey. But since I have here seen the Dutch, I think that if one contemplates defending their possessions it will result in nothing but to their pure loss; for while one is at one place the English could be attacking others. If one goes to Batavia, the squadron runs the risk of being destroyed by disease and without any hope of again being made fit for service. As to the Moluccas, there is not one of them that could not be captured by a frigate, and perhaps at this very moment has been captured. I see one thing only to do if we have the means. That is, to attack Surat. If successful, with the money one could obtain there, sepoys could be raised, we could get the help of the Mahrattas and besiege Bombay. If that were taken, it would be easy to drive the English from the Malabar coast and by the help of Hyder Ali one could attack the Coromandel coast. As to Bengal, nothing is to be looked for there unless revolutions arise in India. If nothing can be done this year (1781), and if peace is not made, operations can be renewed next year. But nothing can be done without troops, less in India, where throughout there are fortifications and troops, than elsewhere, and in practically no part of which ships can approach the shore. The cost of eleven ships is too great to leave them idle or employ them merely in cruising.[15]

Suffren, once Johnstone was no longer on the Cape station, concluded correctly that he was likely to send part of his squadron to India, so he himself made preparations to leave for the Ile de France. The *Annibal* was sent off on 2 August with the convoy, preceded by the *Fortune*, to whose captain he gave orders that when he arrived there he should find and commandeer a suitable mast for the *Annibal*. With the rest of his squadron, he escorted the four East Indiamen in Hout Bay to Table Bay and then on 27 August sailed for the Ile de France. A week later he caught up with the *Annibal* and his convoy. He finally arrived at Port Louis on 25 October.[16]

---

15 Richmond, *Navy in India*, p.184.
16 Cavaliero, *Admiral Satan*, p.82.

10

The Capture of Trincomali

While Suffren was making his way towards his ultimate destination at the Ile de France, the strategic situation in India was beginning to change in a manner very much to the disadvantage of the French. That this was so, was almost entirely due to the persistence of Sir Edward Hughes in his dealings with the Company authorities and their military commanders.

The British strategy for India, which had been laid down once war with the Dutch had broken out, was conveyed in instructions to Hughes from Lord Weymouth, and to the Company from its Secret Committee in London. It was to the effect that attacks should be launched on the Dutch settlements, islands, and possessions in India. These instructions were based on the situation as it was known in London in early 1781, including Hyder's invasion of the Carnatic and the continuing Mahratta war. What was not known at that time was that a strong French squadron was about to sail to India.[1] This meant that it was necessary for those on the spot to interpret the instructions which had been sent in the light of the new situation. Discussions took place between Lord Macartney, the new Governor of Madras, Coote, and Hughes. The first of these meetings

Lord Macartney, Governor of Madras. (Public Domain)

---

1   Richmond, *Navy in India*, p.155.

was held in July, soon after Macartney arrived, and later discussions took place in September and October.

There were effectively three points of view to be considered: those of the Company, represented by Lord Macartney; the military commanders; and Hughes. In interpreting the strategy laid down in London, Macartney had as his first priority the expansion of the company's territory, observing in a despatch of 29 October: 'The overthrow of Indian princes is among us a slighter gratification and a lesser object of national policy than advantages over European enemies.'[2] The military commanders, on the other hand, had their eyes fixed on the situation in the field, and saw the priority as being the defeat of Hyder's army. It was not that they doubted the usefulness of taking Negapatam and Trincomali, but they gravely doubted whether sufficient resources were available for the task without seriously weakening the forces actually engaged with Hyder. Only Hughes grasped the central point of the operations that must immediately be embarked on, which was to seize those two places as soon as possible. In the former case, it would deny the French a port at which to land troops, and in the latter case the possession of Trincomali was particularly important in ensuring the retention of command of the sea. It was the only harbour on the western side of the Bay of Bengal that could give shelter throughout the year:

> As the north-east monsoon sets in on the Coromandel in about mid October, often with a violent gale, shipping in the open roadsteads of the Coromandel coast, lying on the lee shore, is in constant danger until January, and the possession of a secure port, from whence station off Ceylon could immediately be resumed when the violence of the monsoon was over, was a strategical advantage of the highest importance. Hughes, as his letters consistently show, held that command at sea was the factor which dominated the whole military situation. Negapatam and Trincomali were, in his words 'places of the utmost importance in the national interests and the preservation of the Company's possessions on the Coromandel coast.'[3]

The proposal to attack Negapatam had first been raised in June 1781, but it was concluded that before undertaking this it would be necessary to bring to an end the war with Hyder. Both Hughes and Coote agreed that steps should be taken to achieve this and approved a letter to be sent by Macartney to Hyder proposing peace. Hyder, though, was unimpressed. He saw himself in a potentially winning situation, and replied to the effect that he could not trust the Company: 'The Governors and Sirdars who enter into treaties return to Europe after one or two years, and their acts and deeds become of no effect; fresh Governors and Sirdars introduce new conversations.'[4] This response, which was received in July, led to the conclusion that no action could, for the moment, be taken against the Dutch.

Hughes remained convinced that Negapatam could and should be taken, but Coote believed that it would be impossible to detach troops to do so. In July, Coote

---

2   Richmond, *Navy in India*, p.162.
3   Richmond, *Navy in India*, p.158.
4   Richmond, *Navy in India*, p.156.

relieved Wandewash and then marched on Pulicat, where he received a reinforcement of troops from Bengal, and following this won a victory over Hyder at Pollilur. However, a lack of provisions prevented him from following up this success. Hughes had meanwhile remained in his cruising station off Negapatam, while continuing to urge that the army should cooperate in taking action against both that place and Trincomali. His particular concern was that there remained only a limited time before he should leave the Coromandel coast – by mid-October he would ordinarily have to take his squadron around to the west coast. He was willing to remain, though, if any major operation was planned.[5]

Hughes had learned, with the arrival of the *Monarca*, 68, to join his squadron, of Johnstone's failure at the Cape, and that in consequence the three ships of the line sent on from there should shortly be joining him, and he was anxious, in view of the French strength at the Ile de France, to concentrate his force as soon as possible. British policy, however, for the moment was bedevilled both by Macartney's desire to seize Ceylon, not for the strategic naval advantage which Trincomali on its own would provide, but purely for territorial gain, and also by the conviction of the military commanders that Negapatam and Trincomali would require more of their forces than could be spared.

Richmond reviewed in considerable detail the difficulty that Hughes faced in bringing about what to him was the obvious, necessary, and practical step of taking Negapatam and Trincomali. This 'obscure and remote problem' illustrated the conflicting claims that could arise during a joint sea and land campaign, and even more the difficulty of arriving at a reasoned decision in the absence of an authority with the ability to see and understand the position as a whole. In the present instance the problem lay with the members of the Select Committee of Madras, whose decisions were often deplorably wrong: 'A committee is not a body well constituted to direct war.'[6]

In spite of these difficulties, the plan to attack Negapatam was accepted in principle, and Hughes decided to remain on the coast in the hope that action would finally be taken. This still faced opposition from Coote, who gloomily wrote to Macartney on 31 October:

> I will venture to foretell that if the attack on Negapatam is commenced leaving an enemy in the rear to cope with our besieging army, and they move towards its relief, we shall be disgraced, and if we are not more fortunate that we have a right to expect, it will terminate in the loss of Tanjore, Trichinopoly and all the southern countries as well as bring on the ruin of this army.[7]

The attack on Negapatam, when it was finally agreed, was to be led by Colonel Sir Hector Munro, and he arrived off the port from Madras aboard the *Active* on 17 October. The weather was, for the moment, still holding. Hughes had organised a

---

5 Richmond, *Navy in India*, p.161.
6 Richmond, *Navy in India*, pp.167–169.
7 Richmond, *Navy in India*, p.171.

battalion of seamen 827 strong to reinforce his 443 marines, and on 21 October a detachment from the hard-pressed Southern Army arrived to take part in the assault. The ships' battalions went ashore next day. The outer lines were stormed on 29 October and the assault continued with a bombardment, supported by some of the ships of the squadron, on 7 November. By 12 November, it was all over, terms of capitulation being quickly agreed. In this way the military situation on land was considerably improved, while at sea the squadron now had a good watering place to windward, and another anchorage, landing place and source of supply had been denied to the French, if indeed they should arrive on the coast. Coote, meanwhile, was generous in his acknowledgement of the success which Hughes had achieved, writing that it was due 'to the unwearied application and perseverance of the Admiral and to the powerful aid to be afforded by landing so formidable a body of seamen and marines.'[8]

Hughes wasted no time in turning his attention to the capture of Trincomali. In preparing for this, however, he encountered one immediate problem; the Company's battalion of sepoys, which was to have been embarked for the operation, was so afflicted by desertions that it ceased to exist. All the Company could contribute, therefore, were 30 Europeans and 500 sepoy volunteers of very doubtful military value. The next problem came with the expected break in the weather. From 12 November, monsoon gales from the north-east with heavy rain and impassable surf delayed the re-embarkation at Negapatam. It was not until 2 January that the squadron was able to sail with the expeditionary force for Trincomali. However, when it arrived on 5 January, the storm had abated and it was on a calm grey morning in heavy rain that it was possible to disembark a force of marines together with two 16-pounders under Lieutenant Orr at Back Bay, about three miles north of Fort Frederick. The rest of the force, consisting of seamen and marines under the command of Captain John Gell of the *Monarca* were ashore by evening, and the fort was taken by surprise, the bulk of its garrison retreating into Fort Ostenburg, which commanded the inner harbour.[9]

On 8 January the whole force advanced on Fort Ostenburg, and by the following day had got possession of a hill some 300 paces from the fort. This was of relatively modern construction, having been built between 1762 and 1781. Hughes sent Major Geils, the chief engineer, to the governor (who happened to be a personal friend of the admiral) with a summons to surrender. When this was refused, Geils suggested that he should take in another summons so that he might make more exact observations of the fort's defences. This he did on 10 January. When the governor still refused to surrender, it was resolved to launch an assault on the following day.[10]

At dawn, the assault by a column of 450 sailors and marines went in, and in a very short time the garrison was driven back. Terms of capitulation were soon agreed and, in this way, Trincomali fell into British hands at a cost of 21 killed and 42 wounded. Dutch casualties amounted to 13 killed, and 425 prisoners were taken. All the shipping in the harbour was seized, including two richly laden East Indiamen.

---

8   Richmond, *Navy in India*, p.173.
9   Captain L.H.S.C. Cary, 'Trincomali', *The Mariner's Mirror*, (1931) 17:1, p.25.
10 Cary, 'Trincomali', p.25.

Leaving a garrison composed solely of volunteer sepoys with a detachment of artillery, Hughes returned to Madras to refit his squadron.[11]

The possession of Trincomali had gained for Hughes a position of enormous strategic advantage. However, for full use to be made of it, it was necessary that a superior naval force should at all times be available to act against the enemy, and that an adequate garrison should be maintained to hold the place until relieved. The Company made it clear to Hughes that no troops at all could be spared for the garrison, while the strength of his squadron could not be considered a superior force.

He was, though, expecting the reinforcement consisting of the three ships of the line of Johnstone's squadron which had been sent on to India. This did not arrive when he was expecting it. Under the command of Captain James Alms of the *Monmouth*, 64, this force had reached Madagascar on 21 August, but thereafter took an unusual course going to Johanna in the Comoro Islands, instead of direct to Anjengo on the Malabar Coast. By the time it reached Johanna, all three ships were suffering severely from scurvy, and running short of water; 600 men were put ashore to recuperate. It was three weeks before the ships resumed their passage. By December they had only reached the Morabat Gulf on the Arabian coast. From there, Alms, leaving the transports with Medows and his troops to make their own way, sailed for Bombay, where he arrived in January. He then set off as soon as he could to join Hughes at Madras.[12] As events were very soon to show, the capture of Negapatam and Trincomali had been effected only just in time.

Prior to the arrival of the *Fortune* at Port Louis on 6 September, there had been grave concern at the Ile de France as to what might have happened at the Cape. Such news as had been received of the events at Porto Praya and subsequently had suggested that Johnstone would have won the race to the Cape. Now, however, with positive news to the contrary, Souillac could hope that with Suffren's arrival, the French squadron would be able to put to sea and take to India a strong force which, in alliance with Hyder, could establish itself on the Coromandel coast. He was an energetic and determined man, and he succeeded in raising a force of 2,868 men. In command of this, however, he placed one *Maréchal de camp* Duchemin de Chenneville, which proved to be a very unfortunate decision. Duchemin was very inexperienced. He also was to prove himself an extremely irresolute leader. Nevertheless, Souillac had at least managed to put together a respectable force that was in fact substantially stronger than Hyder was expecting.

Suffren, when he arrived at Port Louis on 25 October, almost at once found himself at odds with some of the senior personalities of the French fleet. The captain of the *Brillant*, 64, Bernard de Tromelin, came aboard Suffren's flagship to ask why the command of the *Annibal* had been given to so junior an officer as Morard de Galles. Tromelin had been serving on the Ile de France for 16 years and was extremely experienced. During his time there he had been responsible for the dredging of Port Louis. He now felt that his seniority entitled him to the command of the *Annibal*. The captains of the *Flamand*, 64, (Maurville de Langle) and the frigate *Fine* (Saint Felix),

---
11 Cary, 'Trincomali', p.26.
12 Richmond, *Navy in India*, p.178.

also felt that they deserved the promotions which the new arrivals could provide. When d'Orves asked Suffren for his opinion, he got a terse reply: 'The command of the *Annibal* became vacant by death and I have filled it. It is no longer free.'[13] Regrettably, having first accepted this, d'Orves then bowed to the pressure from his captains, and revoked the appointment of Morard de Galles as captain of the *Annibal*. Suffren was furious, refusing that evening to speak to Tromelin at dinner.

Suffren was far from impressed with the general attitude which he found pervaded the entire society of Port Louis, writing to his cousin:

> Despite the great operations that await us in India, only apathetic languor and indifference reigns here, wholly revolting to a man who professes any patriotism. The military spirit has been forgotten – but what can you expect from the indulgence of commanders and the independence and insubordination of their subalterns, who look on this place as their patrimony and do what they like by making their senior officers afraid of them? Nearly everyone has a wife or a regular mistress. The ladies are charming, life is comfortable.[14]

And to Castries he wrote in similar terms:

> I greatly fear that the spirit which is engendered by great separation of time and distance from authority, by the amassing of money through trade, and by the hope that time and changes in the situation will pass the sponge over anything that may happen, cannot but be highly inconsistent with the military spirit and injurious above all to discipline, which is the very soul of service.[15]

Nevertheless, he threw himself into the task of preparing the squadron for action, making a considerable impression on those who witnessed his unceasing activity. A young officer of the Regiment d'Austrasie, himself impatient to leave for India, described the effect which Suffren was having:

> There was very soon an unaccustomed bustle in the workshops and yards. M. de Suffren was everywhere. The inhabitants, in admiration of his active spirit, supported him with all their power. One sent lengths of timber to the yard, another with those of his slaves who had any skills. The *colons* of Bourbon sent rice, maize and corn. But, believe it or not, all the obstacles he met came from those captains who were here before he arrived ... They were astonished at the way M. de Suffren ordered them about so imperiously and held them responsible for the delays they saw fit to make in carrying out his instructions. They intrigued sullenly against him and tried, with little success, to subvert the junior officers and leading seamen. All they

---

13 Cavaliero, *Admiral Satan*, p.83.
14 Cavaliero, *Admiral Satan*, p.84.
15 Lacour-Gayet, *marine militaire*, p.493.

gained from this was general contempt and obloquy for wanting to upset the operations of a man for whom everyone was filled with admiration.[16]

Suffren's energy and determination began to inspire confidence in the squadron, but he himself continued to feel anxious, as he explained to Mme de Seillans in a letter of 23 November:

> We are going to India with a large force and we should expect success, but there are innumerable reasons which make me fear that we may not achieve it … a spirit of independence and cupidity reigns here among the chiefs and their subordinates, so that it is difficult to hope for anything good. I have the greatest desire to return and I have asked permission for it with all earnestness.[17]

The suggestion that he wished to be recalled to Europe was entirely genuine; when writing to Castries he reminded him that he had been promised that he could return in 18 months.

It took six weeks before all was in readiness to sail, but further delay would have brought with it considerable danger. On 29 November the corvette *Diligente* arrived with an urgent request from Hyder for French support in the Carnatic.[18] By then, the squadron was almost ready for sea, and it finally left Port Louis on 7 December. Suffren was still far from convinced about the quality of its commanders. Two days before the departure of the squadron he poured out his concerns to his cousin:

> I am second-in-command of a beautiful Squadron. M. d'Orves, who is its chief, shows me great consideration, but since he is so good as to be almost feeble, the confidence which he reposes in me is shared with the public. The little prospect that there is of achieving anything good with men of such character has made me earnestly desire to return. I have received a warm welcome from the public here, but not the same reception from the sailors who have been here for five years without having done anything. This country effeminates people, with its large number of beautiful women, and life full of pleasures. The people here make money in commerce and that is much better than making war … Our squadron is well armed for achieving great things, but the qualities we shall lack are intelligence and self-confidence, which are rather rare among us. If we come back from India without doing anything, my decision is made, rather to return to France than remain here in the port for six months. I serve to make war and not to make court to the ladies of the Isle of France.[19]

---

16 Cavaliero, *Admiral Satan*, pp.85–86.
17 Sen, *French in India*, p.236.
18 Caron, *Mythe de Suffren*, p.224.
19 Sen, *French in India*, pp.236–237.

In setting off in the direction of Ceylon, d'Orves took the decision to sail by a new route, pioneered a few years before, which was longer but was swifter; the prevailing winds would take the squadron across the Indian Ocean as far as the Indonesian archipelago, from where it would bear west and approach Ceylon from the south. In this way it was hoped that it would be possible to land Duchemin's force with the benefit of surprise.[20] With 11 ships of the line, the squadron was larger than any that the French had previously assembled in the East. There were three 74s; d'Orves flew his flag in the *Orient*, and Suffren in the *Héros*, while Tromelin commanded the *Annibal*. Of the 64s, Maurville commanded the *Artésien* and Saint Felix, previously of the *Fine*, the *Brillant*. Du Chilleau remained in command of the *Sphinx* and Forbin the *Vengeur*; the remaining 64s were the *Ajax* (Bouvet), *Sévère* (la Pallière), *Bizarre* (la Landelle) and *Flamand* (Cuverville). There were three frigates: *Bellone* (de Cillart); *Pourvoyeuse* (Morard de Galles); and *Fine* (Perrier de Salvert). There were also three corvettes, *Sylphide*, *Subtile* and *Diligente*. The *Fortune* had been left behind at the Ile de France to carry despatches. There were also a fire ship, the *Pulvériseur*, commanded by Villaret-Joyeuse, the hospital ship *Toscane*, and seven transports.[21]

By mid-January the squadron was off Sumatra. En route it encountered the unfortunate 50-gun *Hannibal*, which was taken by the *Héros* on 22 January, which became the *Petit Annibal*. The intention at first had been that the second in command of the *Héros*, Ruyter-Werfusé, should be appointed as its captain, but the decision was reversed following a serious navigation error for which he had been responsible, and Cillart of the *Bellone* was nominated. The illness and subsequent death of d'Orves meant a further round of appointments, which were determined on the basis of seniority, and which cleared the way for Morard de Galles to be appointed to the *Petit Annibal*. La Pallière, of the *Sévère*, was designated as the commander of the *Orient*, and Cillart was given the *Sévère*. Ruyter-Werfusé took the place of Morard de Galles in command of the *Pourvoyeuse*. Pas de Beaulieu of the *Subtile* succeeded to the command of the *Bellone*, and Tromelin the younger was appointed to the *Subtile*, his place in the *Sylphide* passing to de Gallifet.[22]

From the *Hannibal*, it was learned that further reinforcements were expected by Hughes. These were the *Magnanime*, 74, and the *Sultan*, 64, which were escorting a convoy of men and munitions en route from St Helena to Madras. Their arrival would cancel out the French numerical advantage, so the sooner the British could be engaged the better.

D'Orves was by now a very sick man, and on 3 February he gave up the command to Suffren and was transferred to the *Toscane*, and he died six days later. Suffren at once made clear to his captains, whom he assembled aboard the *Héros* on 4 February, how he intended to proceed. In general, he had no intention of seeking their advice, but rather expected instant obedience to his orders. He told them that he would not prescribe an order of battle. Instead, he said that his expectation was that 'the valour and ability of each officer would permit him to adopt any action suggested

---

20 Cavaliero, *Admiral Satan*, p.86.
21 Caron, *Mythe de Suffren*, p.225.
22 Caron, *Mythe de Suffren*, p.227.

to him by the state and position of the enemy's squadron.'[23] However, at this first meeting aboard his flagship, there was a general discussion about the possibility of attacking the British squadron if it was found at anchor at Madras. It was unanimously agreed not to do so if it was drawn up under the guns of the forts. Richmond noted that such an encounter might in fact well have already occurred, had not wind and current carried the French to the eastward, and they therefore missed catching Hughes before the reinforcement reached him:

> If d'Orves had made the usual landfall off Ceylon he would not improbably have met Hughes off Trincomali: if he missed him there, he must almost certainly have caught him off Madras, six strong only, and engaged in provisioning and watering. With such superiority of numbers and circumstances there should be little doubt that all the support which the batteries of Fort St George could give would not have prevented the destruction of the British squadron in the roadstead, if attack were made.[24]

As it was, the decision which had been taken by the French made the point academic.

It was on 4 February that Suffren first learned of the fall of both Negapatam and Trincomali. As he neared the Coromandel coast, he picked up a number of merchant ships carrying rice, which was badly needed in Madras. On 6 February he received confirmation that Hughes had received a reinforcement of three ships of the line, but he was still uncertain where the British squadron actually was. Soon after Suffren had taken command, he had had to endure the extreme frustration of losing his wind, and for eight days was in the grip of a dead calm. When the wind finally picked up on 14 February, at which time he was off Pulicat nearly 40 miles north of Madras, and he was able to move southwards in the direction of that city. He sent Perrier de Salvert on ahead to reconnoitre in the *Fine*. As he neared the Madras, he was soon able to see the British squadron, consisting of nine ships of the line and two frigates, lying at anchor in the roadstead. The game had begun.

---

23 Cavaliero, *Admiral Satan*, pp.88–89.
24 Richmond, *Navy in India*, p.187.

11

Sadras

The news of Suffren's arrival on the coast led to a serious deterioration in the relations between the civil authorities on the one hand and the naval and military commanders on the other. The Committee at Madras saw fit to send Hughes a long letter reciting all the dangers which they saw as currently facing British interests, concluding with the request that Hughes should use the most active exertions to relieve them from those threats. Hardly surprisingly, Hughes took grave offence at the patronising tone of this letter, and resented the apparent assumption that he did not know what he should be doing. His response was immediate and very angry. He told the Committee that all the details contained in their letter were unnecessary 'unless, gentlemen, you suppose me ignorant of the state of affairs on this coast.' He had, he said, prepared and was preparing to do his part: 'Do you, my Lord and Gentlemen, do yours. I meddle not in your department; why will you not trust me in the proper management of His Majesty's squadron since His Majesty and my country have reposed that confidence in me?'[1]

His fury had been considerably sharpened by the discovery that the Company's Resident at Tanjore, a Mr Sulivan, had taken upon himself to open a letter sent to Hughes and Coote by Colonel Humberston, commanding part of the troops of Medows' force, which had arrived at Anjengo on the Malabar coast. Sulivan wrote back to Humberston to say that he should remain there. Both Hughes and Coote were outraged at this interference by the Resident with their plans and intentions and protested in the strongest terms, sending a joint letter to the Committee on 15 February, in which they deprecated the Resident's assumption of a power to make such a decision:

> …a power that we neither have devolved nor will do so on any man or body of men. For as the responsibility of our conduct rests with us only, it is absurd to suppose we can trust the conduct of affairs for which we are responsible to any person or persons whatever, much less to your Resident at Tanjore who must be totally ignorant of our intentions and of the plans of the commander-in-chief in this country.[2]

---

1 Richmond, *Navy in India*, p.189.
2 Richmond, *Navy in India*, p.190.

Between Hughes and Coote working relations remained excellent, and the latter offered to embark at once 300 men of the newly arrived 98th Regiment, who were accustomed to the ships. This offer Hughes gratefully accepted, since the squadron was extremely shorthanded, being 767 men short of complement and with 328 men sick on shore, amounting to nearly 25 percent of his proper strength. He had at once recalled those of his men who were away watering and embarked the troops which Coote had provided. In his subsequent report he wrote: 'In the meantime, I placed His Majesty's ships in the most advantageous manner to defend themselves; and the other ships in the road with springs on their cables, that they might bring their broadsides to bear more effectually on the enemy, should they attempt an attack.'[3] This involved hauling in the squadron and anchoring it in a secure line close to the forts, but ready at once to put to sea if necessary.

Suffren, once he had seen and assessed the position of the British squadron, anchored about four miles out to sea, and convened another council of war to consider whether to launch an immediate attack. Richmond speculated that the calling of this meeting, so alien to Suffren's character, was prompted not by any lack of self-confidence, but by a lack of confidence in his captains caused by their undisciplined behaviour at the Ile de France. He had formed his own view as to what must be done, opening the discussion by saying that it was not without distress that he saw himself as forced to propose that the battle should be postponed. He told the captains that, to ensure the continued goodwill and cooperation of Hyder Ali, the immediate objective must be to put ashore Duchemin and his troops. If an attack was launched on the British squadron in its present position, the enemy would thereafter have immediate access to the resources necessary to effect any repairs. Furthermore, ships at anchor had an advantage over ships attacking them, because their crews had only their guns to serve, while they also enjoyed the added support of the guns of the fortress. In any event the French could compel Hughes to move out from the strong position he had taken up, simply by moving to threaten Trincomali or any other important point; the British would be obliged to put to sea to prevent this.

With one notable exception, all the captains endorsed Suffren's opinion that the secure landing of Duchemin's men must be their first priority. The exception was the youthful Éléonor Jacques Marie Stanislas de Perrier de Salvert, who strongly argued in favour of an attack, contending that this would be the best way to impress Hyder Ali; withdrawing, on the other hand, would suggest timidity. He added that it would be possible for the squadron to sail in and pass inside the two southernmost ships of the enemy line, which were out of reach of the forts, and could therefore be attacked with advantage.

In his study of Suffren, Sir John Knox Laughton explored the question of this intervention by de Salvert, observing that Chevalier considers it doubtful, first, because it was not recorded in the squadron log, and 'secondly and chiefly, because he considers it highly improbable that a young officer of M. de Salvert's rank and position – he was a *lieutenant de vaisseau* – would have ventured on an opinion contrary to that of the commander-in-chief, the hero of Porto Praya.' Laughton,

---

3   Rear Admiral Charles Ekins, *The Naval Battles of Great Britain* (London: Baldwin and Craddock, 1828), pp.180–181.

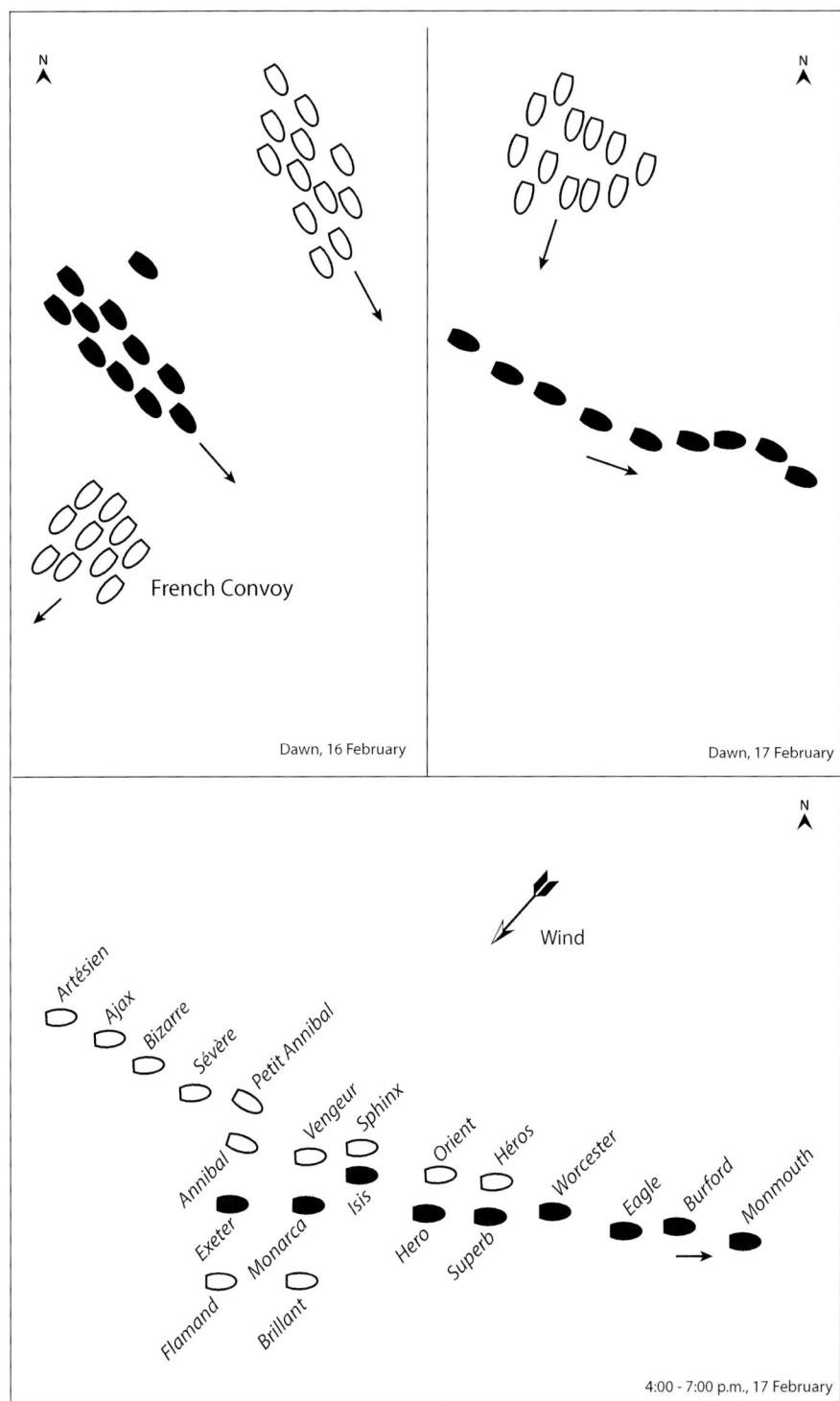

The Battle of Sadras, based on a map in Cavaliero, *Admiral Satan*.

though, considered that it was the supposed impudence of the intervention that led Trublet to include it in his history of Suffren's campaign. Trublet was, at the time, first lieutenant of the *Flamand*.⁴ Regrettably, it appears that a number of senior officers appear to have resented de Salvert's opinions, hinting that it was easy for him to offer bold advice, since as being only in command of the frigate he would not be called upon to put it into effect; and still more regrettably, according to Laughton, some French historians 'taking their tone from the hostile feeling of the fleet, have perpetuated the calumny.'

Caron suggests that 'Suffren, embarrassed and mortified by this reproach on the part of his subordinate, did not let this show, and congratulated the bold commander of the *Fine*.'⁵ At all events, following the discussion, Suffren remained firm in the conclusion which he had reached, having particularly in mind the little wind which there was at that time. Most historians consider that it was, in all the circumstances, the right course to follow. Lacour-Gayet, observing that to launch an attack would have been Suffren's instinctive reaction, wrote that an attack in the prevailing situation would have been of little use and above all dangerous.⁶

Mahan shared Lacour-Gayet's view, considering that Suffren was 'right in not attacking.' He reflected on this first encounter between Suffren and Hughes: 'each curiously representative of the characteristics of his own race, – the one of the stubborn tenacity and seamanship of the English, the other of the ardour and tactical science of the French, too long checked and betrayed by a false system.'⁷ Caron, on the other hand, reckoned that Suffren, still unsure how his attack at Porto Praya would be considered at Versailles, was much affected by a recollection of the outcome of his assault there.⁸

The meeting aboard the *Héros* ended at about 2:00 p.m., and two hours later the French squadron weighed anchor, and sailed south-east in two columns under easy sail.⁹ Hughes, watching them go, knew that he must follow, and his squadron weighed anchor and put to sea. What his intentions were have been a matter of some debate, some French historians considering that his objective was to slip down the coast in order to cover Trincomali. Laughton took a somewhat different view of Hughes's decision to put to sea once Suffren was himself well out to sea:

> His doing so caused great surprise among the French, as they could not conceive it possible that with nine ships he would come out to attack them with twelve; and it is most probable that he had not any such positive intention, but that he wished rather to take, destroy or scatter their convoy, and perhaps also to prevent or obstruct their landing the troops which they had on board.¹⁰

---

4 Laughton, *Studies in Naval History*, p.111.
5 Caron, *Mythe de Suffren*, p.234.
6 Lacour-Gayet, *marine militaire*, p.498; Caron misquotes him as suggesting that it would have been 'suicidal.'
7 Mahan, *Influence of Sea Power*, p.427.
8 Caron, *Mythe de Suffren*, p.236.
9 Richmond suggests that Suffren actually weighed anchor soon after noon.
10 Laughton, *Naval Studies*, p.112.

Certainly Hughes would not have lost sight of a possible threat to Trincomali, but Laughton is probably right in supposing 'that what he actually did first was what he primarily hoped to do.'

Laughton's view that the French were incredulous that Hughes should be putting to sea is of course inconsistent with the fact that Suffren was perfectly well aware that if he made a move away from his position before Madras, it would be seen as a threat to Trincomali or some other important point on the coast. That at any rate was Mahan's view of Suffren's assessment of his position before Madras.[11] Richmond, on the other hand, notes that there was nothing in the terms in which Suffren stated his reasons for not attacking Hughes in his position at Madras which implied that any such consideration was in his mind. It may not have been a reason for not attacking; but Suffren was almost certainly aware that the British would be sensitive to any move to threaten any of their possessions.

Entering this debate, Caron quotes a letter which Suffren wrote on 24 February to the French agent in Ceylon, in which he expressed surprise that the British should leave their secure anchorage in Madras. This, Caron considers, is conclusive evidence that Suffren's intentions were not to provoke the enemy to put to sea.[12] He goes on to speculate as to Hughes's intentions, suggesting that if in fact, despite his numerical inferiority, Hughes, 'was prepared to take the risk of combat in the open sea, it gave credence to Salvert's argument that the British ships were indeed vulnerable in their anchorage.' As usual ready to challenge, with the benefit of hindsight, the decisions that Suffren made, he posed another question:

> Why did Suffren, who witnessed at a distance, and with satisfaction if one is to judge by what he himself wrote, his enemy weighing anchor, not take advantage of this to turn back and offer battle to him before he could form line of battle? Was it not in effect to interfere with the landing of the French troops that Hughes weighed anchor? Was it not preferable to eliminate the risk before attempting the disembarkation?[13]

Caron concedes that night was coming on but suggests that it was an opportunity that should have been grasped. As it was, Suffren was unconcerned and imperturbably continued on his way southwards. The best answer to the questions posed by Caron is probably that Suffren had committed himself to the disembarkation of troops as being his immediate objective, and an unprepared attack at the end of the day could very well have jeopardised that. Suffren can perhaps be more justly criticised, however, for not taking more comprehensive measures to ensure the safety of his convoy.

In making sail to the south, Suffren later explained to Souillac that his object was to touch at Pondicherry to gain information. Hughes, when following, hauled his wind to a north-east breeze with the object of getting the weather gauge. Noting this, Suffren followed suit, in order that he should not find himself to leeward at

---

11 Mahan, *Influence of Sea Power*, p.429.
12 Caron, *Mythe de Suffren*, p.239.
13 Caron, *Mythe de Suffren*, p.240.

dawn, but his convoy continued on its course close inshore, with the result that a wide gap opened between it and the squadron. Suffren had ordered Ruyter-Werfusé in the *Pourvoyeuse* to shepherd the transports so that they sailed between the land and the squadron, keeping in touch as they did so. Unfortunately, he made a mess of it during the night, when he miscalculated the speed with which the wind was carrying the convoy forward, and allowed it to sail too far ahead of him as he hung back to keep in signal distance of the flagship. When he tried to catch it up he found himself alone in the in the dark without a light or sail to guide him and at dawn the sea was empty. He decided to make for the rendezvous at Pondicherry. He had in fact sailed through the gap that he had allowed to develop between the squadron and the convoy and did not see Hughes then sail straight into it.[14]

At dawn on 16 February Hughes was in sight of both Suffren's squadron and of the convoy. The former was some 12 miles off, bearing east, while the latter, which had continued to sail close inshore, was nine miles to the south-west. Hughes made up his mind at once to attack the convoy, 'well knowing the enemy's line of battleships would follow to protect them all in their power.'[15] He detached the *Monmouth*, *Isis* and *Seahorse*, which quickly drew ahead in pursuit of the transports, with the rest of Hughes's squadron following in good order. The move was immediately successful; six prizes were taken, although five of these were actually captured British vessels. The sixth, however, was the transport *Lauriston*, which was carrying 300 troops and a quantity of important military stores. The *Seahorse*, which had taken two of the prizes, next attempted to capture two other armed transports but was beaten off and severely damaged. The rest of the convoy scattered, the hospital ship ran to Negapatam, where it was captured, thus depriving Suffren of both surgeons and medical equipment. Of the others, four sailed to Tranquebar and the rest to Galle and Pondicherry. Subsequently, the French recaptured the five British vessels.

Hughes was perfectly correct in supposing that Suffren would come hurrying down to the rescue of his convoy. By 3:00 p.m., four of the fastest French ships had got as close as four miles from the tail end of the British squadron, whereupon Hughes collected his ships together and steered south-east under an easy sail. Suffren also concentrated his force, following the British at about three miles with the intention of engaging them on the following day.

He had done what he could to ensure that his captains played their part, though he cannot have been entirely confident about this. Three days after he first assumed overall command, he had given Tromelin a letter setting out clearly what he intended:

> The British capture of Trincomali and Negapatam, and perhaps of all Ceylon, requires us to work for a general action. If we are fortunate to find ourselves to windward of the English – who will only have eight or nine ships at the most – my design is to double on their rear division. If your division is in the rear, you will observe from your position how many ships will overlap and order them to double. If on the other hand we find ourselves to leeward, yet our ships by crowding on all sail are still able to

---

14 Cavaliero, *Admiral Satan*, p.105.
15 Richmond, *Navy in India*, p.192.

> double on the enemy, then provided they are not attacked, or if attacked then only feebly or at a distance, you will order them to attack and double to windward. Whatever the circumstances, I ask you to order your division to take what action you shall believe to be the best to achieve the success of the engagement.[16]

He could not have put it more plainly. All the same, as his biographer observed, it was a bold assumption that his captains would overcome their conservative instincts and depart from the traditional commitment to the sanctity of the line of battle.

Mahan noted one significant aspect of Suffren's orders to Tromelin, which was his emphasis on seeking a general action as the most important priority, rather than the recapture of Trincomali and Negapatam, which, he points out would have been the traditional French strategy. It was, though, plain to Suffren that he must above all seek to inflict a decisive defeat on Hughes:

> …and it is therefore safe to say that to avoid such action should have been the first object of Hughes. The attempt of the latter to gain the windward position was consequently correct; and as in the month of February the sea breeze at Madras sets in from the eastward and southward about 11.00 am he probably did well to steer in that general direction, though the result disappointed him.[17]

Reviewing these instructions to Tromelin in the light of the battle that was about to take place, Mahan drew attention to Suffren's conception of the duties of a second in command, which he considered:

> …may fairly be paralleled with that of Nelson in his celebrated order before Trafalgar. In this first action he led the main attack himself, leaving the direction of what may be called the reserve – at any rate, of the second half of the assault – to his lieutenant, who, unluckily for him, was not a Collingwood, and utterly failed to support him.[18]

As dawn broke on 17 February the two squadrons were separated by some nine miles, with the French to the north-east. With the benefit of the squally winds blowing from this direction, they were steadily able to close the gap. However, they were in no sort of line. During the night the ships in the rear had taken the lighting of stern lights to mean that they should turn into the wind, with the result that the rear division had fallen well behind, particularly the *Artésien*.

Hughes subsequently recorded the situation as it appeared at dawn:

> At daylight on the morning of the 17th, the body of the enemy's squadron bore N by E of ours, distant about three leagues; the weather very hazy,

---

16 Cavaliero, *Admiral Satan*, p.108.
17 Mahan, *Influence of Sea Power*, p.433.
18 Mahan, *Influence of Sea Power*, p.434.

with light winds and frequent squalls, of short duration, from the NNE, the enemy crowding all the sail they could towards our squadron. At six in the morning I made the signal to form the line of battle ahead; at twenty five minutes past eight, our line being formed with great difficulty from the want of wind and frequent intervals of calms; I made the signal for the leading ship to make the same sail as the Admiral and made sail; formed in line ahead, intending to weather the enemy, that I might engage them closely.[19]

As the morning wore on, and the gap between the two squadrons continued to close, Suffren did what he could to get his ships into a better line, but his rearmost ships sailed very badly, and the squally gusts of the north-east wind kept blowing them out of line. He was approaching Hughes more quickly than the latter had expected, however. It was soon clear to the British commander that he could not safely delay preparing for action any longer:

At ten, the enemy having the advantage of the squalls from the NNE, which always reached them first, and in consequence continued longest with them, neared us very fast; and I made the signal for our line to alter course two points to leeward; the enemy then steering down on the rear of our line, in an irregular or double line abreast. At half past noon I made the signal to form the line of battle abreast in order to draw the rear of our line closer to the centre, and prevent the enemy from breaking in on it, and attacking it when separated.[20]

This manoeuvre enabled Hughes to hold the French squadron for more than three hours. Suffren was finding it difficult to get his squadron into a better order; managing a squadron of ships of the line was at the best of times an awkward and uncertain process, but in light and variable winds a commander's task became much harder. As Suffren approached the British line, his own squadron was not well placed to deliver the manoeuvre which he had planned, and which would permit the immediate and damaging blow at the enemy for which he hoped. He realised that for his attack to be effective he must take the lead in the *Héros*: 'My uncoppered ships sailed so heavily and several others so badly, that I should not have been able to attack at all had I not taken the lead.'[21]

Watching the French closing on his rear, in what he described as a double line abreast, Hughes at 3:00 p.m. again altered course in order to draw his line more closely together, and 40 minutes later, since it was plainly impossible to avoid Suffren's attack in the prevailing light winds, he made the signal to form line of battle ahead. In doing so, it was his expectation that the attack, when it came, would be delivered line to line. He soon discovered that this was not the case. The rearmost British ship, the *Exeter*, had straggled some way in the rear of the rest of the British

---

19 Ekins, *Naval Battles*, p.181.
20 Ekins, *Naval Battles*, p.181.
21 Cavaliero, *Admiral Satan*, p.107.

squadron. This was led by the *Monmouth*, which was followed by the *Burford*, *Eagle* and *Worcester*. Next came Hughes, in the *Superb*, and behind him the *Hero*, *Isis* and *Monarca*.

Suffren collected his coppered ships into the head of his line, following the *Héros*. Behind her came the *Orient*, *Sphinx*, *Vengeur*, *Annibal*, *Petit Annibal*, *Sévére*, *Bizarre*, *Ajax* and *Artésien*, and then finally the *Brillant* and *Flamand*. His orders to the whole squadron were that they were to engage only at pistol shot range. At 4:00 p.m. he put into effect his long-conceived plan to maximise his superiority of numbers, and ordered the *Annibal*, *Brillant* and *Flamand* to steer to double the enemy's line.

This manoeuvre, Mahan considers that Hughes might have avoided:

> Whether by his own fault or not, he was now in the worst possible position, waiting for an attack by a superior force at its pleasure. The rear ship of his line, the *Exeter*, was not closed up; and there appears no reason why she should not have been made the van, by forming on the starboard tack and thus bringing the other ships up to her.[22]

There were some differences in detail in the way in which each of the commanders described the French attack. Mahan quotes each of them. Hughes wrote of the moment that firing began when the enemy closed on the *Exeter*:

> Three of the enemy's ships in the first line bore right down upon the *Exeter* while four more of their second line, headed by the *Héros*, in which M. de Suffren had his flag, hauled along the outside of the first line toward our centre. At 4:05 the enemy's three ships began their fire upon the *Exeter*, which was returned by her and her second ahead; the action became general from our rear to our centre, the commanding ship of the enemy, with three others of their second line, leading down on our centre, yet never advancing farther than opposite to the *Superb*, our centre ship, with little or no wind and some heavy rain during the engagement. Under these circumstances, the enemy brought eight of their best ships to the attack of five of ours, as the van of our line, consisting of the *Monmouth*, *Eagle*, *Burford* and *Worcester*, could not be brought into action without tacking on the enemy.[23]

In this account which Hughes gave of the manner of Suffren's attack, Richmond detects a hint of resentment that the Frenchman should have acted in this way – 'a suggestion that his opponent had not played quite fair, and had not displayed the chivalry which the conduct of war demands.' Richmond considers that this limitation of Hughes's tactical sense and outlook was a factor not without influence on the way he acted later on.[24] This may be reading too much into the wording of Hughes's report, but certainly he was an entirely orthodox commander who had not so far had reason to appreciate that Suffren was very different.

---

22 Mahan, *Influence of Sea Power*, p.431.
23 Mahan, *Influence of Sea Power*, pp.431–432; Ekins, *Naval Battles*, pp.181–182.
24 Richmond, *Navy in India*, p.196.

Suffren, in his report to Castries of the battle, did put things somewhat differently:

> I should have destroyed the English squadron, less by superior numbers than by the advantageous disposition in which I attacked it. I attacked the rear ship and stood along the English line as far as the sixth. I thus made three of them useless, so that we were twelve against six. I began the fight at 3:30 in the afternoon, taking the lead and making signal to form line as best could be done; without that I would not have engaged. At four I made signal to three ships to double on the enemy's rear, and to the squadron to approach within pistol shot. This signal, though repeated, was not executed. I did not myself give the example, in order that I held in check the three van ships, which by tacking would have doubled on me. However, except the *Brillant*, which doubled on the rear, no ship was as close as mine, nor received as many shots.[25]

By about 4:45 p.m., Suffren's squadron was more or less in the position at which he had aimed. Aboard the *Héros* he now moved up the British line, firing into each of the British ships as he passed. He was closely followed by the *Orient*, behind which came the *Sphinx*, *Vengeur* and *Petit Annibal*. When the flagship reached a position opposite the *Superb*, Suffren checked its progress. At this point it was rather more than a pistol shot away from the British flagship, in the position which he had taken up in order to ensure that the four leading ships of the British line could not tack and then double the *Héros*. In fact, with the wind as it was, there was nothing that these ships could do to take an effective part in the battle. Hughes had, indeed, prepared a signal ordering them to tack, but could see that it would be in practice of little effect. At the same time his centre could not in the state of the wind escape from the van of the French squadron.[26]

What Suffren now required was that Tromelin should act in accordance with the orders which he had previously given him. Suffren confirmed these by signal to Tromelin to lead the rest of the squadron up the leeward side of the British line. He had previously signalled the *Brillant*, *Flamand* and *Ajax* to do this. Not only did Tromelin not do as Suffren expected, he ordered all the rear ships which were under his command to maintain their position in the line, and to continue in the wake of the leading French ships which had followed the *Héros* along the windward side of the British line. When Bouvet, of the *Ajax*, came out of the line in order to comply with Suffren's signal, Tromelin ordered him to return to his place in the line. The *Flamand* was the first to disregard Tromelin's signals and, followed shortly after by the *Brillant*, came up to leeward of the *Exeter*. The *Artésien*, which should, on account of being coppered, have been able closely to follow the *Flamand* and *Brillant*, made no attempt to do so and remained to windward and some way astern of the rest of the French squadron.

The effect of Tromelin's disobedience, apparently occasioned by his sour dislike of his commander, was that five ships in the English rear were engaged, more or

---

25   Mahan, *Influence of Sea Power*, p.432.
26   Ekins, *Naval Battles*, p.182.

less, by eight French ships. Four of these were concentrating their fire on the *Exeter*. The battle continued with the squadrons disposed thus for some two hours, during which the *Exeter*, in particular, suffered a fearful pounding and was reduced to a hulk, though she kept up a return fire on her assailants.

The *Exeter* carried the flag of Hughes's second in command, Commodore Sir Richard King. Several historians have recorded his experience as the *Brillant* and *Flamand* closed in on the stricken ship. At this moment a ball struck his flag captain as he stood beside King on the quarterdeck, splattering the commodore with brains and blood. Almost at once, the ship's master came up to King to report, in an agitated state, that another French ship was closing on the *Exeter*. 'What is to be done?' he cried. 'Done?' said King, as he wiped his face with a handkerchief, 'Why, there is nothing to be done but fight her till she sinks.'[27]

Sir Richard King. (Public Domain)

At about 6:00 p.m., with the British ships suffering rather more heavily than their opponents, there came a decisive change in the wind, which Hughes recorded:

> At six in the afternoon a squall of wind from the SE took our ships, and paid them round, head on to the enemy to the NE; when the engagement was renewed by our five ships with great spirit from the starboard guns; and at 6:25, just before dark, the enemy's ships engaged with ours having visibly suffered severely, the whole of them hauled their wind and stood to the northward. At this time the *Superb* had lost her main yard, had five feet of water in the hold, and several large shot holes underwater, and neither brace nor bowline left entire; and the *Exeter*, reduced almost to a wreck, had made the signal of distress.[28]

With the change in the wind, it soon became apparent to Suffren that to prolong the battle would not provide any chance of a decisive victory, and hauling his wind, he

---

27 Cavaliero, *Admiral Satan*, p.110.
28 Ekins, *Naval Battles*, p.182.

stood to the north-east, allowing Hughes to continue for the moment on his original course. For a while, the *Flamand* continued to inflict further damage on the unfortunate *Exeter*, but when first the *Monarca* and then the *Worcester* and the *Eagle* were able to pull round and come to King's assistance, the *Flamand* broke off the action and turned to join the rest of the French squadron.

The events of this battle have been closely examined by both British and French commentators, who have arrived at very different conclusions. The basic facts are not in dispute. The British lost 32 men killed and 105 wounded, of which the *Exeter* suffered 10 killed and 45 wounded and the *Superb* 11 killed and 25 wounded. These two ships were the most severely damaged of the British squadron. French casualties were very much the same, with 30 killed and 100 injured.[29]

Little adverse comment could be made about the conduct of the British captains and the performance of their ships. Nor has Hughes generally been criticised for the way in which he managed his squadron, although Ekins suggests one way in which he might have acted differently:

> Sir Edward Hughes might have counteracted the attack, by wearing his squadron when it was about to commence. If there was wind enough to bring the enemy's ships into their stations, there was sufficient to enable the British to wear, though not to tack, and thus to have met the attack. The vicinity of the land, in all probability, prevented the British Admiral from performing this manoeuvre. In wearing together, the van would have soon been in a situation to give support to the rear.[30]

For Suffren, responsibility for the disappointing outcome of the battle belonged firmly to his captains and, especially, to Tromelin. He reported to Castries in trenchant terms the way in which a number of individuals had let him down badly. Apart from Tromelin, he was severe in his comments on Landelle, Maurville, Bouvet and Cillart. He was particularly harsh in his comments when speaking to Bouvet who, he told him, had been particularly recommended to him, 'but yesterday's example of subordination [to Tromelin's order to rejoin the line] showed you in your real colours. You little know what it has cost us, retiring when you should have engaged.' Then, perhaps feeling some pity for him, he told Bouvet that he would take care to see that he was not again exposed to such a disagreeable situation.[31] Suffren was, on the other hand, generous in his praise of Saint Felix and Cuverville in particular. And he acknowledged that La Pallière, du Chilleau, Forbin and Morard de Galles had all done their duty, writing of the last named that he had commanded the *Petit Annibal* as he did that of the much larger *Annibal*, and he would do always – very well. Of these, only la Pallière had not come with him from France. In his remarks to Castries, he was cautious: 'I have complained of no one for it would be dangerous to upset these gentlemen, who have been spoiled by the extreme indulgence of M.

---

29 Richmond, *Navy in India*, p.202.
30 Ekins, *Naval Battles*, p.182.
31 Cavaliero, *Admiral Satan*, p.112.

d'Orves and are not at all used to being commanded. I shall have to keep them, for among the junior officers there is no one to replace them.'[32]

It was, of course, Tromelin at whom Suffren's anger was particularly directed. Richmond, observing that initially all went well with Suffren's plan, remarked that 'it only remained for Tromelin to do his duty. There was an overlap of no less than seven ships. Not only had his instructions told the Commodore to double on the rear and engage, but Suffren signalled him to do so. But he did nothing.' After summarising the course of the battle, Richmond went on to pose the question: 'What, precisely, was Suffren's intention and was the misconduct of the Commodore due in any way to want of clearness in his instructions? Were the instructions so worded as to leave no doubt in Tromelin's head as to his chief's intentions, so that however the situation might arise, he could be in no doubt how he should act?'[33]

In considering the answers to these questions, Richmond proceeded to a careful and fair-minded review of Suffren's orders and intentions. He concluded that the wording of his written instructions to Tromelin would leave the impression that Suffren's first intention was to engage ship to ship from van to rear in the ordinary way, and to double only with the surplus or overlap, leaving to Tromelin the adjustment of the doubling force. This suggestion appeared to be corroborated by the signal to only three ships – the *Annibal*, *Ajax* and *Flamand* – to pass to leeward of the British. However, Suffren stopped at the *Superb*, fifth from the van. It was possible that Tromelin, supposing that the whole of the enemy line was to be engaged, expected the *Héros* to move ahead to the van, but the question was not long to remain in suspense once the flagship remained definitely abreast of the *Superb*. His instructions left Tromelin the authority to decide how many ships to send to leeward – either the whole, or only part of the remaining ships. What was unmistakable, however, was that he must take one or other course. In fact, he did neither; and the recall of the *Ajax* to the line was 'rank disobedience.'[34]

For Richmond, therefore, Tromelin's conduct was inexcusable; for a willing and intelligent man, Suffren's instructions provided all that he should need. However, Suffren had already had the opportunity to form an opinion of the commanding officers that he had first met at the Ile de France, and it was not favourable. Richmond considers that he was taking a risk in entrusting to them: 'the conduct of an attack the form of which, being novel, required both a high spirit and professional skill.' Accordingly, he finds that it was impossible to absolve him from some blame.[35] All of which is true, but it is difficult to see what else Suffren could have done in the circumstances in which he was placed. He had to do the best he could with the captains he had, however much he wished that he had inherited an abler, more committed, set of officers.

A separate question does arise, however, and that concerns Suffren's failure to take any steps to renew the action on the following day. Trublet, in his account of

---

32 Cavaliero, *Admiral Satan*, p.111.
33 Richmond, *Navy in India*, pp.197–198.
34 Richmond, *Navy in India*, p.199.
35 Richmond, *Navy in India*, p.200.

the battle, reproached Suffren for not immediately pursuing the British squadron.[36] Certainly Suffren could, if he chose, have used his frigates to keep in touch with the enemy, while the damage that his ships had suffered was not serious enough to prevent them manoeuvring effectively. He told Castries at the end of the battle – when he broke off the engagement due to the coming of night, the change in the wind and the rain, as well as Tromelin's insubordination – that he still hoped to resume the action. On the other hand, he told Souillac that on 18 February his lack of water, his need to rejoin his convoy, and to meet with Hyder Ali, all combined to prevent him doing so. He was well aware that, with the damage that the British sustained, Hughes would not himself wish to renew the action, so that it would be necessary to keep in touch if the battle was to be resumed and he made no use of his frigates to do so. Certainly, he had every possible reason to fight Hughes again as soon as he could, because he knew that his opponent was shortly to be reinforced. Richmond speculates that the explanation might have been that, 'in the tempest of wrath and disappointment which any man would feel at such a frustration of his plans but which would be doubly strong in the case of a man so impetuous and of such a fiery temperament as Suffren, he did not think of doing so.'[37] Since there were already a number of valid reasons for not pursuing Hughes, this suggestion seems entirely possible.

There is an eyewitness account of Suffren's immediate reaction to his disappointment. This comes from the pen of Tillette du Mautort, who wrote: 'When M. de Suffren grasped what had occurred, his anger was terrible, uttering violent threats against those who had so significantly frustrated his endeavours, promising a full enquiry and a demand for exemplary punishment.'[38]

Lacour-Gayet, who quoted this evidence of Suffren's intemperate reaction to the events of 17 February, does make one point in extenuation of those captains who failed to comply with his instruction to close to pistol shot range. His decision, justifiable in itself, to remain further than this from the *Superb* due to his wish to prevent the leading British ships from taking part, led his captains to disregard his signal for close action: 'At the moment that they set eyes on the *Héros*, they could believe that, despite the signals, they were in the right place to engage the enemy.' In other words, it was up to Suffren to correct their misapprehension by making the necessary signals to make the position clear.[39]

Among the French commentators, it is of course Caron who is most critical of Suffren, asserting that once again he had chosen to launch his assault on the enemy in a disordered state. Instead, he contends, it would have been possible to delay his attack until he was sure that he could carry it out successfully before sundown. As it was, he had put himself deliberately into a situation in which he would lose the benefit of the plan which he had prepared. In addition, Caron suggests that for his manoeuvre to have succeeded, it was at least essential for him personally to direct it

---

36 Lacour-Gayet, *marine militaire*, p.505n.
37 Richmond, *Navy in India*, pp.200–201.
38 Lacour-Gayet, *marine militaire*, p.502n.
39 Lacour-Gayet, *marine militaire*, p.503.

by taking up a position in the line from which he could be sure that his orders were being obeyed.[40]

Furthermore, Caron criticises Suffren for not having made clear to his squadron what was required of it: 'The signal books were incontestably insufficient to convey unequivocally all the subtlety of a delicate manoeuvre, but Suffren had had the possibility before and during the battle to send specific orders on board his principal subordinates; why did he not attempt this?' Recalling the problems caused by attacking without having properly prepared at Porto Praya, it might be thought that this was an obvious course; only if he had done so could he have the right to complain of their conduct.[41] Against this, it can be argued that in his previous written instructions he had made himself perfectly clear, and the tactical advantages of what he had indicated as his intention should have been apparent to Tromelin from the moment that the *Héros* brought to opposite the *Superb*.

As to the charge of disaffection on the part of his captains, Caron considers that Suffren's account of the Battle of Sadras contains 'too many anomalies, imprecisions and obscurities' to be relied on for an objective assessment of their alleged shortcomings. He quotes with approval the historian Rene Jouan, who in his *Histoire de la marine francaise* suggested that it was very important to determine the causes capable of winning the respect and affection of his subordinates, or the converse. Such an enquiry, he pointed out, was not conducted by many historians. Caron gives an example of this in Jenkins's *History of the French Navy*, who wrote simply that Suffren was 'angry because he suspected, rightly, that the stupidity had largely been prompted by the most unpatriotic disaffection. The five captains who failed had all been d'Orves' men.'[42]

Although the battle itself had been indecisive, Suffren had nevertheless gained a significant advantage in its wider effects. The French squadron had fought well and bravely against the British, hitherto all-powerful at sea, and had not been beaten. Suffren had shown himself, unlike his predecessor, to be committed to Hyder Ali's cause, and to act effectively in doing so. When, on 19 February, Suffren reached Pondicherry (which had been occupied by Hyder's forces) and was told by Piveron de Morlat that Hyder Ali wished him to proceed to Porto Novo and land his troops there, Suffren readily complied.[43]

However, when he reached Porto Novo on 21 February, he was, to his dismay, held up there, by delays in the disembarkation of his troops, by protracted negotiations with the representatives of Hyder Ali, and by difficulties in procuring provisions and other necessaries. It was not until 10 March that the disembarkation of the troops was complete, but Hyder agreed to supply provisions for these, and to support Duchemin with 6,000 sepoys and a few regiments of cavalry. Suffren was gravely hampered by lack of money. The sale of the prizes which he had taken did

---

40 Caron, *Mythe de Suffren*, pp.252–253.
41 Caron, *Mythe de Suffren*, p.255.
42 Caron, *Mythe de Suffren*, p.270; Jenkins, *French Navy*, p.190.
43 Sen, *French in India*, p.242.

not produce sufficient for his needs, and he was obliged on 12 March to send an urgent letter to Souillac asking for more men, money, and munitions.[44]

Chafing at the thought that these delays almost certainly meant that his chance of encountering the British again before they were reinforced was gone, Suffren may by now have come to regret his mistake in failing to resume the Battle of Sadras on 18 February. As it was, he utilised his time at Porto Novo to refit his ships as well as he could. To their allies, the French naturally represented the Battle of Sadras as a victory, though perfectly aware that at best it was really only a drawn battle. To the Company, it certainly seemed as good as a victory. Warren Hastings wrote to Hughes from Calcutta to say that the outcome 'must excite in the minds of all the powers in India a confirmed opinion of the unrivalled military character of the English nation.' He went on to observe: 'We regard your action with the French fleet as the crisis of our fate in the Carnatic, and in the result of it we see the province relieved and preserved and the permanency of British power in India firmly established.'[45] The coming months were to show that this was a decidedly premature judgement.

Almost at once came the first indication that this was so, with news of a British military disaster. Colonel John Braithwaite, with the small army of 2,250 men with which he had been operating in Tanjore, was trapped on the River Coleroon. On 18 February, after resisting for 25 hours, his defences were overwhelmed by Tipu's cavalry and a body of French mercenaries, and he was obliged to surrender. It was a serious setback; it meant that the whole area of Tanjore, with its crucially important rice fields, was denied to the British.[46]

---

44 Sen, *French in India*, p.242.
45 Cavaliero, *Admiral Satan*, p.113.
46 Cavaliero, *Admiral Satan*, p.115.

12

Provedien

Before proceeding to Porto Novo after the Battle of Sadras, Suffren had proposed that Duchemin's troops should be employed in an attempt to seize Negapatam. This was altogether too bold a proposal for the timorous Duchemin, whose immediate priority was the negotiations with Hyder Ali, which were conducted at the latter's camp by two French officers, Moissac and de Canaple. Duchemin was extremely reluctant to agree to the disembarkation of his troops until these negotiations were concluded, and it was not until 10 March that he finally agreed that they could go ashore. The negotiations, now conducted by Duchemin's brother, Poncin, dragged on until in the end Duchemin agreed to accept the conditions insisted on by Hyder. These included a requirement that the French should not withdraw from the alliance even if the war between France and Britain should come to an end, and that the French should at all times ensure that their forces on land and sea should be superior to the British.[1]

Hyder Ali had conducted these negotiations in a spirit of considerable distrust of Pierre Duchemin, which was why his negotiating position remained adamant. The terms of the treaty which Duchemin negotiated (which was apparently not signed at that stage) were strongly disapproved by Castries when they were reported to him. The conditions about the maintenance of the alliance, and the guarantee of French superiority, clearly went beyond Duchemin's authority. In addition, Castries objected to the provisions which entitled the French to retain some territories when conquered from the British:

> It was, he declared, going against the wishes of the King, who wanted the liberation of the Indian Princes from the yoke of the English and not making any territorial conquests. It was necessary to avoid giving the impression to the Indian Princes that the French only wanted to take the place of the English. Castries also did not like the peremptory demand made by Souillac to maintain the independence of the French army from the control of the Mysore ruler. Such a tone betrayed distrust of Hyder and was bound to displease him. Finally, Castries did not favour the demand, as an essential condition of the treaty, for an advance of 24 lakhs of rupees by Hyder.[2]

---

1   Cavaliero, *Admiral Satan*, p.116.
2   Sen, *French in India*, p.276n.

The terms of the treaty which Duchemin was empowered to negotiate had been laid down by Souillac. Castries learned of them only on 10 April, when he wrote to the governor to express his disapproval, by which time of course the negotiations had been concluded. It seems surprising that, well before this, Castries had not specifically laid down the terms which should be put forward to Hyder; or, if he did, that Souillac proposed a treaty that did not follow his instructions.

Suffren was not a party to these negotiations. He recognised that the disembarkation of the troops must await the outcome of the discussions, and that he must for the moment remain at Porto Novo. When the disembarkation finally began, it took until 10 March for it to be completed. The news which reached Suffren overland on 12 March that Hughes had returned to Madras sharpened his determination to put to sea. Even more serious was information that reached him on 19 March to the effect (incorrectly) that Hughes now had been joined by the *Sultan* and the *Magnanime*, which would mean that he now had a force equal to Suffren's squadron.

While waiting for the conclusion of the negotiations with Hyder Ali, Suffren was engaged in the slow process of watering his squadron, as well as refitting it after the damage suffered on 17 February. He had been rejoined by those ships of his convoy that had gone to Tranquebar. It was his intention, when he finally put to sea, to sail to Galle, in the south west corner of Ceylon, to pick up the rest of his convoy that had gone there. Meanwhile, he was pleased with the arrival of a convoy from the Ile de France that brought him stores, spars and some seamen. Nevertheless, the squadron was still considerably short of its full complement.[3] Suffren enjoyed one other piece of good fortune when the *Bellone*, on 1 March, captured the sloop *Chaser*, which was found to be carrying no less than 12 lakhs of rupees from Bengal to Madras.

Suffren finally, to his great relief, was able to put to sea on 23 March. He had an open mind as to the next step which he should take. The most tempting objective was Trincomali, but he did not know the strength of the garrison there, or whether he could count on any support from the Dutch if he should attempt to take it. On 27 March he wrote to Souillac to set out the possible courses of action which he had in mind: 'I might try to retake Trincomali; or I might attack the settlements in Sumatra or those to the northward of Madras except Masulipatam; and, according to circumstances go up the Ganges ... But in the end no plan can possibly be made until I have had a second action with the English squadron.'[4]

Once he was at sea again, Suffren's spirits had risen considerably. He intended to keep up the pressure on the British, notwithstanding the orders which he carried requiring him to return to the Ile de France in March to refit and strengthen, before returning to the Coromandel coast in April. In not returning to Port Louis, Suffren was taking a different course from his predecessors in their cruises in the Indian Ocean:

> Suffren had made this promise to himself when he sailed from Port Louis; he would remain permanently in the waters of Coromandel and Ceylon. This was a true strategic conception. India, like all colonial territory, could

---

3 Richmond, *Navy in India*, p.205.
4 Richmond, *Navy in India*, p.206.

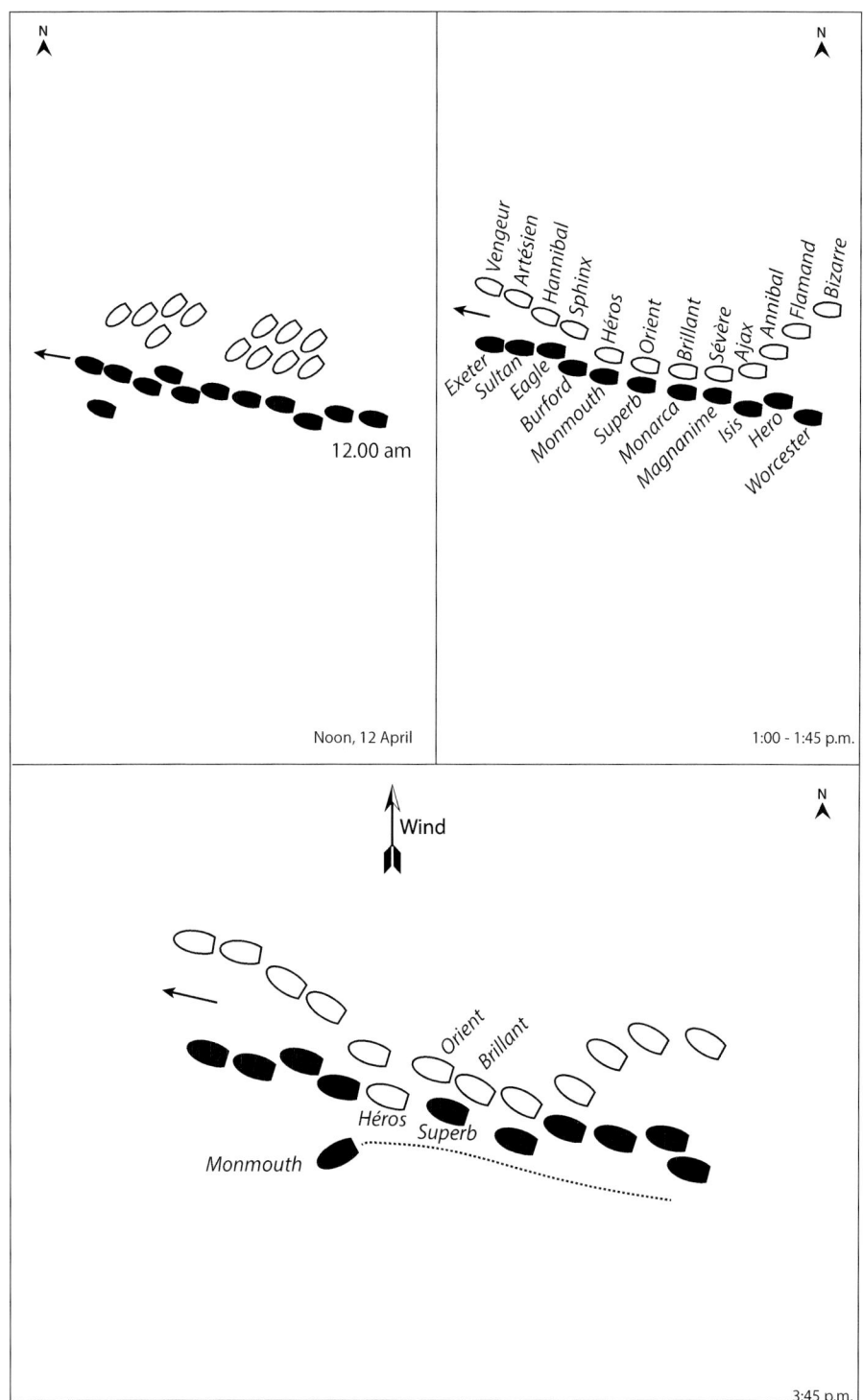

The Battle of Provedien, based on a map in Cavaliero, *Admiral Satan*.

not itself confer naval power; to hold an empire in India, it was necessary to begin by commanding the sea, with squadrons. These truths, which Suffren perceived in the application of his military intelligence, convinced him of the absolute necessity not to depart from the boundaries of the Bay of Bengal; there he was, and there he would remain.[5]

Suffren preferred to seek out Hughes as soon as he could, and not waste time proceeding to the Ile de France and back. He was perfectly aware that this course of action, as well as being an act of disobedience, would be most unwelcome to those of his officers who would be glad to exchange the demanding task of seeking and fighting Hughes for the opportunity to remain in Port Louis. Remaining on the coast would be a significant reassurance to Hyder Ali, and his combative spirit yearned to have another crack at the British squadron.

The improvement of Suffren's morale appears from the letter which he wrote to Mme. de Seillans on 1 April:

> The English have not appeared again since the combat of 17 February. I am on the sea; I would very much like to give you good news shortly, but for that it is necessary to meet and fight the English. I am in a superb position, commanding 12 ships of the line ... I now very much fear that M. de Castries may grant my prayer to return which I had made to him, as nowhere else could I be employed in such a brilliant way.[6]

As Suffren made his way southwards down the Coromandel coast, Duchemin, at Porto Novo, was finally preparing to embark on operations with the force under his command. Rather than Negapatam, the target which Suffren had suggested, he proposed to march north from Porto Novo on Cuddalore. This was a small British outpost garrisoned by a force of some 400 sepoys under the command of Captain James Hughes, and it did not take long to reduce it. By 8 April it was in French hands. There are two views as to just how valuable an acquisition this was. Sen described it as so unhealthy that the French made their camp some four miles to the north of Cuddalore at Manjukuppam. Richmond, on the other hand, regarded it as of major importance: 'The French were thereby put in position of an anchorage of great value, more convenient for the embarkation of supplies than Madras, in consequence of the sheltered river into which the boats could come. With the whole district in their hands, the squadron could now be supplied from the resources of the country which the Mysoreans had at their disposal. Without Cuddalore, Suffren could not have remained on the coast. His nearest base must have been Batticaloa.'[7]

Meanwhile Hughes had also been subject to considerable frustration in the weeks that followed the Battle of Sadras. Once the action had ended, he took his battered squadron southward to Trincomali, towing the dismasted *Exeter* all the way. In consequence of this, it took him some eight days to reach his destination

---

5   Lacour-Gayet, *marine militaire*, p.507.
6   Sen, *French in India*, p.244.
7   Sen, *French in India*, p.280; Richmond, *Navy in India*, p.209.

where, in the space of a week, he was able to refit the squadron. Before leaving, he was encouraged by Major General Medows to strengthen the garrison, which was palpably inadequate, and Hughes landed two officers and 50 men, a step which was subsequently disapproved by Coote. Hughes, on leaving Trincomali, set off at once for Madras to which he returned on 9 March. There, he found that the situation on land had not improved since the disaster to Braithwaite's force. Though Coote had successfully fought three times against Hyder's army, and had relieved Vellore, Hyder still occupied most of the Carnatic. Duchemin was ashore at Porto Novo, a large number of the badly needed grain vessels had been destroyed, and the army was short of pay and on the verge of mutiny.[8]

As soon as he arrived in Madras, Hughes wrote to Macartney to tell him of his immediate intentions which were:

> … to attack the squadron if by position I can bring them to an equal combat, to compleat the stores and provisions of the squadron, to receive such reinforcements as may be sent me from England, and to cover the arrival of our transports that may hourly be expected from Bombay, and if possible keep open the communications with Bengal. These are my present objects.[9]

The transports from Bombay were those which Captain Alms had left behind him when he set off to join Hughes with the *Monmouth*, *Hero* and *Isis*. These had soon followed Alms, reaching Bombay on 22 January, and then setting off for Anjengo. Here, they learned of Suffren's appearance on the Coromandel coast, and paused in view of the obvious danger. Subsequently, after conducting an operation against Cochin, they were ordered by a joint letter from Coote and Hughes to come round to the Coromandel coast.

Hughes, meanwhile, continued to be anxious for the safety of the ill defended Trincomali. In a further letter to Macartney, he insisted that he must sail for its protection, and that he must be given troops with which to strengthen its garrison. This, he now considered, must take precedence over his previous intention to await the arrival of the transports and the reinforcements from Britain. Coote, reluctantly, agreed to part with some troops. When, on 26 March, Hughes learned that Suffren had put to sea, he realised that he could wait no longer, and he sailed for Trincomali on 28 March. His intention was to land his troops there and then cruise in the offing to pick up the transports coming from Anjengo.

Two days later, as he struggled southwards against light winds and northerly currents, a fleet was sighted ahead. To his very great relief, it proved to be the long-awaited *Sultan* and *Magnanime*, escorting a convoy of seven transports carrying the 78th Regiment. Of the 975 rank and file originally embarked, 247 had died of scurvy en route and only 369 were fit to bear arms.[10] They were also accompanied by the East Indiaman *Hinchinbrook*, briefly taken at Porto Praya before her recapture,

---

8 Richmond, *Navy in India*, pp.202–203.
9 Richmond, *Navy in India*, p.203.
10 Anon., *Historical records of the 72d Highlanders, now 1st battalion Seaforth Highlanders, 1777-1886* (Edinburgh: Blackwood, 1886), pp.3–4.

and a small French prize, the *Necker*. Their progress had been slow, having towed the *Necker* all the way from St Helena. At this, Hughes was furious, when he considered what might have been if they had reached him before Sadras: 'Had these ships been conducted with common prudence and the least attention to the orders they were under our superiority would have been decisive.'[11]

If fortune had smiled on Suffren, he might well have been able to intercept the convoy, but if Hughes was lucky that he had not done so, he was disconcerted by the condition in which he found his reinforcements. They were plagued with scurvy, and it was at once apparent that the many sick must be put ashore as soon as possible. Thus, although the addition of two ships of the line brought him up to virtual equality with Suffren, they were both seriously undermanned.[12]

By the time that Hughes met with the *Sultan* and the *Magnanime* and their convoy, Suffren had already been at sea for a week. He could be anywhere. For Hughes, the immediately most vulnerable point was Trincomali, and it was there that he must go as fast as he could. He certainly could not spare the time to return to Madras to offload his scorbutic patients there.

Thus it was that the two commanders were, during the first week of April, sailing southwards towards Ceylon in complete ignorance of each other's movements. For his part Suffren, though he regarded the capture of Trincomali as being an objective of the greatest importance, did not at this time feel strong enough to attempt it. If its garrison was not strong, it seemed to him that with the troops in the missing transports he might be able to attempt it, but it would be helpful if the Dutch could assist with the forces which they had in Ceylon, and during March he wrote twice to the governor of Colombo to ask if he could support an operation against Trincomali.

It was Hughes's hope that he would be able to reach Trincomali before Suffren, in time to secure it against the assault which he correctly divined would be in Suffren's mind. Although Suffren had set off five days before Hughes, he spent a week cruising off Negapatam in the hope of picking up an expected convoy. This did not materialise, and he resumed his journey southwards. He opted to steer to the east of Ceylon and Hughes, bound for Trincomali, naturally did the same. Suffren was some way ahead when the transport *Brisson*, which he had sent off on a separate mission, signalled him at noon on 8 April reporting 14 sail to the north north-west, roughly abreast of the northern tip of Ceylon. Suffren turned north and followed them through the night and on the following morning was able to see for himself that it was indeed the British squadron.[13]

Suffren's immediate objective was quite straightforward; he aimed to fight what he hoped would be a decisive action against the British. Only after that would he be able to consider the alternative courses of action open to him. Hughes, on the other hand, had a problem. He had 11 ships to Suffren's 12, but the new additions to his squadron had had their complements heavily reduced by scurvy. His force carried a total of 724 guns compared to Suffren's 780. Once he knew that he had been spotted by the French, it was apparent to him that he was not going to be able to fight from

---

11 Cavaliero, *Admiral Satan*, p.119.
12 Richmond, *Navy in India*, p.204.
13 Cavaliero, *Admiral Satan*, p.120.

the position of advantage that he had set himself. He must now, therefore, decide what would be the best course of action.

His correspondence and his movements during the next three days leave no doubt that that which dominated his mind was the security of Trincomali, which he regarded as the principal object of the moment to get his reinforcements into the fortress. We have seen how the weakness of the garrison had been his constant anxiety, how he had pressed the government for additional troops ever since he had obtained possession of the place. Nothing was more deeply impressed upon his mind than that if he were worsted in an engagement with the superior forces of the enemy, Trincomali would fall like a ripe fruit into the hands of the French, who had not only the forces of the squadron at their disposal but might be expected to receive further help on land from the Dutch at Jaffna.[14]

Hughes's fears were entirely justified. Even before he left Porto Novo, Suffren had formed the opinion that once he had collected his missing ships at Galle he would probably have sufficient strength to take Trincomali. He was in correspondence with Governor Iman Willem Falck at Colombo, and although their letters had crossed and no plan had yet been made, the Dutchman, when learning of Suffren's departure from Porto Novo, had given orders for the force which he had on standby at Jaffna to move towards Trincomali. In his last letter to Suffren, dated 5 April, which did not arrive until after the imminent battle, Falck had written: 'Never would the moment be more favourable for an attack. Pagoda Hill would probably surrender without firing a shot, while Ostenburg, manned by a garrison composed of Swiss mercenaries and discontented and discouraged sepoys, would certainly never expose itself to the penalties of being taken by assault.'[15]

In addition, Suffren learned by a stroke of good fortune on 10 April all that he needed to know about the garrison at Trincomali, when he captured a brig carrying Hugh Boyd, Lord Macartney's secretary, who was returning from an abortive mission to the King of Kandy. Macartney had sent him to carry a proposal for a joint offensive against the Dutch to drive them out of Ceylon. Once this was done, he planned for a joint offensive against Hyder by landing on the Malabar coast, which would not only secure Trincomali but would result in a large and rich island falling under the influence of the Company and would lead to Hyder's abandoning the Carnatic. Unfortunately, the King was unimpressed by the plan, so Boyd was returning empty-handed when his brig was captured by the *Fine*.[16] Boyd was carrying all his papers and despatches, which disclosed to Suffren just how weak was the garrison of Trincomali, with 60 European troops and 450 sepoys of doubtful fighting value.

The problem which confronted Hughes was extremely difficult, which was how, with 11 ships, nine of which had left Madras 600 men short of complement and two more seriously weakened by disease, he was to get into Trincomali in the face of what was manifestly a superior force. He could achieve this in one of two ways; he must either attack this superior squadron and beat it so that he could then force his

---

14 Richmond, *Navy in India*, p.211.
15 Richmond, *Navy in India*, p.212.
16 Cavaliero, *Admiral Satan*, p.120.

way into Trincomali or he must circumvent it. For the moment, he had the weather gauge:

> To force his way in he must defeat the enemy who lay directly in his path. A defeat of that enemy could result only from superiority in some form; tactical skill, technical skill, or personal or individual skill, which singly or in combination, would counterbalance the superior numbers in ships, and their supposed superiority in numbers and health of the personnel. Hughes was not a man of original tactical ideas. All of his fighting makes it clear that he was simply a man of his time whose tactical doctrine was summed up in a well locked up line of battle with his strongest ships in the centre.[17]

Hughes was not, therefore, the man to attempt anything in the way of a tactical innovation, such as concentrating his whole force on part of the enemy, which would be the only way which he could overcome Suffren's superiority. He may or may not have formed any conclusion as to the likely performance of Suffren's captains based on what he had seen of them on 17 February at Sadras. As it was, to attack Suffren in the traditional manner was unlikely to produce the result he needed. Hughes accordingly decided that he must endeavour to circumvent the enemy in order to get into Trincomali. He might be able to do this by drawing Suffren in pursuit in the hope of being able to gain some kind of advantage or alternatively by out sailing the French and slipping into Trincomali across their track. Richmond, reviewing what happened over the next few days, considers that the latter course is the one that Hughes had decided to take:

> It offered greater prospects of success than fighting against odds where he then was. Once Trincomali was rendered secure and his sickly crews restored to health he could act as he said he would, and as at a later time he did; and seek the enemy. In the meantime to fight at a disadvantage when by a postponement the disadvantage would be reduced, was not only to risk a reverse but the loss of the British possessions in India.[18]

Suffren had applied a similar principle in February, when he first came upon Hughes at Madras, which was not to risk a defeat which might ruin his whole campaign.

As the two squadrons manoeuvred for position, Suffren might have been able to force an action on 10 April if he had had all of his ships in hand, but his rear division was lagging behind. By the following morning Hughes and Suffren had reached the latitude of Trincomali, and the British admiral made an attempt to dash into the port, setting studding sails and beating to quarters. However, the wind failed, and at sunset he was obliged to turn south and attempt to work his way to windward of the French. He was approaching the coast of Ceylon and unluckily misjudged how close he was to the shore, which he only realised at dawn on 12 April, by which time

---

17 Richmond, *Navy in India*, p.215.
18 Richmond, *Navy in India*, p.216.

Suffren was only seven or eight miles away.[19] Hughes was now obliged to accept that his efforts to evade the enemy had failed. In his later report of the battle, he wrote:

> On the 12th, at daylight, the position of the enemy's squadron being altered by my bearing away, so as to give them the wind of ours, I discovered them crowding all the sail they could set after us; and their copper bottomed ships coming fast up with the ships in our rear; I therefore determined to engage them. At nine in the forenoon I made the signal for the line of battle ahead on the starboard tack, at two cables' length distance; the enemy then bearing N by E, distant 6 miles, and the wind at N by E.[20]

Suffren, therefore, thus firmly had the windward gauge, and it would only be a matter of time before the squadrons engaged. As he approached, dark clouds heralded an approaching storm; in the sultry air, and there were occasional rain showers. The two squadrons were now close to a small coral island, known to the Dutch as Provedien, which lay some 30 miles to the south of Trincomali: 'The distance between the squadrons, which lessened with each minute that passed and the proximity of the land gave the English Admiral no chance of avoiding battle.'[21] All Hughes could do was wait.

Perhaps in the hope of avoiding any misunderstanding on the part of his captains, Suffren determined to engage Hughes in a classic ship for ship action, intending that his rearmost ship should then be free to double the last ship in the British line. With the north-east wind behind him, he bore down on Hughes's squadron in line abreast, intending that it should not turn into line ahead parallel with the enemy until it had closed to pistol shot range. As the French approached, Hughes was sailing west north west; it was now plain that he could not avoid an engagement. He described the enemy as 'manoeuvring their ships, and changing their positions in the line, till a quarter past noon; when they bore away to engage us.'[22]

In preparing for the French attack, Hughes had got his squadron into a reasonably well-ordered line. Suffren, on the other hand, owing to the light wind and the fact that his squadron had become somewhat scattered, and perhaps also because his captains were once again demonstrating that they were not as good seamen as their opponents, was experiencing some difficulty in getting his ships into position as they bore down. As they neared the British line, the fitful north-east wind somewhat strengthened, which tended to increase the disordered state in which the French were approaching. Suffren had posted his coppered ships so that they would constitute his van, the *Vengeur* and *Artésien* leading the *Petit Annibal* and the *Sphinx*. Next came the *Héros*, followed by the *Orient*, *Brillant*, *Sévére*, *Ajax*, *Annibal* and *Flamand*, with the *Bizarre* bringing up the rear in position to double the last British ship, which was the *Worcester*.

---

19 Cavaliero, *Admiral Satan*, p.121.
20 Ekins, *Naval Battles*, p.185.
21 Lacour-Gayet, *marine militaire*, p.509.
22 Ekins, *Naval Battles*, p.165.

As the French squadron stretched out, the distances between the ships increased, and the faster coppered ships drew further ahead, while the rearmost ships fell further and further behind. The *Vengeur* and *Artésien* were the first to come within range of the leading British ships, the *Exeter* and the *Sultan*. These were followed by the *Eagle* and the *Burford*. Forbin, in the *Vengeur*, prematurely luffed in order to bring his broadside to bear, but well short of the close range intended by Suffren. The *Artésien* followed suit, and both ships held off at a distance. Suffren signalled to them to resume their original tack in order to close with the British, but neither did so.

Aboard the *Héros*, Suffren made for the British centre, which he closed to pistol shot range before luffing to take up a course parallel to the British. In the first instance he headed for Hughes's flagship *Superb*, sixth in the British line. Immediately ahead of her was the *Monmouth*, while behind her came the *Monarca* and the *Magnanime*. The *Héros* was soon supported by the *Orient* and the *Brillant*, while ahead of her the *Petit Annibal* and *Sphinx* complied with Suffren's signals to close the range, engaging the *Eagle* and *Burford* respectively. Firing had begun at about 1:30 p.m.

Suffren's worst sailers were accordingly well behind the stations intended when firing commenced. Mahan quotes Chevalier as he described the position of the French rear:

> Breathing the letter, and not the spirit of the Commodore's orders, the captains of these ships luffed at the same time as those preceding them. Hence it resulted that the French line formed a curve, whose extremities were represented in the van by the *Artésien* and *Vengeur*, and in the rear by the *Bizarre*, *Ajax* and *Sévére*. In consequence, these ships were very far from those which corresponded to them in the enemy's line.[23]

In fact, the *Sévére*, following the *Brillant*, was the closest of the rear division, and was then herself followed by the *Ajax*, *Annibal*, *Flamand* and finally the *Bizarre*.

As a result of the disposition of the French ships, the engagement began with a fierce action between the five ships each of the British and French centres, with the *Petit Annibal*, *Sphinx*, *Héros*, *Orient*, and *Brillant* engaged with the *Eagle*, *Burford*, *Monmouth*, *Superb* and *Monarca*. This chance distribution gave Hughes an unexpected advantage; with one 74, two 70s and two 64s he could deliver a broadside of 163 guns, while the French ships, consisting of two 74s, two 64s and one 50 had a collective broadside of 141 guns. As the battle developed, however, this theoretical advantage in numbers of guns was cancelled out by the French concentration of fire, which was largely directed at the *Monmouth* and *Superb*.[24]

Hughes formed a slightly different impression of the way in which the battle began. Perhaps not able to see entirely clearly what was going on ahead and astern of the action in the centre, he described the opening phase in these terms:

---

23 Mahan, *Influence of Sea Power*, p.440.
24 Richmond, *Navy in India*, p.219.

> Five ships of their van stretched along to engage the van of the British squadron, and the other seven steered directly on our centre ships, the *Superb*, the *Monmouth* and the *Monarca*. At 1:30 the engagement began in the van, and I made the signal for battle. The French Admiral and his second bore down within pistol shot of the *Superb*; the *Héros* then stood on to attack the *Monmouth*, at that time engaged with another ship; making room for the ships in his rear to come up to the attack of our centre, where the engagement was hottest.[25]

The concentration of fire on the British centre resulted in particularly heavy damage being suffered by the *Monmouth*. The *Héros*, at first engaged with the *Superb*, had one of her braces severed and, unable to back her topsails in time, she shot up and found herself closely engaged with the *Monmouth*. Suffren was now flying the signal for all his squadron to engage close action, and first the *Orient* and then also the *Brillant* were concentrating their fire on the *Superb*, which also began to sustain heavy damage. The *Héros* continued to hammer the *Monmouth*, whose master described her ordeal:

> As soon as within gunshot we engaged the enemy's third ship which passed under a press of sail. The French Admiral lying upon our Admiral's bow and his second ahead of him [the *Sphinx*], we being our Admiral's second and ahead of him on that tack and supposing that the French Admiral was going to board ours, luffed up to rake him, backed our mizzen topsail which brought us within pistol shot of M. de Suffrein and in that situation we engaged him and two more ahead from three quarters after one to three when our mizzenmast fell over the stern and soon after the mainmast over the larboard quarter.[26]

The *Monmouth* fought the *Héros*, *Sphinx* and *Petit Annibal* for the best part of an hour and a quarter, and had a very hard time of it, her colours being twice shot away. Seven of her guns were dismounted, and Captain Alms was struck in the face by splinters, while two musket balls went through his hat, his hair was set on fire, and his coat torn between his shoulders. By now only two people remained on the quarterdeck.[27] With two of her masts gone, the *Monmouth* was reduced to an unmanageable wreck, and drifted slowly out of line, 'floating like a piece of flotsam.'[28] In an effort to protect her, Hughes, in the *Superb*, edged to windward of the *Héros*, but was then thwarted as a violent explosion shook his flagship, and the *Orient* and *Brillant* came up between her and the *Héros*. The *Monmouth*, meanwhile, drifted slowly to the rear, and as they passed her the remaining French ships each poured their fire into her.

---

25 Ekins, *Naval Battles*, p.185.
26 Richmond, *Navy in India*, pp.220–221.
27 Cavaliero, *Admiral Satan*, p.124.
28 Lacour-Gayet, *marine militaire*, p.514.

Hughes was by now becoming concerned that his ships were approaching dangerously close to land, and at 3:40 p.m. he made the signal to wear, and to form line of battle on the port tack.[29] His ships executed this order with admirable precision, but when Suffren also gave the order to wear, it was much less efficiently carried out. The *Vengeur* and *Artésien* were much too slow in completing the manoeuvre, leaving them out of touch with the enemy, while the *Ajax* turned the wrong way, so that she was temporarily blown out of line altogether. The mainsail of the *Orient* caught fire, and her crew became fully engaged in extinguishing it.

While these manoeuvres were taking place, and before the engagement was fully renewed, the *Hero* succeeded in getting a towline aboard the *Monmouth*, so that for the moment she was out of danger. Suffren shouted orders through his speaking trumpet to the *Artésien* to intercept them, but to his frustration this was to no avail. He was soon in trouble himself, when at 5:30 p.m. the *Héros* lost her foretopgallant yard. Accordingly, leaving Moissac in command of the *Héros*, Suffren transferred to the *Ajax*, and could now see from her quarterdeck just how close to the land the two sides were.

At 5:40 p.m. Hughes, who continued to be anxious about the proximity of the shoreline, and in particular the risk to the *Monmouth*, took action. The squadron was at that time in 15 fathoms of water, but it was shelving fast, and he made the signal to the squadron to prepare to anchor. An hour later, according to his report, 'the enemy drew off in great disorder to the eastward, and the engagement ceased; and soon after I anchored with the squadron, the *Superb* close to the *Monmouth*, to repair our damages, which were very great; and all the ships had suffered considerably in their masts, sails, and rigging etc.'[30] It was not a moment too soon; the *Monmouth* had already touched bottom by the time Hughes gave the order to anchor. What he did not, however, mention in his report of the ending of the battle was that the storm, which had been threatening all day, now burst, with torrential rain, and soon the crews of both squadrons were more heavily engaged in preserving their ships than in taking any notice of the enemy in their midst.

Some of the French ships had already grounded briefly. As darkness fell the intensity of the storm increased. The *Orient* and the *Héros* dropped anchor in seven fathoms. So close were they to the British ships that they could hear their crews calling to one another.[31] Suffren now ordered Salvert in the *Fine* to take the *Héros* in tow, and the frigate succeeded in getting a line aboard her. However, in the darkness the *Fine* became entangled with the *Isis* and caught her bowsprit in the British vessel's shrouds. At first no one aboard her knew what had happened. It was only the men aloft who realised that they had run into a British vessel, while in the chaotic situation a number of British prisoners on the *Fine* endeavoured to escape. Running to the quarterdeck, Captain the Honourable Thomas Lumley of the *Isis* shouted through his speaking trumpet that if the French gunners fired, he would blast the *Fine* out of the water. Receiving no reply, he thought that Salvert had surrendered and prepared to send men aboard the *Fine*. At that moment the *Orient* appeared and

---

29 Ekins, *Naval Battles*, p.185.
30 Ekins, *Naval Battles*, p.186.
31 Lacour-Gayet, *marine militaire*, p.512.

sliced through the tow rope and thus rescued the frigate from her entanglement.[32] In the confusion the *Ajax* grounded briefly, and for a moment Suffren believed that she might be lost.[33]

Moissac now found himself aboard the *Héros* at the mercy of the winds; he put a spring on his cable and hoped for a change in the weather. Luckily for him, at 9:30 p.m., this came when the wind went round to the south-west, and cutting his cable he sailed clear and anchored alongside the *Ajax*. It had dropped anchor, with the rest of the squadron, at about two miles east of the British. The weather now relented, and when the sun came up the respective admirals were able each to take stock of their opponent.

To Hughes, it seemed that the French appeared to be 'in much disorder and apparent distress, but they had lost no lower masts', while in his own squadron 'all the ships had suffered considerably in their masts, sails and rigging etc.'[34] On 13 April, and in the days following, both squadrons were busily engaged in effecting such repairs as they could. Hughes was still particularly anxious for the safety of the *Monmouth*, which he feared that Suffren might attempt to capture. He re-anchored his ships in a good line with springs on their cables to secure himself against attack and continued the work of repair. He sent to the *Monmouth* all the carpenters and artificers of the squadron to prepare her for a journey in the open sea.

Losses during the battle had been considerable. Total British casualties were 137 killed and 430 wounded. These were unevenly distributed, those suffered by the *Monmouth* and *Superb* accounting for 104 killed and 198 wounded. The *Isis* had suffered total casualties of 57, the *Exeter* 44, the *Monarca* 35, the *Worcester* 34 and the *Burford* 32. The remaining ships got off much more lightly. In the French squadron the total losses of 138 killed and 357 wounded were much more evenly shared. Not surprisingly, in view of the ineffective part she had played, the *Vengeur* had suffered least, with just two men wounded. Hardest hit had been the *Sphinx* and the *Orient*, each with 98 total casualties. Whatever Suffren may have thought of Tromelin, it is noteworthy that the next highest loss was suffered by the *Annibal*, which sustained total casualties of 45, suggesting that she had been heavily engaged.[35]

Hughes considered that the outcome of the battle had been a draw. Reviewing the damage suffered by each squadron, he thought it about equal, adding 'nor had either side any just cause to brag of a victory over the other. Night brought an end to the battle at the time it had become most critical by both squadrons being disordered and both having disabled ships to protect.'[36]

Mahan, on the other hand, regarded the battle as having been a success for the French. He based this conclusion on Suffren's despatches and on the accounts of various French historians:

> The practical advantage gained by the French must also be tested by comparing the lists of casualties, and the injuries received by their

---

32 Cavaliero, *Admiral Satan*, pp.125–126.
33 Lacour-Gayet, *marine militaire*, p.511.
34 Cavaliero, *Admiral Satan*, p.126; Ekins, *Naval Battles*, p.186.
35 Richmond, *Navy in India*, p.220.
36 Richmond, *Navy in India*, p.222.

individual ships; for it is evident that if both the squadrons received the same total amount of injury, but that with the English it fell on two ships, so that they could not be ready for action for a month or more, while with the French the damage was divided among the twelve, allowing them to be ready again in a few days, the victory tactically and strategically would rest with the latter.[37]

Against this, of course, it could be claimed for Hughes that he eventually attained his principal purpose, when he was later able to take his squadron into the harbour at Trincomali.

Mahan noted also that there was subsequently some unfavourable criticism of the management of the battle by Hughes 'because he refrained from attacking the French, although they were for much of the time to leeward with only one ship more than the English and much separated at that. It was thought that he had the opportunity of beating them in detail.' He added that 'the accounts accessible are too meagre to permit an accurate judgement upon this opinion.' In his view, Hughes was adhering to his basic objective in declining any opportunity to attack the enemy, since this was to get in to Trincomali and reinforce the garrison. The fact that, having put this first, he then could be criticised, indicated 'how strongly the English held that the attack of the enemy's fleet was the first duty of an English Admiral.'[38]

During the following days, the two squadrons worked energetically at making repairs. It was not until 17 April that Suffren felt that his squadron was in a state to renew the action, but in the meantime he had written to Castries on the day before to explain why he had not ventured an attack on the British in the position which they had taken up at anchor:

> I owe you a justification for not having attacked the enemy in the position he had taken up on the coast.
> 1. The uncertainty as to a coral shoal to seaward of them, on which the *Ajax*, *Orient* and *Fine* struck on 12 April.
> 2. In operations of this kind, all is lost unless one succeeds.
> 3. I have at present enough ammunition for one battle only.
> 4. Shortage of men.
> 5. No means of repairing my rigging.
> 6. The squadron is lacking in 12 spare top masts.
> 7. I intend first to go to Galle where I shall find cordage, some ammunition and some men.
> 8. To make that attempt with any real hope of success, capacity, goodwill etc are needed; and assuredly I have experienced the want of them too greatly thus to risk all for all.[39]

---

37 Mahan, *Influence of Sea Power*, p.434.
38 Mahan, *Influence of Sea Power*, p.442.
39 Richmond, *Navy in India*, pp.224–225.

Of these eight reasons, Richmond took the view that only two were really weighty. These were 'the difficulty and risk of failure in an attack on a fleet in an anchorage, and the want of confidence in his captains.' A well anchored fleet was always to be regarded as a serious deterrent, but it was the question of confidence in his captains that was the most serious. They had failed him again on 12 April in an attack that was entirely orthodox; an attack in the present circumstances would require much more of them. Two were particularly deficient; five others had behaved indifferently, and although Tromelin appeared to have behaved better this time, Suffren still had his doubts.

A serious consideration was the extent to which his squadron was shorthanded; Suffren was some 600 below complement after the battle and he had a considerable number of sick. He was not aware of the situation in Hughes's squadron, which had been reduced to half strength, and the fact that Suffren landed a large number of men, including his wounded, when he did finally make port shows that his situation in this respect was extremely grave. Trublet described the condition of the squadron after the battle of Provedien, when it finally reached Batticaloa:

> Scurvy was making frightful ravages in the fleet: 1,500 men suffering from it were landed; the medicines on board the ships had all been used; the capture of the hospital ship had deprived us of all further supply. The country (round Batticaloa) was unhealthy; and though there was plenty of fish and game; though we obtained, through the Dutch governor, a few wretched bullocks, it was impossible to get either fruit or vegetables, things which are the most powerful, if not the only remedy against the disease. In addition to this, the damage sustained by many of our ships, rendering it necessary for them to be docked; our supply of rope exhausted; the provisions running short; the crews, sadly diminished in number, overworked; the certainty of more battles, in which we could not promise ourselves any advantage more decisive than those in which we had fought – all these were considerations which threw a dark cloud over our future prospects, and gave rise to the most embarrassing reflections.[40]

Nevertheless, on 18 April Suffren got under sail and stood off and on the British anchorage in the hope that Hughes might come out and fight. But the *Monmouth* had not yet been re-masted and rigged, and Hughes was not tempted to do so; only if Suffren directly made for Trincomali would he take the risk of fighting in his present state. On 19 April Suffren tried again to provoke a combat, but Hughes remained at anchor. Accordingly, at 3:00 p.m. the French bore away to Batticaloa to refit. Suffren sent the *Diligente* round to Galle to call the convoy waiting there to come to meet him at Batticaloa. Hughes watched Suffren go philosophically. He later reported:

> Both squadrons continued at anchor till the 19th in the morning, when the enemy's got under sail with the land wind, and stood out to sea close hauled;

---

40 Laughton, *Naval Studies*, pp.122–123.

and at noon tacked with the sea breeze and stood in, as with an intent to attack us; but after coming within two miles, and finding us prepared to receive them, they tacked again and stood away to the eastward; nor have I been able to learn certainly where they have gone.[41]

Suffren's departure meant that Hughes was now free to make his way into Trincomali and thus attain his original object. Jury masts were rigged to the *Monmouth* to get her into harbour, but in fact there had not been time to establish Trincomali as an arsenal or supply port, and when he got there he was obliged to re-mast the *Monmouth* with some difficulty from the spare stores aboard the other ships. Hughes remained in Trincomali until 23 June, when he sailed for Negapatam.

Before leaving Providien, it is appropriate to consider Caron's view of Suffren's conduct of the battle, which, predictably, was extremely critical. Referring to the way in which the squadron approached the British, he writes: 'This unfortunate disposition leads one to consider the manner of Suffren's command. This last militates in favour of considerable autonomy on the part of his subordinates. At least, so Castex affirms, even though his hero had most often displayed a decided taste for authoritarianism.'[42]

Caron goes on to point out that Suffren, when serving as a subordinate, had demonstrated an extremely independent spirit, notably when commanding the *Fantasque* under d'Estaing, to whom he frequently conveyed his views in strong terms, 'but as for the opinion of his own subordinates, he took not the slightest interest.' Caron suggests that throughout the battle he paid no attention to their movements, without conceding to them any freedom of action, yet felt able seriously to criticise them after the end of the battle: 'It is necessary either to give precise orders or to delegate authority. Suffren never did either.' This, like a number of Caron's other conclusions, is scarcely fair. He did give instructions, but they were not faithfully carried out by all his subordinates and the course of his battles would have been very different if they had done so.

---

41 Ekins, *Naval Battles*, p.186.
42 Caron, *Mythe de Suffren*, p.293.

13

Negapatam

Suffren had very good reason to be discontented with the performance of some of his captains during the battle of Provedien. Particularly disappointing had been the timorous performance of his cousin Forbin, in the *Vengeur*, whose failure to engage the enemy properly was indicated by the fact that he suffered only two men wounded during the course of the battle. The *Artésien*, under Maurville, did manage to get rather closer to the enemy, as her casualty list of 12 men killed and 20 wounded showed. But if these two ships had played the part expected of them, Hughes would have found himself in a much graver situation. At the other end of the French line, Tromelin in the *Annibal* did ultimately become seriously engaged with the *Isis*, and suffered considerable casualties as evidence of this, but the *Flamand* and *Bizarre* were even later in closing with the enemy.[1]

In his letter to Castries of 16 April, Suffren had spelt out his extreme dissatisfaction:

> I cannot go into detail; but if, in this squadron, we do not change five or six captains – that is to say, half – we will never achieve anything and perhaps miss every opportunity. M. le Comte du Chilleau, the captain of the *Sphinx*, vigorously attacked the *Burford*, which was the ship ahead of the *Monmouth* – M. le Comte du Chilleau, with whom I was discontented at La Praya, who conducted himself well on 17 February, conducted himself in this last affair with the greatest distinction; and if all the ships had done the same, the English squadron would be no more. We are still in their presence. We are going to have a third affair. I do not know what I shall do afterwards.[2]

He went on gloomily to add that he would perhaps have no more masts, rope, powder or shot, and that he had lost about 500 men, of whom half were dead or dying. But this pessimistic report had not prevented him from offering battle on 18 and 19 April, and by the time he sailed for Batticaloa he was turning his mind to his next thrust at the enemy.

He was handicapped by the fact that Batticaloa offered only a reasonable anchorage, but was entirely without facilities or stores for repairs, so that he was largely obliged to do the best he could from his own limited resources. The Dutch did let him have some quantities of ammunition and rope, though they expected to

---

1 Richmond, *Navy in India*, p.220.
2 Lacour-Gayet, *marine militaire*, pp.512–514.

receive payment for this, but they could provide none of the larger spars which he needed.³

When Suffren arrived at Batticaloa, he was dismayed to find the *Pulvériseur* there with despatches from Souillac. The governor of the Ile de France passed on to him the orders from Versailles that Suffren should leave the Coromandel coast and return to Port Louis to await the arrival of the expeditionary force which the French government had decided to send out to India. This was led by Charles Joseph Patissier, Marquis de Bussy, who had retired two decades earlier after a 20-year career of glittering military success in India. In that time he had become the effective ruler of the central plateau of southern India that constituted the Nizamate of Hyderabad.

These orders, with the information relating to the composition of the force which Bussy would be bringing, had been drafted as long ago as November 1781, and of course took no account of what had been happening in the meantime. Bussy had spelt out to the government the minimum strength of the force that would be needed. In the event, Castries was only able to promise 6–7,000 men, rather than the 9,000 which Bussy had specified, and a budget of five million livres in cash, compared to the 10 million for which Bussy had asked. He also guaranteed naval superiority. Bussy was, however, given a commission as *lieutenant-général* with the command of all French land and sea forces in the East.⁴

Suffren had no intention of carrying out the orders to leave the Coromandel coast. He explained in a trenchant letter to Souillac his reasons:

> At Batticaloa … I found the *Pulvériseur* which handed over to me the duplicate of the despatches sent by the corvette, *Expédition*. Let us pass over the regrets of the past and examine the present situation. The intention of the King was that the squadron should return (to the Isle of France) in March and start back at the end of April, reinforced and repaired; that is no longer possible. Forty five days carrying the troops to Ceylon; forty for the voyage, forty five for repairs, thirty for the return voyage, in all 160 days. That would mean a loss of six months, and God alone knows what the enemies can undertake during that time. It would be wrongly interpreting the intentions of the King and of yours to undertake at the end of April what you had thought of at the end of February; and if after my repeated assurances not to leave the coast, and if after the certainty that you might arrive at from the news sent by the *Bons Amis* and the *Chasseur* that the corvette had not arrived here yet, you had thought it too late and had sent the convoy already in response to my repeated demands, what would I do in the Isle of France? Moreover, if I quit the coast after my combats, M. Hughes, whom I had defeated on 17 February and 12 April, would not fail to declare that I myself had been defeated.⁵

---

3 Richmond, *Navy in India*, p.230.
4 Cavaliero, *Admiral Satan*, p.131.
5 Sen, *French in India*, p.247.

In particular, Suffren was concerned that leaving the coast meant the abandonment of Duchemin, the possible capture of Ceylon by the British (a threat which was greatly agitating Falck, the governor of Colombo), the possibility that Hyder might come to terms with the British, and effectively ceding to Hughes complete control of the Bay of Bengal. These considerations seemed obvious, but Suffren was not surprised to receive representations from some of his captains, who had not yet heard of the orders to return to the Ile de France, that this would be the right course to adopt. At first, he firmly refused to call a council of war to discuss the issue, which is what they had suggested, but on thinking it over decided to do so, in order to spell out to them, in terms incapable of being misunderstood, what he intended to do:

> I have, gentlemen, only a few words to say to you. I have decided to remain in India and you know why as well as I. What, perhaps, you do not know is the tenor of His Majesty's general instructions which dictate what we should do. I know them by heart, and they run like this: The wisdom of His Majesty does not attempt to determine any particular operation. He knows that, 4,000 leagues away, it would be unwise to do so, and he limits himself as a result to informing M. le Comte d'Orves that the inactivity of the squadron is what he principally forbids ... It would be better to sink the squadron under the walls of Madras than to retire from before Sir Edward Hughes. If anyone of your men believe that I am capable of such an act of cowardice, let him come and tell me, and I shall tell him what I have decided. You may inform your officers and men that these are my orders.[6]

To his credit, Souillac entirely accepted Suffren's reasoning. He wrote to Castries on 18 June, justifying Suffren's decision to remain in Indian waters:

> Consider, Monseigneur, the turn that affairs in India might have taken during this long interval; Hyder Ali would have surely made peace with the English; all the other Indian Princes, who are watching the issue of the conflict to decide their policy, would have shown themselves more submissive than ever to a nation whom they do not love but fear; our troops on the mainland would have been faced with a grave danger and it would have been rather fortunate if they could have passed on to Ceylon, against which all the efforts of the English would have been directed. It may then be said that the bold policy which M. de Suffren has adopted has saved India and prepared the success of M. Marquis de Bussy.[7]

The progress of Bussy's expedition was, however, very disappointing. He sailed from Cadiz on 4 January 1782 aboard the *Saint Michel*, 60. Accompanying this vessel were the *Illustre*, 74, the frigate *Consolante*, the cutter *Lezard*, and three transports. The intention was that these would join a convoy sailing from Brest under de Guichen, part intended for the West Indies, and part for India. Bussy and his squadron

---

6   Cavaliero, *Admiral Satan*, p.133.
7   Sen, *French in India*, p.248.

arrived at the agreed rendezvous at the Canary Islands to find the convoy had not arrived there. Two of the transports from Brest, carrying his heavy artillery, turned up later at the Cape. The rest had fallen victim to an attack by Rear Admiral Richard Kempenfelt's squadron, which took a dozen prizes, the remainder of the convoy returning to Brest. Bussy decided not to wait for another attempt to be made to get the rest of his expedition to sea, and sailed for Table Bay. However the *Illustre* was such a poor sailer that by the time that he arrived there he was well behind schedule; he should by then have already reached the Ile de France. He decided to wait there for the rest of his convoy, and was in the meantime implored by the Dutch governor of the Cape to leave half his force behind in order to defend the province against an anticipated attack by the British. Bussy, who was a martyr to gout, now fell ill, and it was not until 28 April that he finally sailed for the Ile de France, leaving behind 650 men to strengthen the Dutch garrison.[8] Bussy arrived at Port Louis on 31 May.

Another attempt was duly made to send out the rest of Bussy's expeditionary force, which sailed as part of a convoy escorted by another squadron under de Guichen on 11 February. The component destined for India included four ships of the line – two 74s, the *Fendant* and *Argonaute*, and two 64s, the *Hardi* and *Alexandre* – together with the frigate *Cleopatre* and the corvette *Chasseur*. With them sailed 35 transports carrying 2,500 troops and a huge quantity of stores and munitions. This convoy, having lost only one small transport while en route (captured by the *Sceptre*, 64) arrived at the Cape on 19 May. By the time that they got there, however many of the vessels were suffering severely from scurvy, and it was to be a considerable time before they resumed their journey to the Ile de France.[9]

Meanwhile, at Batticaloa, Suffren was completing his repairs and preparing to put to sea. He had been kept informed of the situation of the British squadron at Trincomali. On 2 June it was reported to him that Hughes was still there, that three ships had entered the harbour to refit, that a new mast was being made for the *Monmouth*, and, most importantly, that the squadron had lost a lot of men from sickness, as well as the casualties sustained at Provedien.[10]

Suffren had been joined by his transports from Galle. On 3 June he sailed for Tranquebar and Cuddalore. He paused two weeks at Tranquebar where he sought provisions and naval stores. Three Dutch vessels had arrived there, having sailed from Batavia, heading in the first instance for the east coast of Ceylon, but, finding the British squadron still in Trincomali, had come on to Tranquebar. These supplied some of Suffren's wants, having brought money, munitions, provisions and naval stores. From Hyder Ali there also came a quantity of provisions. On 20 June Suffren sailed on to Cuddalore.[11]

While Suffren had been at Tranquebar he had sent out the *Artésien* and *Sphinx*, with the frigates *Bellone* and *Fine*, to cruise off the coast in search of British merchant shipping. They encountered a small convoy of Company ships, sent by the governor of Fort St George carrying reinforcements for the army operating in Tanjore and

---

8   Malleson, *Final French Struggles*, p.54.
9   Cavaliero, *Admiral Satan*, p.185.
10 Cary, 'Trincomali', p.26.
11 Sen, *French in India*, pp.248–249.

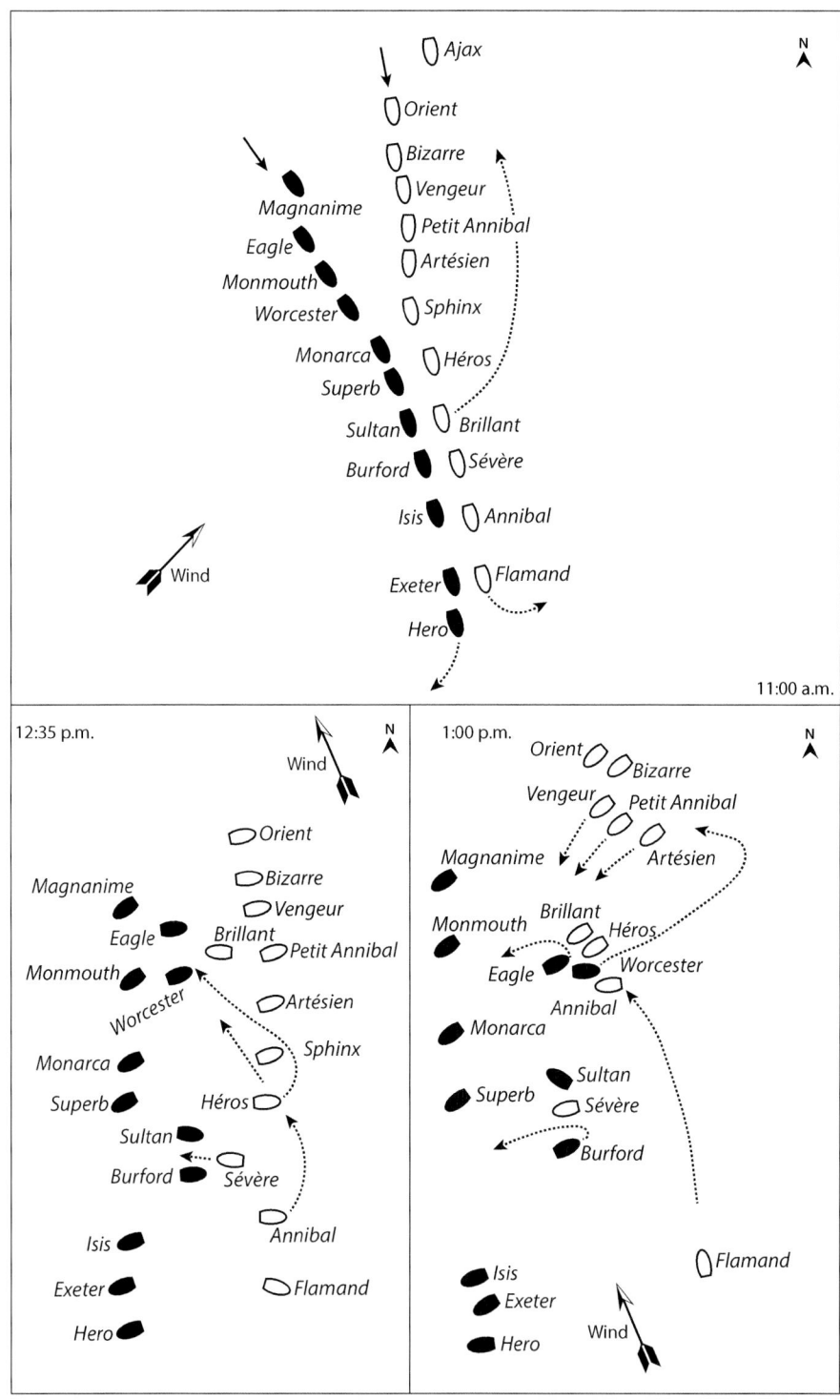

The Battle of Negapatam, based on a map in Cavaliero, *Admiral Satan*.

also for Trincomali. The convoy became divided, and on 7 June the French met three of them. One, carrying a cargo of muskets and field artillery, was quickly taken. The *Artésien* pursued another, carrying 44 guns, and should have captured her, but Maurville called off the chase just as he was about to close with her.[12]

Not surprisingly, Suffren was furious when he heard what had happened, demanding an explanation from Maurville for his failure to capture the enemy transport. According to Lacour-Gayet, du Chilleau, as senior officer in the *Sphinx*, had ordered Maurville expressly to continue the pursuit.[13] Whether or not this was so, there had certainly been no signal from the *Sphinx* ordering him to abandon the chase. If Maurville thought he needed an order to continue, Suffren angrily asked, why did he not ask for one? Maurville was far from contrite in the manner in which he responded, and this made up Suffren's mind; at the first opportunity he would send him back to France in disgrace.

Anchoring off Cuddalore, Suffren strengthened the crews of his squadron with troops from Duchemin's force. He then received news that the British had assembled a force of 2,000 British troops and 5,000 sepoys in the Southern district, which he took to mean that they had been concentrated for a descent on Ceylon. This appeared to confirm the fears which Falck had been repeatedly expressing to him, in which case, he wrote to the governor, 'I observe with sorrow that my position on the east coast will be of no help to you. This makes me urge the generals and the Nabob to send you help, which could go via Jaffna. If my fears are unwarranted let me know, and what the English are doing.'[14]

Suffren was, nevertheless, determined on an offensive, and he now decided to make an attempt to recapture Negapatam, the Dutch settlement previously taken by the British. This was an operation which had been strongly urged by Hyder Ali, and which would have the naval advantage of providing a defended anchorage. Suffren's reasoning in making this his objective may have included the possibility that it might divert British attention from launching an attack on Ceylon. In the event that this did materialise the troops would be available to reinforce Ceylon if it became necessary. He sent Moissac to Hyder Ali to ask if he might borrow 400 European troops and a sepoy battalion. This was readily agreed, and it brought the total strength of the force to attack Negapatam to 3,000 men.

Hyder Ali's willingness to comply with Suffren's request was in marked contrast to his attitude to Duchemin, for whom he felt a scarcely concealed contempt. He had been greatly impressed with the news of Suffren's battles against the British squadron, saying to Piveron de Morlat, the French agent at his court: 'Write to this extraordinary man that I have the greatest desire to see him, to embrace him and to express to him all my admiration for his heroic valour.' And to his generals he said that 'at last the English have found a master. Here is the man who will help me in exterminating them.'[15]

---

12 Cavaliero, *Admiral Satan*, p.140.
13 Lacour-Gayet, *marine militaire*, p.519.
14 Richmond, *Navy in India*, p.231.
15 Sen, *French in India*, p.249.

For their part, the French were hugely impressed by Hyder's court and particularly by his army. Young *Lieutenant* Mautort wrote that he was struck

> … by the beauty of the troops composed of so many different nations, the order which reigned in the Nawab's camp and, above all, by his intelligence and mighty resources. He alone gave all the necessary orders to his ministers for the direction of this great machine and for the provisioning of a camp of 100,000 combatants, of whom about 60,000 were cavalry. His army, including camp followers, numbered 300,000 but he made no special distribution of supplies. He saw to it that the bazaars were daily supplied with the necessities of life, with clothing and with entertainment. Even curios, which no one would have expected to find in the middle of an army, could be bought there. What a head! What a genius![16]

Before he arrived on the Coromandel coast this time, Suffren was concerned to hear about Hyder Ali's attitude to Duchemin, and it was substantially the need to cement the relationship with the Nawab that he proposed to strike at Negapatam. He was relieved, therefore, to hear from Moissac when he returned from his mission of the great admiration which Hyder had expressed for Suffren and his exploits. It was in part a response to the support which Hyder Ali was providing that Suffren now took a step for which he has been roundly criticised by British (but not by French) historians.

Immediately following the battle of Provedien, Suffren had written to Hughes to propose an exchange of prisoners. He had some 60 officers and 400 men on his hands. Hughes, either because he preferred to leave these as a burden for Suffren to bear, or because he supposed that he did not have the authority to agree to the exchange, referred the matter to Macartney, who in his turn passed the matter on to Coote. The general, aware that there were also some British prisoners in the hands of Hyder Ali, suggested that the exchange cartel should extend to the allies of the French, and that those who had suffered longest in the appalling conditions in which they were held should be the first released. Macartney did nothing. He was either indifferent or he saw the opportunity to embarrass the French by them being obliged to keep a large number of prisoners on board which would severely deplete the squadron's supply of provisions. Suffren was of course aware that there was nowhere ashore where they could conveniently be housed and was conscious of the military commitment that would be involved in guarding them. In the face of the British refusal to agree to the proposed exchange, Suffren took the decision to hand them over to Hyder Ali. French officers and civilians at Pondicherry protested, but Suffren proceeded to land them, where they were taken first to Chillumbrum and then subsequently marched to Mysore.

Suffren, in a letter to Souillac of 2 July, gave as his reason for taking this step: 'It is more in order to increase his confidence in me than as a reply to the proceedings of Macartney, Coote and Hughes that I am entrusting the English prisoners to him.'[17]

---

16 Cavaliero, *Admiral Satan*, p.142.
17 Rouv, *Le Bailli de Suffren*, p.116.

This was not consistent with the explanation that it was unavoidable in view of the failure of the British to respond, since it was a military necessity to divest himself of the burden of carrying the prisoners. His candid admission to Souillac appears to be the real reason for the transfer, since shipping was available, taken from his enemy prizes, sufficient to have conveyed these prisoners to the Ile de France or Batavia if it was impossible to guard them on the territory in occupation of the French army.

Roderick Cavaliero, Suffren's British biographer, was extremely censorious in condemning his decision: 'It was an act for which the British never forgave him and which even his humanity lived to regret.' He went on to recite Suffren's conversation with William Hickey, several months later, when Suffren, 'troubled in his conscience' explained that while Hughes had behaved in a manner 'that did honour to his feelings as a man, Macartney had treated him with contumely. Hughes, he said, while explaining his powerlessness to do anything, had begged him not to send the prisoners to Mysore, which 'would be worse than condemning the unfortunate men to death.' What else, Suffren told Hickey, could he do, short of provisions, without a port or shipping to send them to the yield to France? 'It would have been unreasonable in the extreme to suppose that I was to set at liberty near 500, the greater part able seamen. Common justice to my sovereign forbade such a measure.'[18]

Sen wrote that 'Suffren took every care to assure proper treatment of them', adding that 'it was his ignorance of Hyder Ali's methods of dealing with prisoners of war that led him to take the step.'[19] It seems that he did negotiate with Hyder's officers a generous rate of subsistence, and assigned an officer to oversee their treatment, but the latter was ignored and the prisoners suffered fearfully from 'capricious jailers, brutal marches in the broiling sun, infested dungeons.' Suffren was not solely responsible for this humanitarian disaster; Macartney's denials of having received specific proposals are wholly unconvincing, and there was plenty of opportunity for terms of an exchange to be agreed. But Suffren's own observations are more than enough to demonstrate that he was blameworthy in the matter. Laughton put thus:

> Suffren, however, was not a man to be burdened in this way. Of resolute will, and unflinching determination, when he found that he could not exchange his prisoners, he handed them all over to his ally, Hyder Ali. This was clearly contrary to the custom of civilised war; for whatever the French may pretend, Hyder Ali was in reality a barbarian, and his treatment of his prisoners was such as might have been expected from his savage nature. At the same time, we must remember that Suffren's resources were extremely limited; and the providing for a large number of useless mouths was a severe tax on his slender stores … Suffren was undoubtedly a hard man; but in this lies a great part of his merit; a man of a softer and more genial nature, even with equal talents, would have been overwhelmed in the course of the campaign.[20]

---

18 Cavaliero, *Admiral Satan*, pp.147–148.
19 Sen, *French in India*, p.251.
20 Laughton, *Naval Studies*, pp.121–122.

There, perhaps, the matter may be left.

On 2 July, just as he was ready to depart for Negapatam, Suffren received the unwelcome news that Hughes had appeared off Tranquebar. In his letter to Souillac of that date, previously referred to, he wrote:

> I have embarked seven hundred Europeans and eight hundred sepoys; that is quite sufficient to attack the English and take Negapatam, if we beat them and assist Ceylon if necessary. I did not wish to embark a single man without the knowledge of the Nawab. I have left on shore 800 sick; send me men and money; with this all will go well but without it nothing can be done. Misery in this country is so great that even with merchandise it is difficult to procure money … I leave tomorrow to attack them; if I am lucky I will at once besiege Negapatam, but whatever happens, I will have the wind for Ceylon.[21]

It took a considerable time for Hughes to emerge from Trincomali and proceed north in pursuit of his enemy. As a matter of fact, though, he had experienced difficulties quite as great as those faced by Suffren. His crews were barely half their proper complement, reduced by death, wounds, and sickness. He had found it extremely difficult to procure fresh meat and vegetables, and he had to send foraging parties far inland to obtain what they could. He was, though, somewhat better able than Suffren to complete the repair of his ships. He too was kept well informed of the situation of his opponent at Batticaloa. When news came that Suffren had sailed north, he embarked all the men fit to sail and fight, and set off on 24 June to Tranquebar and Negapatam. To Macartney, he wrote on the following day to say that his intentions were 'to watch their motions, neither seeking nor shunning an engagement till I am reinforced, which by all accounts I have received must be soon; when I doubt not I shall be able to drive them from these seas.'[22]

Reporting to Castries, Suffren was in much more bullish mood than his opponent: 'Since my arrival in Ceylon, partly by the help of the Dutch, partly through the prizes we have taken, the squadron has been equipped for six months' service, and I have rations of wheat and rice assured for more than a year.'[23] He sailed from Cuddalore on 3 July, optimistic as ever that he would be able to inflict a decisive defeat on the British squadron.

On 5 July the French squadron came in sight of the *Eagle* at 10:30 a.m., as Hughes lay at anchor off Negapatam. The *Eagle* reported at first 10 ships bearing north-east. The sea breeze was still fresh, and Hughes decided to wait until the breeze came off the land, since it was not at first clear how strong the enemy squadron was. In the meantime, he cleared for action. By 12 noon the French could be seen in greater detail, when it was apparent that they had 12 ships of the line compared to Hughes's 11. He opened his subsequent account of the battle:

---

21 Roux, *Le Bailli de Suffren*, p.118.
22 Richmond, *Navy in India*, p.235.
23 Mahan, *Influence of Sea Power*, pp.444–445.

> I continued with the squadron at anchor in Negapatam Road till the fifth of this month; when, at one pm the French squadron, consisting of 18 sail, twelve of which of the line, came in sight. At three pm I weighed with his Majesty's squadron, and stood to the southward all that evening and night, in order to gain the wind of the enemy.[24]

What Hughes did not mention in this report was that at 3:00 p.m., with the land breeze blowing in gusts from the west and southwest, when he was beginning to weigh anchor, a sudden heavy squall hit the French squadron. It was so severe that it caught the *Ajax* lying along with her lowest tier of gun ports opened ready for action. The water poured in, and she was nearly overset until her main top mast and mizzen top gallant mast went over the side, upon which she slowly righted herself, and she fell back to the tail of the French line. Hughes felt it was 'too late to do the business properly' and continued to the southward to be sure of keeping the wind next morning.[25] Suffren ordered the squadron to anchor and sent the frigates *Bellone* and *Sylphide* to assist the *Ajax* in effecting the necessary repairs.

Next day, at 5:45 a.m., Suffren was outraged to receive from Bouvet, the captain of the *Ajax*, a request that he should remain at anchor, as he had succeeded only in replacing the mizzen top gallant mast. Without a maintopmast he felt unable to take his place in the line. Suffren bluntly refused, ordering the *Ajax* to take up her proper place in the line, and take station as closely as she could. In the event, when the squadron did weigh anchor, Bouvet cut his cable and drifted helplessly to the rear and took no part in the ensuing action.[26]

At dawn the two squadrons were some six or seven miles apart, the French bearing north north-east of the British. At 5:50 a.m., Hughes made the signal for his squadron to bear away towards the French in line abreast. Ten minutes later he could see Suffren getting under sail, and he ordered his ships to form line of battle. Just before 7:00 a.m., Hughes ordered them to bear down to attack the enemy, ship to ship, with the exception of the *Monarca* which was to attack the same ship as the *Superb*, which was to fight Suffren's flagship. At this time Suffren was sailing close hauled on the port tack. The British were sailing with four of their largest ships in the centre of their line, with the evident intention of concentrating the heaviest fire on the French centre. For an hour, the two squadrons sailed about four miles apart, both steering north-west, the wind continuing south-westerly.

At about 8:00 a.m. it seemed to Suffren that he had an opportunity to pass across the British rear, and he tacked in succession to do so. Hughes continued on his course for about an hour, and then tacked in succession from his rear. A few minutes later, however, seeing that Suffren's movement was bringing him past more quickly than he expected, he changed his order to one of tacking together. His line had, in the course of these manoeuvres, become somewhat disordered. At 9:20 a.m., being now more or less abreast of the enemy Hughes tacked together and formed his line

---

24 Ekins, *Naval Battles*, p.187.
25 Richmond, *Navy in India*, p.237.
26 Cavaliero, *Admiral Satan*, p.153.

ahead on the starboard tack. The French, meanwhile, for once in a good line, were sailing south south-east on the starboard tack.[27]

At about 10:00 a.m., although his rear had not yet been able to get into the wake of his van, Hughes ordered his squadron to bear up together and attack the French ship to ship. Hughes was now concerned that it might be Suffren's intention to attempt to outrun him and make for Trincomali, so he felt he could put off his attack no longer. It was the first, and only, time in the series of battles which he fought with Suffren when he was the attacker.

At 10:40 a.m., the *Exeter* and *Hero*, at the head of the British line, began to exchange fire with the *Flamand*, leading the French squadron. It was going to be an unequal encounter, the British ships both being 74 s, and the *Flamand* being only a 50 gun ship. However, as the British ships closed, the *Exeter* ran into the *Hero*, with the result that they both shot too far ahead and neither was able to close with the *Flamand*, which kept up a concentrated fire on both of them. The *Isis*, meanwhile, holding back in order not to collide with the *Exeter*, came under fire from both the *Sévère* and the *Annibal*. Aboard the latter ship, Tromelin might have taken the decision to press forward to relieve the *Flamand*. As it was, he chose to engage the *Isis*, only to find that she was proving a vigorous opponent, inflicting about four times as many casualties as she suffered.[28]

As the rest of the British van and centre closed and came into action, the *Burford*, 74, engaged the *Sévère* with more or less equal results, while the *Sultan* took on the *Brillant* to great effect, ultimately bringing down her mainmast. Following these, the two flagships were locked in a fierce combat, of which the *Superb* had much the better. Behind her, the *Monarca*, ordered to support the flagship, in the opening phase of the battle engaged the *Sphinx*, inflicting twice as many casualties as she suffered.[29]

The ships astern of the *Monarca* failed to close, rather as the French rear had done at Provedien. First of these was the *Worcester*, which engaged to the *Petit Annibal* at long range. Next came the *Monmouth*, which at a similar range did succeed in inflicting considerable casualties on the *Artésien* but suffered few itself. It was followed by the *Eagle*, which also suffered little. Finally, the *Magnanime* was engaged, again at long range, by the *Bizarre* and *Orient*, neither of which lost any men at all, while the *Magnanime* lost two killed and 19 wounded. In the case of these last four British ships, Richmond suggests that being four ships to five, 'their captains deliberately refrained to engage the superior force and elected to act on a containing force while the action was decided at close range in that part of the line where superior guns were concentrated.'[30] That may well have been the case, but Hughes, in his report, made no mention of this aspect of the battle.

In the van and centre the battle raged with great intensity. The *Flamand*, which continued to put up a fierce resistance to the battering she suffered from the *Hero* and *Exeter* had her sails and rigging extensively damaged, and she began to edge away.

---

27 Richmond, *Navy in India*, pp.238–239.
28 Cavaliero, *Admiral Satan*, p.154.
29 Richmond, *Navy in India*, p.241.
30 Richmond, *Navy in India*, pp 241-242

Behind her the *Annibal* continued to be heavily engaged with the *Isis*. Cuverville, aboard the *Flamand*, expected to be followed, but the *Hero*, at the head of the British line, had suffered so severely aloft that she was herself pulling out of line and making for Negapatam.

Meanwhile the *Brillant*, with no less than 234 casualties, had lost both her mainmast and her mizzen, and was also forced out of line, enabling the *Sultan*, which had engaged her to such effect, to turn attention to the *Sévére*, which had continued her duel with the *Burford*. With both the *Brillant* and *Flamand* falling out of line, the four ships of Hughes's centre were now able to concentrate their fire on the *Héros*, *Sévére* and *Annibal*, inflicting considerable casualties. The *Monarca* had previously been able, in her duel with the *Sphinx*, to inflict on her twice the losses which she herself had received.

At this point there occurred an incident which led to considerable controversy after the battle had ended. Aboard the *Sévére*, her captain, Cillart, panicked at the prospect of being taken on by two opponents. Both his second and third officers were down, wounded. As the *Sultan*'s guns began to score hits on his ship, he lost his nerve entirely, and ordered that her colours be struck. He first gave the order to an auxiliary officer named Bonvallet, who refused to carry it out. Cillart was now alone on the quarterdeck of the *Sévére*, and according to Captain James Watt of the *Sultan* 'began … to run up and down, waving and dropping his hat and shouting at the top of his voice that he wished to surrender.' He found a sailor willing to haul down the flag, but at this point two other auxiliary officers, Dieu and Rosbo, who had heard from Bonvallet what was happening, ran up to Cillart calling on him to raise the flag again. Dieu cried that they would never accept the shame that Cillart wished to lay on them, and Rosbo hauled the flag to the masthead amid shouts of 'Vive le Roi.'[31]

Watt, aboard the *Sultan*, seeing the colours come down, had ceased fire and was on the point of sending a boat to take possession of the *Sévére*, but that moment his second officer reported a signal from Hughes to the whole squadron to reform his line. Dieu and Rosbo, meanwhile, had taken command of the lower tier of the *Sévére*'s guns and delivered a shattering broadside at the *Sultan* which Watt, understandably, regarded as a breach of the customs of war.

The signal which Hughes had made was occasioned by a sudden, violent squally change in the wind at 12:35 p.m.; it changed from south-westerly to south south-east. Both fleets were taken aback. Some ships paid off towards the enemy, and some away. Most of the British ships paid round to leeward, away from the French, but the *Burford* and the *Sultan*, together with the *Worcester* and *Eagle* in the rear, which had suffered less damage to their rigging, turned their heads towards Suffren's line. The *Sévére*, together with the *Brillant* had alone of the French turned their heads to the east, towards the British; both had suffered considerable damage aloft and were less manageable. As a result, the two fleets were now in considerable disorder, and their commanders were faced with the task of sorting out the confused situation which had arisen.

---

31 Cavaliero, *Admiral Satan*, p.157.

This was not easy. The *Burford*, *Worcester* and *Eagle* pressed on towards part of the French squadron, further separating in this way from the rest of the British. Hughes described what happened when the wind changed:

> At this time the sea breeze set in at SSE, very fresh, and several of our ships in our van and centre were taken aback, and paid round with their heads to the westward; while others of our ships, those in the rear in particular, which had suffered much less in their rigging, paid off and continued on their former tack. Some of the enemy's ships were also paid round by the sea breeze, with their heads to the westward; the Admiral's second ahead in particular, which I supposed to be the *Ajax*, but it proved afterwards to be the *Sévére*, fell alongside the *Sultan* and struck to her; but, while the *Sultan* was wearing to join me, made what sail he could, fired on and raked the *Sultan* without showing any colours and then got in amongst his own ships.[32]

Hughes, seeing that the *Worcester*, *Eagle* and *Burford* were all still on course for the enemy squadron, and closing fast, at 12:50 p.m. made the signal to wear, hauling down the signal for the line, intending instead to make the signal for a general chase. However, Captain John Gell of the *Monarca* at this point hailed him to tell him that all his standing rigging had been shot away, and that she was ungovernable. At the same time the *Hero*, on the opposite tack, was hauling in for the land flying a signal of distress. Suffren, meanwhile, had been able to bring the *Héros* between the *Worcester* and *Eagle* and the badly damaged *Brillant*. Tromelin, in the *Annibal*, came up in close support and raked the *Worcester* with a savage broadside. Suffren next turned upon the *Eagle*, calling the *Vengeur* and *Artésien* to support him. After half an hour of this Hughes realised that a general chase was out of the question, and made the signal to wear, standing to the west.[33]

Hughes's intention at this point was to resume the action once he had collected his ships and the *Monarca* had been brought under control, and 10 minutes after making the signal to wear he made the signal for line ahead on the port tack. He also ordered the *Exeter* to take station astern of the *Sultan*. The wind then dropped, and for the next 30 minutes Hughes was occupied in collecting his ships into some kind of order.

By 2:30 p.m. the wind had almost died away completely. The British squadron, except for the crippled *Hero* which was heading south and the *Worcester* which had turned out to sea to escape the French ships firing on her, were more or less collected. Both squadrons were now heading towards the shore, but making only very slow progress, and Hughes concluded that it would not be feasible to renew the battle that day. At 5:30 p.m. he anchored the *Superb*, in six fathoms of water, between Negapatam and Nagore. In this position he was joined by the other ships of the squadron as they came into the land, apart from the *Worcester*, the movement of which had taken her a considerable way to the westward; she rejoined on the

---

32 Ekins, *Naval Battles*, pp.187–188.
33 Cavaliero, *Admiral Satan*, p.158; Ekins, *Naval Battles*, p.188.

following day. Suffren, meanwhile, had anchored at 6:00 p.m. off Karikal, about 12 miles to the north.

Next morning, 7 July, Suffren got his squadron under way, with the remasted *Ajax* in position in line and the battered *Brillant* under tow. His attempt to take Negapatam had been frustrated, and in terms of casualties he had suffered more severely than his opponent, losing a total of 178 men killed and 602 wounded; the British losses amounted to 77 men killed and 244 wounded. It seemed to Suffren that Hughes had virtually conceded that he had had the worst of it by standing south-west with his squadron. Hughes himself took a very different view, though acknowledging that his ships had suffered severely:

> On the 7th, in the morning, the damage sustained by the several ships of the squadron appeared to me to be so great that I gave up all thoughts of pursuing the enemy; and at 9.00 am the French squadron got under sail, and returned to Cuddalore Road, their disabled ships ahead, and those less so covering their retreat in the rear. I am extremely happy to inform their Lordships, that, in this engagement his Majesty's squadron under my command gained a decided superiority over that of the enemy; and, had not the wind shifted, and thrown his Majesty's squadron out of action, at the very time when some of the enemy's ships had broken their line, and were running away, and others of them greatly disabled, I have good reason to believe it would have ended in the capture of several of their line of battle ships.[34]

One can hardly blame Hughes for putting such a favourable spin on the battle's outcome, but he was somewhat overstating the case. It was certainly not true that he had been deprived by the change of wind of the opportunity to capture several of the French ships. Neither the *Flamand* nor *Brillant* were near to striking, and if the *Sévére* had struck she must at once have been recaptured.[35] At best, the two squadrons had fought yet another indecisive action, and if Hughes was really as convinced as he claimed of having secured such an advantage, it is not unreasonable for Richmond to observe that 'it is not easy to understand why he did not press that advantage.' He had the wind, and so would have been able to attack; although the *Hero* and *Monarca* were out of action both were to windward and in safety, while Suffren's two crippled ships, the dismasted *Brillant* and the badly damaged *Flamand* were to leeward. Although the wind was light, it was not so light as to prevent him considering the possibility of pursuit. There were still nearly four hours of daylight left after 2:30 p.m., and Suffren, at least, expected that Hughes would renew the attack.[36]

Although it had been a fierce and very expensive encounter, Suffren was still bullish about his prospects. His immediate task was, of course, to gain the temporary security of Cuddalore and get his ships repaired as soon as possible before he

---

34 Ekins, *Naval Battles*, p.188.
35 Cavaliero, *Admiral Satan*, p.160.
36 Richmond, *Navy in India*, pp.246–247.

again took the offensive. In the meantime, he had to attend a meeting with Hyder Ali, which was crucial to the continued maintenance of the now absent goodwill.

Before this, however, he had to deal with the fallout from the incident involving the *Sévére*. Hughes, when he heard from Watt of what had occurred, sent him in the brig *Rodney* to Suffren under flag of truce to claim his prize, which he mistakenly believed to have been the *Ajax*. Suffren refused to receive Watt. He had not yet heard of the incident, and he dictated a reply that none of his ships had struck; if the colours had come down it was due to the halyards being shot away. He went on: 'but if your claim is as well-founded as it appears to you to be, I doubt not that the King my master will attend to it; but as to myself, who do not see things with the same eyes, I think that I neither can nor ought to do so.'[37]

In his account Richmond dealt with this incident in considerable detail, pointing out that though Hughes's claim for the surrender of the *Sévére* might have 'a fantastic appearance to modern eyes, but it was in accordance with those still existing survivals of the old chivalrous laws of war.' He went on to cite other instances in which the question of surrender was raised, such as one during the Battle of Quiberon Bay, another during the Battle of Trafalgar, and another during the battle of 6 February 1806, when Vice Admiral John Duckworth claimed that the French ship *Dioméde* had struck before her captain had then burned her. Subsequently in that instance, Duckworth concluded that the *Dioméde* had been mistaken for another vessel, and he withdrew the charge. But it was still a tradition of honourable conduct that once a ship had struck she became a prize, and could neither seize an opportunity to escape, as the *Sévére* had done, nor to rob her captors by burning, as it had been supposed that the *Dioméde* had done.[38]

Suffren, on his return to Cuddalore, instituted an enquiry into what had actually happened aboard the *Sévére*, and when he did so was furious to discover the truth of the matter. He had been turning over what to do about his unsatisfactory captains for some time, and now he could defer action no longer. He wrote to Souillac on 24 July to tell him:

> There are three captains who have to be sent to France: (1) M. de Cillart for having shamelessly brought down his flag; (2) M. de Maurville who on the 6th far from effacing only aggravated the wrongs which had committed on 17 February 12 April and 5 June; (3) M. le Comte de Forbin who far from mending his bad conduct of 12 April had conducted himself equally badly.[39]

Bouvet, of whom he said that age had paralysed his energy, was removed from the command of the *Ajax*.

These actions were, in Suffren's mind, essential if discipline was to be restored in the squadron, and it appears that they were generally approved by officers and men. Suffren also reported to Castries what he had done:

---

37 Richmond, *Navy in India*, p.246; Cavaliero, *Admiral Satan*, p.160.
38 Richmond, *Navy in India*, pp.248–250.
39 Roux, *Bailli de Suffren*, p.127.

You will perhaps be annoyed that I have not made an example of them sooner; but I must ask you to take into account that the ordinances do not give this right to general officers, which I am not one, and no general has done so before me ... I have not done it before but I believe that the service requires it absolutely and that it is the surest means that I have to make the best of my squadron.[40]

In another letter to Castries, Suffren wrote warmly of those who had distinguished themselves during the battle, including those officers of the *Sévére* who, in spite of their captain, had not wished to surrender; these he deemed worthy to be rewarded with promotion. He also particularly commended Tromelin, La Pallière, du Chilleau, Saint Felix and Cuverville.

Suffren's decisions necessitated a number of command changes. Cuverville was appointed to the *Vengeur* and was succeeded as captain of the *Flamand* by Perrier de Salvert. Saint Felix became captain of the *Artésien* and was followed as captain of the *Brillant* by Pas de Beaulieu, previously of the frigate *Pourvoyeuse*. Another member of Maurville's family, Maurville de Langle, was appointed to the *Sévére*, and Suffren's nephew Pierrevert was given command of the frigate *Bellone*. Bouvet left the *Ajax* and went back to Port Louis and was succeeded by Beaumont de Maitre. It had been a considerable reshuffle, but Suffren had reason to hope that it would result in an improved all-round performance.[41]

It remains to consider Caron's assessment of the battle:

Whatever else may be said, on the evening of the battle, even though he enjoyed parity with Hughes, Suffren could not claim a victory. He had done no better than his predecessor d'Orves eighteen months earlier, and if the English feared him, it was due less to his abilities than the power of the instrument put into his hands with which to dispute command of the sea. During the battle he had suffered three times as many casualties, and the damage to his ships had been greater than the English.[42]

Against this it should be noted that it was Suffren who was the first to be ready to return to sea. As so often is the case, Caron does not conceal the animus he feels towards Suffren, which here appears in the scornful (and absurd) comparison with d'Orves.

A fairer comment, perhaps, is to be found in Mahan's account: 'It is immediately after the action of 6 July that Suffren's superior energy and military capacity begin markedly to influence the issue between himself and Hughes. The tussle had been severe; but military qualities began to tell, as they surely must.'[43]

---

40 Lacour-Gayet, *marine militaire*, p.524.
41 Cavaliero, *Admiral Satan*, pp.163–164.
42 Caron, *Mythe de Suffren*, p.339.
43 Mahan, *Influence of Sea Power*, p.450.

14

The Madras Committee

Once the French squadron had returned to Cuddalore on 8 July, the work of repair was immediately put in hand. There was a great deal to be done. The squadron was short of 19 top masts, and none were available. The remasting of the *Brillant* was the most urgent priority; and the main mast, topmast yards and sails of the *Pourvoyeuse* were removed to fit out the *Brillant*. The frigate found replacements from the captured Indiaman *Fortitude*. From the corvette *Sylphide* came its mainmast to provide another topmast, and two more came from the lower spars of the *Pulvériseur* fire ship. The spars from the *Yarmouth*, another captured Indiaman, were shared out between the *Sylphide* and the *Pulvériseur,* and once the work on these was completed the latter was sent off to Malacca to obtain a new mainmast and other spas from the Dutch. The *Sylphide*, once a jury mast had been fitted, was sent to the Ile de France with despatches. The *Fortitude* was to go to Pegu, there to replace her mainmast. The *Resolution*, which had been captured on 10 June, was famous for having taken Captain Cook to the South Seas. It was now sent to the Pacific where her mission was to obtain, in addition to spars and other stores, some Filipino sailors in Manila.[1]

As always, Suffren recognised the urgency of the repairs. Uncertain about the extent of the damage suffered by the British squadron, he could not be sure when Hughes might appear. Day and night he threw himself into supervising the activity of his artificers and carpenters, going from ship to ship to ensure that there was no letting up in the work. Lacking sufficient materials in the squadron, he sent some of his carpenters ashore to procure timber, even demolishing some of the wooden houses there. He overcame all obstacles by his extraordinary personal energy, as Cunat, one of his biographers recorded:

> Notwithstanding his prodigious obesity, Suffren displayed the fiery ardour of youth; he was everywhere where work was going on. Under his powerful impulse, the most difficult tasks were done with incredible rapidity. Nevertheless, his officers represented to him the bad state of the fleet, and the need of a port for the ships of the line. 'Until we have taken Trincomali', he replied, 'the open roadsteads of the Coromandel coast will answer.'[2]

---

1 Cavaliero, *Admiral Satan*, p.161.
2 Mahan, *Influence of Sea Power*, p.402.

Given the lack of enthusiasm of some of his senior officers, Suffren's performance at Cuddalore was particularly remarkable. Astonishingly, on 1 August, only 25 days after the ferocious battle of Negapatam, the French squadron was ready to sail.

Suffren's other priority was to meet with Hyder Ali. He had written to the Nawab to tell him that Bussy was on the way with a substantial force. Wishing to put to sea again as soon as he could, he was reluctant to leave the oversight of the repairs of the squadron, but Hyder had insisted on a meeting. This, the French entirely accepted. In correspondence with Souillac, Piveron de Morlat was always at pains to stress the importance of this: 'The interests of our nation are absolutely and entirely in his hands at this moment and it is above all essential to convince him of the imminent arrival of our reinforcements.'[3] Suffren understood that, however reluctant he might be to abandon for a while the supervision of the repairs, he must comply with Hyder's request for the meeting, and he went ashore to await the Nawab's arrival at a point close to Cuddalore.

On 25 July Hyder's army, 100,000 strong, made camp at Manjikuppam, some six miles north of Cuddalore, and on the afternoon of the following day Suffren, in full dress uniform, set off for the meeting. He took with him a delegation of his captains consisting of Moissac, Cuverville, la Pallière, Saint Felix and Beaulieu. At 9:00 p.m., after having been greeted by the French mercenary officer Bouthenet and his sepoys, and by Ghulam Ali Khan, Hyder's senior general, Suffren made his way to Hyder's camp, escorted by a company of Austrasian Grenadiers: 'His reception was magnificent … The appearance of Hyder Ali was the signal for a general presentation of arms on the part of the troops drawn up in battle array. The drums beat, the trumpets sounded, the attendants sang hymns recording the prowess of the French. Not a single mark of respect or of honour was omitted.'[4]

This first meeting between the two men lasted three hours. Apparently Suffren's considerable bulk made it difficult for him to sit comfortably on the seat provided, as Mautort recorded:

> The extreme grossness of his body … His gallic vivacity, the continuous heat of the tent made him very uncomfortable. Several more cushions were brought with which to prop him up at the sides when he threatened to keel over, but these mountains of stuff made him sweat more and more until the Nawab, noticing his embarrassment, called for a divan, remarking that 'while it was always better to sit down than to stand, it was better still to lie down.'[5]

After a prolonged and mutual exchange of compliments, there followed a lavish exchange of gifts. Among these was an aigrette feather set in a diamond clasp which Hyder took from his own turban and pinned to Suffren's tricorn hat.

Next day, the two men met over a ceremonial banquet, in the course of which Suffren astonished his hosts by the impressive way in which he disposed of the richly

---

3   Cavaliero, *Admiral Satan*, p.166.
4   Malleson, *Final French Struggles*, p.42.
5   Cavaliero, *Admiral Satan*, p.167.

Suffen meeting Hyder Ali. (Public Domain)

spiced meal that was set before him. It was not until their third meeting on 28 July that Suffren and Hyder got down to business, but this produced the most important results. In the course of their discussion Hyder made a number of significant commitments. First, he undertook that his army would remain in the Carnatic to await Bussy's arrival, sending to the Malabar coast only such a force as was necessary to cover any threat from Lieutenant Colonel Thomas Frederick Mackenzie Humberstone. The latter, who had sailed to India after Johnstone's coup at Saldanha Bay intending to go to Madras, had on learning that Suffren might be awaiting him off Ceylon, thought it wiser to proceed to the Malabar coast, where he landed 1,000 men at Anjengo. He had been successful in defeating a force under Mukhdum Ali. Second, Hyder promised to keep the French garrison at Cuddalore fully supplied. The most important aspect of these meetings between the two men was that they had cemented an alliance which had, in the previous months, become decidedly shaky.

That evening Suffren had further good news, when de Launay, Bussy's *Intendant des Affaires*, arrived with the information that *Capitaine de Vaisseau* Louis-Esprit d'Aymar, with two ships of the line, the *Illustre*, 74, and the *Saint Michel*, 64, and the frigate *Consolante*, had arrived at Galle with a convoy of six transports and 600 troops.

On the following day Suffren went to Hyder Ali to take his formal leave, and to announce the arrival of the first instalment of Bussy's expeditionary force. He invited Hyder to come down to the sea shore to witness the French squadron dressed overall in his honour, but the Nawab declined, saying that he 'had left his camp for one object only, that of seeing so great a man, and that now that he had seen him there was nothing remaining that he cared to see.'[6] The two men parted with further mutual expressions of esteem, and Suffren returned to his squadron, feeling glad that he had after all agreed to meet with Hyder Ali: 'He treats me like a brother and takes my advice … If we had known how to deal with him from the start we could have had him do anything we wanted. My only cunning in dealing with him was to use none and to tell him always what was strictly true.'[7]

Back aboard his flagship, Suffren prepared to put to sea. His first objective was to pick up the reinforcements which had arrived at Galle, which were crucial if he was to take on Hughes in another battle. Time, as ever, was of the essence. If, by the speed at which he had been able to complete his repairs, he had gained some advantage over the British squadron, it was vital not to lose it now. If he had the opportunity to defeat Hughes before the British reinforcements arrived, it must not be missed. On 1 August, therefore, he put to sea, heading for Batticaloa, where he arrived eight days later to await his reinforcements from Galle.

Before leaving Cuddalore, Suffren wrote to Bussy. He had been told by de Launay that it was unlikely that Bussy could arrive on the Coromandel coast before the monsoon – in other words, by 15 October. If this was indeed the case, Suffren suggested that it might be better for the expeditionary force to land on the Malabar coast. Bussy, who received this letter on 14 September, was in a gloomy frame of mind, as he contemplated the various setbacks which the French might possibly face, but he recorded in his diary a somewhat more hopeful comment: 'Perhaps M. de Suffren's activity at sea will overcome both the hazards of war and of the sea.'[8]

At Batticaloa, Suffren did not have long to wait. The *Consolante* arrived there on 16 August, and was followed by the rest of the ships and convoy from Galle five days later. The squadron was now composed of 14 ships of the line, and Hughes, so far as Suffren knew, still had no more than 12. Now he was in a position to make his attempt to seize Trincomali. There was not a moment to lose:

> One of the most marked of Suffren's military traits was his promptness, his grasp of the value of time. It was in his careful husbandry and economy of time, in his never depreciating the value of a minute or a day, that his superiority over Hughes displayed and proved itself. He left as little as possible in this respect to the chances of foul winds and calms. Haste and ever more haste, to act quickly, dominated his thoughts. Therefore, when d'Aymar with his two ships of the line arrived at Batticaloa, Suffren's predominant thought was to get to Trincomali without the least delay.[9]

---

6   Malleson, *Final French Struggles*, p.43.
7   Chevalier, *Histoire de la Marine Francaise*, p.429.
8   Cavaliero, *Admiral Satan*, p.160.
9   Richmond, *Navy in India*, pp.267–268.

It remained to be seen, of course, just how soon Hughes might appear, and interfere with Suffren's plans.

For the British commander, things had not been going so well. Following the battle of Negapatam, Hughes had expected that if he remained there he would be able to carry out a large part of the repairs which the squadron needed from the stores which he had on board, but after several days it became apparent that the resources of the squadron were quite inadequate for the purpose, and that he would have no choice but to go to Madras, as he later reported in a despatch of 12 August:

> Finding it impossible to repair the loss of top masts and the other damages the ships of the squadron had sustained in the engagement without a supply of spars, fishes and cordage, and the ammunition of the squadron, as well as its provisions being nearly exhausted, I was under the necessity to proceed to this road (Madras) where our stores and provisions are deposited … When I left the windward station of Negapatam the French squadron was at anchor off Cuddalore repairing their damages.[10]

While at Negapatam he had at least managed to repair the *Superb*'s main mast sufficiently for her to undertake the journey to Madras.

Repairing his squadron's damages, however, had not been the only reason that Hughes had intended to remain at Negapatam. By remaining in the windward position there, he would be best placed to meet with the reinforcements which he was confidently expecting, and thus avoid any risk of their being intercepted by the French squadron at Cuddalore. Like Suffren, he did not know how long it would take his opponent to complete his repairs and put his squadron in a battleworthy condition. He was perfectly aware, however, that both Negapatam and Trincomali were weakly garrisoned, and hence vulnerable to an assault by Suffren.

The question of the arrival of reinforcements had been one which had dominated the thinking of both commanders. For Suffren, these were the ships accompanying Bussy's expeditionary force. For Hughes, an even more substantial reinforcement was now en route. A squadron under the command of the experienced and able Commodore Sir Richard Bickerton had sailed from England for India on 5 February, after a considerable and quite unnecessary delay. This consisted of the flagship *Gibraltar*, 80, which had been taken by Rodney from the Spanish in the Moonlight Battle of 1780, two 74s, the *Cumberland* and *Defence*, three 64s, the newly built *Africa* and *Sceptre*, and the almost new *Inflexible*, and the 50-gun *Bristol*. There were two frigates, the *Juno*, 32, and the *Medea*, 28. With the squadron also went a convoy of transports carrying 4,000 troops. Bickerton's arrival would shift the balance of strength decisively in favour of Hughes.

Bickerton's instructions, dated 22 January 1782, were to proceed as quickly as possible to Madras. He was ordered to keep well away from the coasts of France and Spain and follow a course 40 or 50 leagues to the west of Madeira and the Cape Verde Islands. If obliged to stop at Rio de Janeiro for water or provisions, he was to move

---

10 Richmond, *Navy in India*, pp.252–253.

on with the minimum of delay. After rounding the Cape, he was to send a frigate ahead to Bombay to ascertain the current situation in India. After he had reached Bombay himself, he was to sail down the Malabar coast, with the object of joining Hughes. If he did not meet the latter's cruisers off Ceylon, he was to make his way direct to Madras.[11]

Bickerton, however, did not have a fortunate passage. The *Sceptre* and *Medea* became separated from the squadron on 11 February in gales off the Irish coast and made their own way independently to Rio de Janeiro. They left there on 21 April and proceeded to India. Bickerton reached Rio de Janeiro eight days later. By then, scurvy was already

Sir Richard Bickerton. (Public Domain)

rife among the troops in the convoy, and it was not until 3 June that he was able to resume his passage eastwards. He finally arrived off Bombay on 3 September, where he learned that Hughes had already fought three battles against Suffren, and that the *Sceptre* and *Medea* had themselves reached Madras.

In their journey eastwards the *Sceptre* and *Medea* had encountered the convoy carrying 2,500 of Bussy's troops and succeeded in capturing one transport with 96 troops and stores. This vessel proving to be a very poor sailor, Captain Samuel Graves of the *Sceptre* decided to leave the *Medea* with the prize, while he pressed on to Madras, where he arrived on 13 July and was able to announce that Bickerton was on his way.[12]

Hughes had lingered at Negapatam for as long as he could, reluctant to abandon the windward position while hoping for Bickerton's appearance. On 18 July, however, he set sail, arriving at Madras two days later. Thereafter he began the considerable task of repairing and refitting his squadron. He had to repair or replace 16 lower masts, 17 top masts, 18 lower and topsail yards, and four bowsprits, together with much rigging and sails. Many of his spare spars on the booms had been shot to pieces. Like Suffren at Cuddalore, he can have been no less aware of the need for haste; but as it turned out, the work of repair took him a good deal longer.

While the work was going on Hughes was obliged to consider with the Madras Committee, and with Coote, the strategic decisions which now must be taken. Foremost among Hughes's concerns was the safety of Trincomali, but as he pointed

---

11 Richmond, *Navy in India*, p.305.
12 Richmond, *Navy in India*, p.257.

out to the Committee, 'Far other services fall to me than the matter of the security of Trincomali.' It was necessary, he said, for him 'to attend to the operation of the enemy squadron on this coast, which brought on the engagement of July 6 last, as the protection of Trincomali had brought on that of April 12 last.'[13]

Since Madras itself now appeared safe from attack, the Committee had been looking at ways to go over to the offensive. For this to be undertaken effectively, there must be close cooperation between army and navy, and the operation in which this might most usefully be achieved was, it was suggested, to launch an attack on Cuddalore. Success here would burnish British prestige, dispose of the larger part of the French army, and deprive Suffren of a port from which he was able to draw supplies, but from which he could also recruit men from the army to make good losses among his crews. That was all very well, but for Hughes it was absolutely necessary for Trincomali to be secured if other projects were to be undertaken.

Hughes was convinced that Suffren would make an attempt to capture the port. He was also convinced that its garrison was inadequate. Strengthening it must, he considered, be an essential part of any programme of action. It was necessary to do all that could be done to prevent Suffren obtaining a base in which he could winter from October to January, make necessary repairs, and operate against the food supplies, vital to Madras, that passed along the Coromandel coast.

However, he was only partly successful in persuading the Madras Committee to act in accordance with his views of the situation. A small reinforcement of 200 troops, with a junior officer in command, was embarked aboard the *Sceptre* and *Monmouth*, and they left Madras on 1 August carrying also 3,000 bags of rice for the garrison. There is no explanation for the fact that the Committee was not prepared to do more. Lord Macartney wrote to St John McPherson, a member of the council, on 26 July making clear his own concerns about Trincomali: 'It runs strongly in my head that Suffrein will attempt it.'[14]

So the two ships set off on their mission, only narrowly missing Suffren's squadron which had sailed southward heading for Batticaloa. Suffren, indeed, had thought on his journey south from Cuddalore of exploring the bay of Trincomali, but he thought better of it and proceeded directly to Batticaloa, thus missing the opportunity of capturing the *Sceptre* and *Monmouth*.[15] As it was, they returned safely to Madras 10 August with the news that Suffren had sailed past Trincomali three days earlier. In the meantime, the Committee went ahead with planning its proposed operation against Cuddalore. This, it was intended, should proceed without the cooperation of Hughes's squadron, still in the midst of its repairs. Hughes had only 68 artificers available to him, while he reckoned that Suffren probably had between 200 and 300. Nevertheless, his lack of progress in getting his squadron ready for sea compared very unfavourably with the despatch that Suffren had shown.

The members of the Committee were discontented with Hughes and expressed it in terms which reflected their lack of confidence in the admiral, a feeling which he reciprocated. The Committee seriously annoyed Hughes, writing: 'Your desire, so

---

13 Richmond, *Navy in India*, p.256.
14 Cavaliero, *Admiral Satan*, p.170.
15 Sen, *French in India*, p.261.

often instanced in overtaking and engaging the enemy wherever the public safety required it, leaves us only to observe on this occasion to you, as our duty binds us, that we consider the public safety never more concerned than it is at present.'[16] Hughes's response to this was terse; he would sail with the squadron when it was in a condition for service.

The criticism faced by Hughes for the slow progress of the repairs was, to some extent, unfair. The British did suffer from a shortage of stores, and the conditions at Madras for repairing the squadron were far from ideal; the boatmen were fickle and lazy, and everything moved slowly and laboriously. Suffren, on the other hand, had received store ships with cordage and smaller spars, and the physical circumstances at Cuddalore were rather more convenient. Hughes's mistake was to tarry as long as he did off Negapatam, which had given Suffren a head start.

Hughes originally thought that he would be ready to sail by 11 August, but well before this he realised that this would not be possible. He was not, however, unduly concerned, since the report that Suffren had sailed on 1 August had been contradicted. When he announced this to the Committee at Madras, however, it had provoked the letter of protest in extravagantly critical terms previously quoted, which Hughes described as 'very extraordinary':

> That description is not inappropriate when it is considered that the Committee was vested with no authority over the King's squadron; possessed no means whatever of forming an opinion as to the state of readiness of his squadron to engage a superior force; and were themselves the persons who, by their constant refusal to place Trincomali in a state of security, exposed to danger from the French squadron.[17]

In drafting his reply Hughes was, understandably, very put out. As well as repeating that he would sail when he was ready to do so, he observed that he was 'by no means ignorant of the state of public affairs in every part of India, and needed not your information.' He added caustically that while declining to provide adequately for the garrisons of Trincomali and Negapatam, the Committee had preferred 'to keep 10 or 12,000 men and 60,000 followers, at enormous expense, parading around the Mount, eating up the small supplies of provisions that came to Madras, without any material attempt on the enemy.' Observing bitterly that the Committee had seen fit to praise Suffren, he remarked that those comments were far from unacceptable to him, but that the Committee complimented Suffren at his expense.[18]

Hughes was not alone in the dislike and contempt which he felt for the Madras Committee. Sir Eyre Coote shared these feelings. Macartney had continually interfered with the general and his conduct of operations, notwithstanding the fact that the governor general in Calcutta had given Coote complete and unfettered discretion over the operations on land. When Hughes returned to Madras after the battle of Negapatam, one of the first communications that he received came from Coote,

---

16 Cavaliero, *Admiral Satan*, p.172.
17 Richmond, *Navy in India*, p.261.
18 Richmond, *Navy in India*, pp.263–264.

with whom he continued to enjoy an excellent professional relationship, and who was anxious for a meeting: 'In three or four days more I shall have had such an opportunity when we must have under contemplation a plan of joint cooperation without which it is at present altogether impracticable for the army to act in any shape against our natural enemy.'[19] Although Coote had succeeded in winning victories against the forces of Hyder Ali, he was unable to exploit them due to the lack of supplies.

Meanwhile the frigate *Coventry* arrived in Madras on 16 August, bringing a company of troops from Bombay. En route it had encountered the French frigate *Bellone*, and a brisk engagement lasting two hours had caused each vessel some 40 casualties, among whom was Suffren's nephew *Lieutenant* Pierrevert, the *Bellone*'s commander, killed by the *Coventry*'s first volley. The *Medea* had also now arrived at Madras, and Hughes was almost ready to leave. He announced on 18 August that he would be putting to sea on the following day. The latest news he had was that Suffren was still at Batticaloa; that being so, he might still be in time to pre-empt any assault on Trincomali.

---

19 Richmond, *Navy in India*, p.254.

15

Trincomali

Once d'Aymar had arrived at Batticaloa, Suffren wasted no time in preparing his assault on Trincomali. There was much to be done; the troops must be allocated, sick men put ashore, and the ships watered. It was also necessary to take on board provisions, since if the attack should fail, and he also lost Cuddalore, he would no longer have a base from which he could be supplied. On 21 August all was ready, and he put to sea. Four days later, having looked into Trincomali to assure himself that it was unoccupied by the enemy squadron, he was tacking into Back Bay. The landing place selected was three miles to the north of Fort Frederick, and at 2:00 a.m. on 26 August the force of 2,410 men went ashore, under the command of *Lieutenant colonel* Baron d'Angoult. This included 1,200 regular troops brought down from Cuddalore, together with 600 sepoys and Malays supplied by the Dutch, and 500 men from the squadron which were commanded by *Lieutenant* Dupas.[1] The landing was covered by the cutter *Lezard*, anchored close inshore, but no attempt was made by the garrison of Fort Frederick to interfere.

The French at once began to prepare batteries with which to bombard the fort. Gabions brought from Batticaloa, and sacks of earth made on the spot, were duly laid. From a number of houses which had been occupied planks were taken to form platforms. After the first battery of four guns, consisting of three 18-pounders and one 12-pounder, had been completed, a second battery, of three mortars, was prepared. This was followed by a third battery, the work being supervised by *Capitaine* Desrois, the artillery commander. On 27 August the garrison, which was commanded by Captain Hay Macdowall of the 42nd Regiment, launched a half-hearted sortie, which was easily beaten off. Meanwhile work on the batteries continued, and by dawn on 29 August they were ready to open fire; to this the guns of the fort responded vigorously. On the following day, with all three batteries in action from 6:15 a.m., there were lively exchanges of fire; the French suffered some casualties which were sent on board the ships of the squadron. That night, they were occupied in repairing their batteries, which opened up again on the following morning. At 9:00 a.m., an officer who spoke English was sent into the fort to call upon it to surrender. Although no breach had so far been made in the walls of the fort, its south-west bastion had been seriously damaged.[2]

---

1 Cary, 'Trincomali', p.27.
2 Cary, 'Trincomali', p.28.

The envoy returned at 11:00 a.m. accompanied by two British officers, who were ready to discuss possible terms of surrender, but the terms which they put forward were rejected as excessive. Suffren told them that he was ready to grant all the honours of war if, but only if, they capitulated promptly. One of the British officers went back into the fort with the draft of a capitulation document, while the other remained to dine. Macdowall attempted to negotiate, but Suffren would not budge, ordering the attack to recommence as soon as the British officers had returned to the fort. This was enough for Macdowall, and he came out himself to sign the articles of capitulation. He complained bitterly that Suffren had besieged him and battered a breach without first summoning him according to the laws of war. Suffren brushed this aside, saying that he had not done so as he would have considered it an insult to have expected the British to surrender without firing a shot. He agreed to grant the honours of war, and to provide shipping to take the garrison to Madras.

The terms of capitulation having been quickly agreed, Suffren now prepared to move against Fort Ostenburg, which was on a promontory across the bay, jutting out into the entrance to the harbour. Orders were issued that night for the French infantry to march against it before dawn on 31 August. Fort Ostenburg had the potential to be a difficult place to capture. It was perched high on a wooded hill, approachable only along a narrow ridge which was swept by the guns of the fort, and provided no space to deploy for an attack. However, the stonework of the fort had been allowed to fall into disrepair, and not much had been done since the British captured it. Nevertheless, it was still capable of withstanding a considerable assault if it was properly defended, and such an assault could cost men that Suffren could not afford. But even more importantly, he could not afford the loss of time, and he ordered that the assault should go forward. The attacking troops were able to reach the hill after a brief exchange of fire with only slight loss, whereupon d'Agoult summoned the fort to surrender. It has been suggested that he added that if Captain William Kelso (98th Regiment), the garrison commander, did not surrender at once he would be sent as a prisoner to Hyder Ali. There was no further resistance; Kelso promptly surrendered and was granted the honours of war.

The capture of the two forts yielded a considerable reward. In Fort Ostenburg there were found 50,000 piastres, 20,000 pounds of powder, 1,650 cannonballs, victuals sufficient for six months, 1,200 muskets, four field pieces, 10 mortars and 30 cannon. Fort Frederick was even better provided; 40 cannon, half of them brass, were found there.[3] Suffren at once set about putting the two forts into a state of defence calculated to last at least 15 days, as he told Falck in Colombo. Suffren was under no illusion about the need for haste and worked feverishly not only to strengthen the forts, but to complete his preparations for the battle with Hughes which he knew was sure to come. By 1 September the British garrisons had been embarked on transports to take them to Madras, and the attacking force, save for the garrisons to be left to hold the forts, was re-embarked. Command was given to Desrois, who had a force consisting of the 3rd Battalion of the Ile de France Regiment, together with 400 sepoys and 500 Malays. The operation to take Trincomali had been a resounding

---

3   Cary, 'Trincomali', p.30.

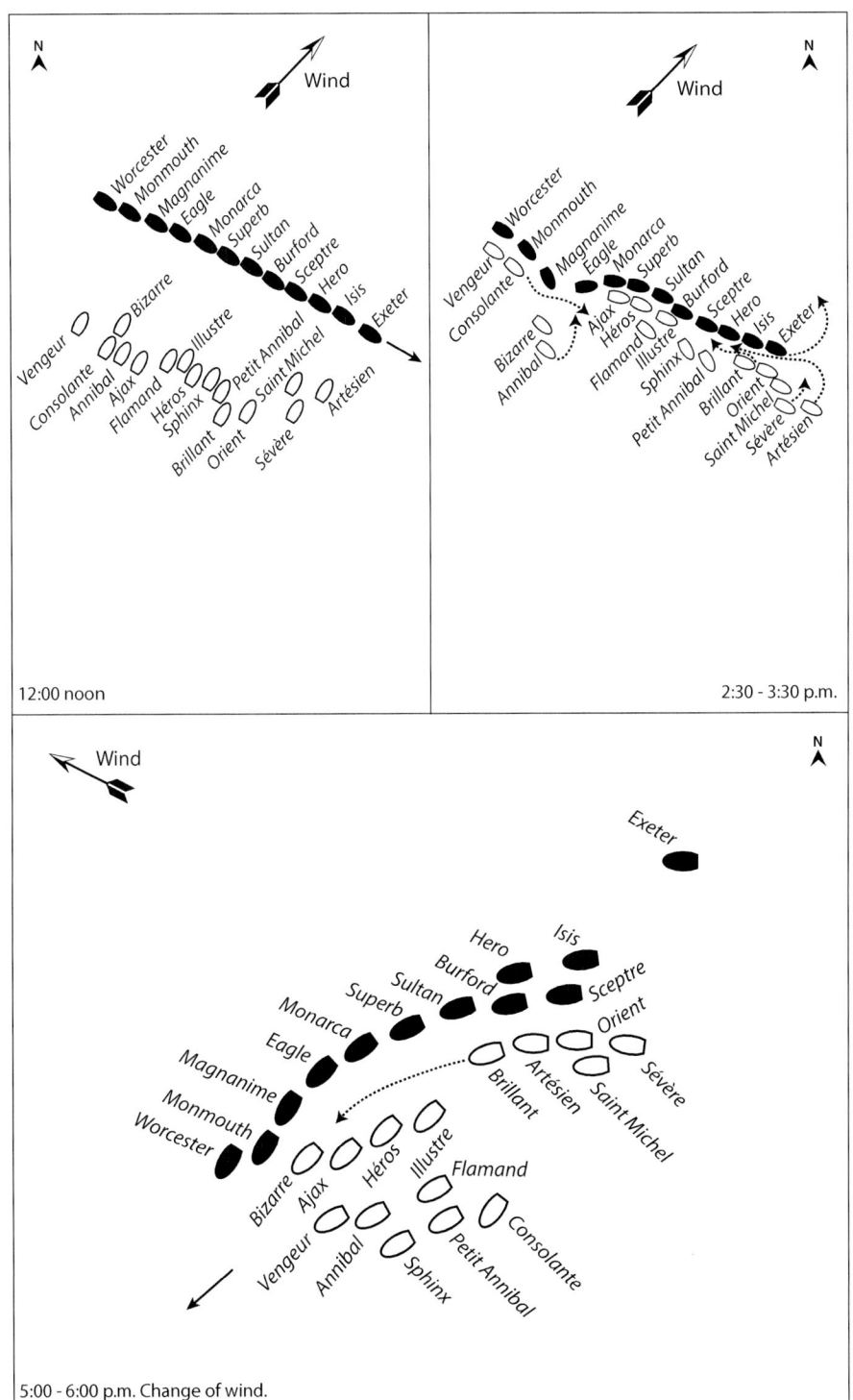

The Battle of Trincomali, based on a map in Cavaliero, *Admiral Satan*.

success; French casualties during the operation amounted to no more than 25 men killed and wounded.[4]

On the afternoon of 2 September, Suffren entertained the captured British officers to dinner. In the course of this, news was brought to him at 3:00 p.m. that 16 or 17 sail had been sighted bearing east south-east. These could only be the ships of Hughes's squadron, and Suffren bid his captives farewell and returned to his ship. Those of his seamen who were ashore were quickly re-embarked, together with some of the troops. Within a couple of hours the squadron was ready to put to sea and Suffren hoisted a signal to prepare for action.

Hughes had indeed arrived, but as he had feared might be the case found that he was too late. When he first came in sight of the coastline he could see no sign of the French, and he had briefly cherished the hope that all was well, but dawn of the following day revealed an unpleasant surprise when he saw the French flag flying over the two forts. In his subsequent despatch, he sadly wrote:

> The squadron having completed its provisions, and being in a tolerable condition for service, I left the road with the squadron under my command, and used all diligence possible to get to the southward, to Trincomali; being apprehensive the enemy would endeavour to make themselves masters of that harbour in the absence of the squadron. But, the wind blowing strongly from the southward, I did not arrive with the squadron off Trincomali until the night of the second of this month.[5]

Hughes had been very unlucky. The 280-mile journey from Madras, which the *Sceptre* and *Monmouth* had been able to complete in seven days, took him 14; Suffren had come south from Cuddalore in eight days. The logs of the ships recorded the sequence of calms and drifting, and even of days when the strong north running current set the squadron 12 miles further off than it had been the day before. In the first week the actual distance covered in the direction of Trincomali was only 16 miles; and thereafter the average run was no more than 50 miles.[6]

However, for all the urgency of Suffren's first reaction to the news that the enemy was in sight, the French squadron was on the morning of 3 September far from ready. Some ships had not got their yards crossed, some were bending sails, while others were in the act of raising anchor. Hughes saw a chance of attacking them before they got into proper formation, and as he approached the port, he made the signal to engage the enemy as the British ships came up with them. But at that moment the wind dropped away. Only the lightest of breezes now blew from the south-west, which effectively meant that Suffren held the windward position, and was unapproachable. Hughes accordingly hauled his wind, and at 6:10 a.m. signalled to his squadron to form line of battle at two cables' distance. He shortened sail, edging away from the wind, in order that the ships of his van could more quickly take up their stations.

---

4   Cary, 'Trincomali', p.30.
5   Ekins, *Naval Battles*, p.191.
6   Richmond, *Navy in India*, p.271.

At Trincomali, however, all was not well. The news that Hughes was in sight with 16 or 17 ships had caused great concern among some of the French captains. A number of them came to Suffren to urge upon him that in the circumstances it would be better not to put to sea. They pointed out that to do so would put at risk all that had been achieved. If they were beaten, Trincomali would be lost. The wiser course, therefore, they said, would be to remain in port, where they would be safe from injury, and where their presence ensured that Hughes could not retake it.

Suffren, for once, reacted calmly to a suggestion which instinctively he was inclined to reject out of hand. Instead, he sent out the *Bellone* to obtain an accurate picture of the enemy, which soon returned with the information that Hughes had only 12 ships of the line. Suffren had heard all that he needed to know, as he at once made clear, saying to his captains: 'If I had inferior force, it would be difficult to resist the temptation to fight the English; with equal force the honour of the flag would demand my fighting them; with superior force we must fight. Repeat the signal immediately to form line and bear down on the enemy.'[7]

There seems little doubt that the apparently persuasive military arguments put forward against putting to sea were by no means the sole reason for the advice proffered by these captains. Once Suffren had made his position clear, there could be no further argument:

> But the resentment felt by the recalcitrant captains cost Suffren very dear in the action which followed. From the point of view of national interest he had no doubt made the wisest decision in not losing this opportunity of destroying the English squadron, weaker in both the number of ships and of guns, before it was joined by the expected reinforcement under Bickerton ... It was an opportunity not to come again, and in spite of all his past glories Suffren would have incurred severe condemnation if he had decided to miss it. On the other hand he should have known from his past experience that success depended to a very large extent on the cooperation of all the captains, and he should have considered whether that cooperation would have been forthcoming in view of the feeling of extreme resentment on the part of many of them.[8]

Suffren might have given consideration to this; but in the circumstances in which he found himself there could have been no question of not fighting. He was perfectly aware of the strength of the resentment which he faced, as well as of the longing of some to return to the easy life of the Ile de France, and of the fatigue which some were suffering. But he had to do the best he could with what he had.

At the same time, looking at the history of the squadron since it originally left the Ile de France, it is difficult not to attach some blame to Suffren for the lack of discipline of so many of his captains. There had been opportunities to exercise the squadron to improve its performance in manoeuvring in battle, and he seems not to have done as much in this respect as might have been expected. On the other

---

7   Richmond, *Navy in India*, p.274.
8   Sen, *French in India*, p.262.

hand, from the moment that Hughes was reported in sight on the afternoon of 2 September each captain had plenty of time to prepare, and none should have been found unready at dawn on the following day.

As the French were sorting themselves out, Hughes, who could depend on the professionalism and seamanship of his captains, had his squadron in good order, sailing eastwards under topsails, hoping that further out to sea he might catch any change in the wind. For the moment, all he could do was to endeavour to draw Suffren so far from the port that any French ships that might be disabled in the coming action would find considerable difficulty in regaining it.

Suffren meanwhile had decided to make a change in the deployment of his squadron. The French line consisted of 15 ships, of which 13 were ships of the line. The other two were the *Petit Annibal*, 50, and the frigate *Consolante*, 40. Hughes had 12 ships in his line, the only one not a ship of the line being the *Isis*, 54. On this occasion Suffren decided to employ his fast coppered ships differently. In the previous actions he had grouped them together in one body, using them as a fast van division in the actions of 17 February and 12 April, and as the centre division in the action of 6 July. In the battle about to be fought he seems to have given up the idea of using a fast division, for in the order adopted – his *ordre naturel No 1* – he located two coppered ships in the van, one in the rear and the remainder in the centre.

Hughes, on the other hand, massed four of his five heavy ships in the centre. Since Suffren's distribution of his heavy ships meant that they were now scattered all down his line, this gave Hughes a preponderance of firepower in the centre. On this occasion Suffren was not going to attempt any complex manoeuvres as he approached the British line. Once his squadron was at sea the only orders other than those for the squadron as a whole were at 11:30 a.m. for the *Vengeur* and *Consolante* to concentrate on the rearmost British ship. Suffren appears to have reached the reluctant conclusion that the lack of order that prevailed in the French squadron denied him the opportunity of achieving a more complex tactical concentration on a part of the enemy.

As Hughes continued to lead Suffren further away from the land, the French squadron began gradually to close, but even when it got to within four miles of the British, it was still in very poor order. The van, headed by Saint Felix in the *Artésien*, which was closely followed by the *Sèvère* and *Saint Michel*, steadily drew ahead of the French centre, while at the rear the *Vengeur* was falling behind.

Nevertheless, Suffren approached the battle in as optimistic frame of mind as ever. He had a superiority in numbers, much of the day lay before him giving plenty of time to win a victory; and he had at least rid himself of some of the captains who had previously let him down. But his innate enthusiasm should not have blinded him to the extremely disadvantageous manner in which his ships were approaching the enemy. As on previous occasions, many were sailing badly, and were poorly handled, and although he displayed signal after signal in an effort to get his squadron into position, they remained in a serious state of disorder. Watching them, Hughes noted that they were 'sometimes edging down, sometimes bringing to, and in no regular order, as if undetermined what to do.'[9] For his part, Suffren did not at all accept that

---

9   Ekins, *Naval Battles*, p.192.

different sailing qualities would account for the continuing disorder of his line. In his view, these differences could not, or should not, have prevented the ships from keeping up with the centre since, as he wrote, three of the ships comprising it came into action simultaneously: 'the *Héros* sails very well, the *Illustre* passably, and the *Ajax* very badly. Nothing shows more clearly than this that all could have closed the enemy and kept the line.'[10]

At 2:00 p.m., despairing of getting his ships into a better line, Suffren ceased bearing down, hauled his wind somewhat, and signalled for the squadron to follow in the wake of the *Artésien*. His hope was that she would continue to lead on parallel to the enemy, and thus enable the rest of the squadron to form a line astern of her. This manoeuvre did not achieve his object, however, because the *Artésien* also luffed, and this carried the van further away, the *Artésien* being carried too far forward to bear down on the *Exeter* at the head of the British line. Suffren now saw himself as having no choice but to order the squadron to bear up together and stand down on the enemy: 'Since I cannot establish order, let each ship bear down on the enemy, choose his ship, and do as I do.' To draw attention to the signal, Suffren ordered a gun to be fired. Unfortunately, the gunners aboard the *Héros*, impatient for action, took this to be a signal to fire a broadside, and the rest of the squadron opened fire. The *Héros* was not yet in pistol shot range. With its broadsides blazing away at a longer range, it was assumed by the other ships that on this occasion Suffren was not intending close action.

At the tail of the French line the *Consolante* and *Vengeur* endeavoured to carry out Suffren's instructions to double on the British line and bore up towards the *Worcester* in order to pass under its stern. This move was thwarted, however, by the prompt action of the *Worcester*'s captain, Charles Wood. Seeing what was intended, he at once threw his maintopsail aback to block the way and was supported in this by the *Monmouth*. As a result, these four ships dropped astern of the rest of the squadrons and carried on an action between themselves at long range.

At the head of the line, the five ships that constituted the French van had by now drawn a considerable distance ahead of the centre. These five were the *Artésien, Sévére, Saint Michel, Orient* and *Brillant*. The first two had overshot the *Exeter*. The *Saint Michel* was abreast of the British ship, and at close quarters. The *Orient* was almost abreast, but slightly abaft the *Exeter*'s beam, and the *Brillant*, further back, was firing with her bow guns into the *Exeter*'s quarter. In its turn the *Brillant* was assailed by the *Isis*, the second ship in the British line. As a result of the concentrated enemy fire which it received, especially from the *Sévére*, the *Exeter* was obliged to bear up and turn away to leeward. It was pursued by the four leading French ships.

This first phase of the battle was described in Hughes's report:

> At 2:30 pm the French line began to fire on ours, and I made the signal for battle; at five minutes after, the engagement was general, from our van to our rear; the two additional ships of the enemy's line falling furiously on our rearmost ship, the *Worcester*, were bravely resisted by that ship, and the

---

10 Richmond, *Navy in India*, p.278.

Monmouth, her second ahead, which backed all her sails to assist her. About the same time, the van of the enemy's line, to which five of their ships had crowded, bore down to the *Exeter* and *Isis*, the two headmost ships of our line; and, by an exerted fire on them, forced the *Exeter*, much disabled, out of the line; then tacked, keeping their wind, and firing on the *Isis*, and other ships of our van, as they passed.[11]

The *Exeter* ultimately ran at least a mile to leeward of the line; its main mast and foretopmast were incapable of bearing sail, and its rigging and sails had been cut to pieces. In spite of the heavy pounding which it had suffered, the *Exeter*'s casualties were surprisingly slight, amounting to six killed and 19 wounded. It is evident from this that the *Exeter*'s adversaries were, on this occasion, deliberately firing high. When, after some time spent battering the *Exeter*, the leading French ships were ordered to tack so that they could come to the support of the centre, the wind had dropped away to such an extent that they were obliged to tow their heads round with their boats. In all, the seven leading ships of the French line had, by reason of drawing so far ahead, been effectively unable to play a significant part in the development of the battle.

It was in the centre that the engagement was at its fiercest. Here, three French ships, the *Héros*, *Illustre* and *Ajax* were in action against five British, the *Burford*, *Sultan*, *Superb*, *Monarca* and *Eagle*. Casualties aboard these ships mounted quickly. The British ships carried a combined broadside of 176 guns compared to the French 106, and the disproportionate weight of metal took its toll. Total casualties in the five British ships amounted to 26 men killed and 169 wounded; the three French ships lost 64 killed and 178 wounded.[12]

This particularly savage engagement raged for over two and a half hours. With the wind having dropped almost completely, Suffren found it impossible to gain support for the hard-pressed centre from those of his ships following him that had not become closely engaged. These were the *Flamand*, *Annibal* and *Bizarre*. It was accordingly now that he signalled his van ships to tack in order to assist the centre. At this stage of the battle, therefore, Hughes had won for himself a favourable position, largely due to the mistakes and poor seamanship of the French, but also partly due to chance. He was subsequently criticised for his tactics in not now going about, doubling on the French centre, and crushing it. Richmond dismisses this assessment:

> This, however, fails to take into account the lightness of the wind, the damage aloft, and the fact that if he should have worn – for the wind was too light to tack – he must have exposed his ships to a raking fire for a long time while the boats, if they could be got into the water, would be towing the ships' heads round.[13]

---

11 Ekins, *Naval Battles*, p.192.
12 Richmond, *Navy in India*, p .278n.
13 Richmond, *Navy in India*, p.280.

Apart from the heavy casualties which the three ships of Suffren's centre had sustained, they had all suffered considerable damage aloft. The mainmast of the *Héros* was so badly wounded, and its shrouds so cut to pieces, that it went over the side later. The *Illustre* lost its maintopmast and mizzen mast, and the *Ajax* lost its mizzentopmast. They had, however, inflicted considerable damage on the five British ships with which they were engaged. The *Burford*, in addition to its rigging being badly cut about, was leaking badly from shot holes and was making four feet of water an hour and was reported as sinking. The *Sultan*'s upper spars and rigging were badly damaged, as was its mainmast; four guns been dismounted. The *Superb* had suffered extensive damage to its hull, and some damage aloft. The *Monarca* had also been extensively damaged, particularly below the waterline, and was leaking heavily, and it had also been seriously damaged aloft. The *Eagle*, too, was in a bad way and was making to three feet of water an hour, all its seams being opened by the battering it had undergone.

It must be said, though, that the difficult situation of the French centre was one which they had brought on themselves, and Suffren must take a share of the blame for allowing his squadron to go into action in such a disordered state. He could have deferred his attack somewhat longer to improve the state of his line, and he appears not to have had any overriding concept of the way in which the battle was to be fought. Reflecting on its conduct, Mahan was critical of both commanders:

> A military operation could scarcely be worse carried out. The French ships in the battle did not support each other; they were so grouped as to hamper their own fire and needlessly increase the target offered to the enemy; so far from concentrating their own effort, three ships were left, almost unsupported, to a concentrated fire from the British line … In this disorder such gaps existed as to offer a great opportunity to a more active opponent. 'Had the enemy tacked now', wrote the chief of staff in his journal, 'we would have been cut off and probably destroyed.'[14]

The French centre was, accordingly, in an extremely vulnerable state. The frigates were too far off to be able to come to the assistance of the badly damaged ships, while although Tromelin in the *Annibal* belatedly attempted to come up in support, there was not enough wind and neither his ship, nor the *Flamand* and *Bizarre*, could be of any help. Their casualty lists reflected their ineffectiveness, and Suffren noted caustically his opinion of their performance. The *Annibal* suffered no casualties at all (*Trés mal*), the *Flamand* had one man killed and 13 wounded (*Mal*), and the Bizarre two killed and 16 wounded (*Mal comme toujours*).[15]

At the head of the British line, the Exeter continued to drift slowly away, the French van allowing her to go as they strenuously used their boats to bring their heads round. In the case of the *Saint Michel*, d'Aymar nearly came to grief. Having opened his lower gun ports, the ship listed steeply as it came round, and the lower gun deck was immediately swamped. Meanwhile at the other end of the line, the

---
14 Mahan, *Influence of Sea Power*, p.455.
15 Richmond, *Navy in India*, p.280n.

Monmouth and the *Worcester* were getting much the better of their duel with the *Consolante* and *Vengeur*, and at about 4:00 p.m. the latter turned out of line with her mizzen topsail in flames.

This phase of the battle came to an end at about 5:35 p.m., when the wind shifted suddenly from south-west to east south-east. Hughes at once signalled his squadron to wear, which it did in good order, although enduring raking fire while the turn was being made. During this manoeuvre the *Burford* suffered particularly, as several of the French ships which had already got on to the other tack passed under her stern in the gathering sea breeze as she was going round. Hughes described what followed: 'The engagement was renewed, on the other tack, close and vigorously on our part. At 6:20, the French Admiral's mainmast was shot away by the board, and soon after his mizzenmast; and about the same time, the *Worcester*, one of our line of battle-ships, lost her main topmast.'[16]

By the time that the *Héros* lost her mainmast, the ships of the French van, now the rear after the change of direction, had been able to come up to support their admiral. At 7:00 p.m., Suffren concluded that he could do no more and hauled his wind to the southward. Although fighting continued in the rear, which was still in action for another 20 minutes, it then ceased, and the French squadron moved away. As darkness fell, Hughes made no attempt to follow. This, as he explained, was unavoidable. He wrote that 'the ships of our squadron had apparently suffered so much as to be in no condition to pursue them.' At midnight he signalled for the squadron to lie to on the port tack. When dawn broke on the following day, there was no sign of the French, and Hughes took stock of his situation: 'The *Eagle*, *Monmouth* and *Burford* were reported to me to be in a sinking condition and the *Superb* and several other ships making much water from shot holes so very low down as not to become at to be effectively stopped and the whole had suffered severely in their masts and rigging.'[17]

Hughes was therefore entitled to feel a very grave concern for the badly damaged ships of his squadron. The news that three ships were making water so heavily as to be in a sinking condition was itself enough to make up his mind, though other damage was also a cause for anxiety. The *Worcester* had lost a topmast, the *Exeter's* mainmast and foretopmast could not bear sail, and although the *Magnanime* had not been heavily engaged, she reported that its mainmast, maintopmast, and main yard were so cut through that sail could not be made on the mast. Hughes, when he arrived there, explained his decision to return to Madras:

> Under these circumstances, and Trincomali being in the enemy's possession, and the other parts of the west coast of Ceylon unsafe to anchor on at this late season of the year, when the NE winds often blow strong there, I was under the necessity of steering with the squadron for this coast to get anchoring ground, in order to stop the shot holes underwater; and, from the disabled state of the ships, I fell in with the land very few leagues only to windward of this port, on the 8th instant, and anchored in this road on

---

16 Ekins, *Naval Battles*, p.192.
17 Richmond, *Navy in India*, pp.281–282.

the 9th, and am now closely employed in repairing the damages the several ships have received.[18]

As the battle in the centre raged, Suffren had become predictably emotional, furious at the lack of support he was receiving from the rest of his squadron. At one point he addressed Bruyères aboard the *Illustre* through his speaking trumpet aboard shouting that 'since he had been betrayed and abandoned he would rather perish alone than bring the *Illustre* to destruction with him.' Bruyères replied to say that he would rather sink than desert him.[19] When the mainmast of his flagship came down, Suffren could be heard shouting for 'flags, more flags. Bring me every white flag aboard and hang them over the ship.'

Six months after the battle William Hickey was able to record in his diary the generous comments made by Hughes on what he had seen of his opponent during the battle:

> Mr Suffren is as gallant a man as ever lived. After fighting his ship in a manner bordering on desperation and performing wonders the superior fire of the *Superb* and *Sultan* completely silenced that of the *Héros* These two British ships continued pouring their broadsides into her without her being able to return a single shot. My ship being within pistol shot, I could distinctly see all that occurred. Her upper deck was more than once completely cleared, scarce a man remaining on it except Mr Suffren himself who ran up and down like a lunatic, crying out most earnestly for some fortunate shot to take him off. I have never thought of the scene but with astonishment and how the *Héros* sustained such a tremendous galling fire is still incomprehensible to me.[20]

While the British squadron was lying-to during the night after the battle, the French had made their way south-eastward. Suffren was now concerned to return to the safety of Trincomali as fast as he could. The *Petit Annibal* took the *Illustre* in tow; its badly damaged mainmast finally came down at about 8:00 p.m. The squadron arrived off Trincomali on the following day, though it was several days before all the ships were safely at anchor, and the considerable work of repair could begin.

In the meantime, Suffren suffered a wholly avoidable setback. At the end of the battle he had transferred his flag to the *Orient*. This was now one of the ships awaiting its turn to enter the anchorage. When, on 7 September, it endeavoured to do so, a misjudgement by *Lieutenant* La Pallière, a son of the captain, grounded the ship on a coral reef at Foul Point at the southernmost tip of Back Bay. There was a rough swell running, and in the nine days that followed, in spite of all efforts to refloat it, it sank deeper and deeper. It was a relatively old ship, dating from 1756. The rocks had pierced its bottom, and there was nothing that could be done to save it. All that could be salvaged were its guns and spars, and that was by no means

---

18 Ekins, *Naval Battles*, pp.192–193.
19 Cavaliero, *Admiral Satan*, p.180.
20 Cavaliero, *Admiral Satan*, p.182.

easy, since it had heeled over on its bilge, and the heavy swell continued to knock the vessel about. In the end its foremast served to replace the mainmast of the *Héros*, and other repairs saw the mainmast of the *Bizarre* transferred to the *Illustre*. That of the *Consolante* was fitted to the *Bizarre*, being replaced by the mainmast of a Dutch ship.

While the work of repair of the French squadron got under way, the fallout from the battle was considerable. One of the earliest developments had been a visit to Suffren by Tromelin, Saint Felix, Landelle and Morand de Galles to ask leave to give up their posts. Suffren kept them waiting an hour; when he finally saw them, he was almost too angry to speak. Tromelin said that he had had news of the death of both of his parents and was suffering early onset of scurvy. Saint Felix, with whose performance Suffren had no quarrel, said that he was ill, and reminded Suffren of a promise that he could return to the Ile de France after the next battle. Suffren had been perfectly satisfied with Morand de Galles as well, but he was a sick man. As for Landelle, he had failed, and Suffren was not sorry to see him go. He was even more profoundly relieved to be rid of last of Tromelin, whom he correctly saw as the fount of much of the resentment expressed by officers from the Ile de France. When Tromelin returned there, Souillac made it clear that he was well aware of Tromelin's malign influence.[21]

Suffren wrote to Souillac on 23 September to give him an account of the battle, in which he made no secret of his belief that some of his captains had abandoned him due to 'une bonne jalousie':

> I began the combat fifteen against twelve, as I had put the *Consolante* also in the line. But what you will not believe is that there were only the *Héros*, the *Illustre* and the *Ajax* which fought close quarters. Yet all, yes all, had the greatest facility to approach, and you, who are a sailor, how can you be persuaded that having gained the head of the line anybody can fail to approach it, and that for vessels with good speed?[22]

On 30 September Suffren sent Castries a report of the battle, reiterating his discontent with the way in which he had been supported:

> I have just missed an opportunity to destroy the English squadron. I had fourteen ships and the *Consolante* which I had put in the line. Admiral Hughes was escaping without a fight, or to put it better fleeing in an orderly manner ... It was not till half past two in the afternoon that I could join him. My line having been nearly formed I attacked and gave the signal (to my ships) to approach (the enemy) ... Only the *Héros*, the *Illustre* and the *Ajax* fought at close quarters and in line. The others, without any regard to their posts and without making any manoeuvre, fired from a long distance, or is it better to say outside the range of a cannon?[23]

---

21 Cavaliero, *Admiral Satan*, p.185.
22 Roux, *Bailli de Suffren*, p.156.
23 La Varende, *Suffren et ses ennemis*, pp.251–252; Lacour-Gayet, *marine militaire*, pp.532–533.

Suffren went on to reflect on the reasons for the loss of his chance to finish off Hughes and his squadron:

> I can only attribute this horror to a desire to have done with the campaign, to ill will and to ignorance, for I dare not suspect worse. The result has been terrible. The damage we have suffered would have been appalling in Europe. Judge how much worse it is in India where we have no resources. I must say this to you, Monseigneur, that those officers who have been there a long time are neither sailors nor soldiers. They are not sailors because they never do any sailing, and not soldiers because the spirit of merchandise, independence and insubordination are absolutely opposed to the spirit of fighting. The masters there have contracted the spirit of avarice which it is impossible to eradicate. You cannot imagine what little ruses they have got up to persuade me to return.

He added, sadly: 'It is frightful to have had four times in our power to destroy the English squadron, and that it still exists.'

Reviewing Suffren's accounts of the battle, Mahan noted that many of the officers he condemned had done well on other occasions and drew attention to the irregular order of the French squadron. He suggested that Suffren's signals had followed each other with confusing rapidity, and concluded that chance, as well as the inexperience of several captains, was against Suffren: 'It is pretty certain that some of the mishap must be laid to the fiery and inconsiderate haste of Suffren who had the defects of his great qualities, upon which his coy and unwary antagonist unwittingly played.'[24] In Mahan's judgement, credit must be given to Hughes who, 'though lacking in enterprise and giving no token of tactical skill or *coup d'oeil*, showed both judgment and good management in the direction of his retreat and in keeping his ships well in hand.' He might have added that the superior seamanship of his captains gave Hughes a distinct advantage.

Thus it was, for a fourth time, that an engagement between Suffren and Hughes had ended indecisively, with each squadron both inflicting and receiving considerable damage during the course of the battle. But its outcome still left Suffren in possession of Trincomali, while Hughes had to nurse his badly damaged squadron all the way back to Madras. On the other hand, the monsoon season was approaching, and Suffren knew that he must soon make his plans for the winter.

When he returned to Trincomali after the battle of 3 September, Suffren had found awaiting him news of the campaign on land. Coote had begun a march on Cuddalore, and was apparently only awaiting provisions by sea before he embarked on a siege of the place. Its capture, and the consequent destruction of the French land forces, would be a major blow. It was indeed a serious threat; the total garrison of Cuddalore was no more than 2,700 men, of which 1,200 were European troops. Hyder Ali was at least two weeks' march away, and Tipu, west of Pondicherry, could do nothing to help. Confronted by this disturbing information, Suffren sent off the

---

24 Mahan, *Influence of Sea Power*, p.467.

Bellone to find out the current situation at Cuddalore, while he hastened the repairs to his squadron. Waiting anxiously for the frigate's return, such news as he did receive suggested that Cuddalore was in real danger. At the same time, the weather was seriously delaying the progress of his repairs. He had written to Castries on 22 September to tell him that at that moment he had only 10 ships fit to go to sea; the *Héros*, *Illustre* and *Vengeur* would not be ready for another week. To his relief, however, the *Bellone* sailed in on the following day with reassuring news; Cuddalore was for the present safe from attack, though in need of food and reinforcement.

Coote had now retreated, in the absence of support from the sea. Thus the battle of 3 September had had the effect of saving not only Trincomali but also, for the moment, Cuddalore. When he reached Pondicherry, Coote was disconcerted to find no sign of Hughes or his squadron. Without the cooperation of the navy, which he had always maintained was indispensable, Coote decided to retreat and he fell back towards Madras. It was an extremely low point for the East India Company and for British interests generally. A major famine was effectively depopulating the Carnatic, the garrison of Fort St George was reduced to iron rations, and most of the villages in the neighbourhood had been devastated by Hyder Ali's troops.

Suffren, once his repairs had been completed, decided to sail for Cuddalore. He had with him the troops of the Ile de France Regiment and the Bourbon volunteers, and he decided to return them to the army in the Carnatic. He sailed on 29 September, pausing on 3 October at Negapatam Bay, where he sank the 20-gun armed ship *Prince William* which was carrying munitions for the British forces in Tanjore. Then, after exchanging cannon fire at long range with the fortress, he went on to Cuddalore, arriving on the following day. He there suffered another, quite unnecessary, misfortune, when the *Bizarre*, on entering the anchorage, ran on a shoal. Attempts to haul her off all failed, and she became a total wreck. It was, however, possible to salvage her masts. The disaster was due to the misjudgement of another inexperienced officer, Trehouret, her captain, had sailed too close to the shore and had failed to tack in time.[25] The loss of the *Orient* and the *Bizarre* meant that Suffren was once more reduced to parity with Hughes in ships of the line and his weight of broadside was somewhat less.

By now, the monsoon season was at hand, and he wrote to Falck at Colombo to tell him that he would have to leave the Coromandel coast before the next full moon. While at Cuddalore he received news that Bickerton had sailed from Bombay for Madras on 18 September, which meant that he might appear at any time, giving Hughes an advantage of 17 ships to 12.

Suffren's visit to Cuddalore had been of great value in reassuring Hyder Ali, who had once again begun to lose faith in the value of the French alliance. Suffren's appearance restored his confidence. Piveron, at Hyder's headquarters, had written from there on 3 October to pass on to Suffren the Nawab's concerns. Since he had first attacked the Carnatic, he reckoned that he had lost 20,000 horses, and many elephants, camels, cattle and men, as well as a great deal of money. He was not

---

25 Cavaliero, *Admiral Satan*, p.193.

prepared to launch an attack on the British until Bussy arrived, and he was beginning to doubt if this would ever happen.

Suffren sent to Piveron instructions to tell Hyder Ali that Bussy was expected at the end of November, though privately feeling that this was over optimistic, and this news was sufficient to reassure the Nawab. He agreed to remain in the Carnatic in order to unite his army with that of the French. Hyder also agreed to supply timber for spars from Mangalore and have it sent round to Trincomali, and would arm five or six ships of from 40 to 50 guns to join Suffren's squadron. These might not be of much use in a fleet action, but would certainly prove a powerful threat to the Company's Bombay Marine.

16

Winter

Hughes finally brought his battered squadron into the roadstead at Madras on 9 September, considering it to be the only suitable place in which to stop the leaks from which his ships were suffering. Once there, he could make a proper review of their condition, and when he did so he had little difficulty in concluding that he could not remain during winter on the Coromandel coast, writing: 'most of the ships must absolutely be docked to put them in a condition for the next years' service, which is not to be wondered at considering the four severe engagements they have sustained within eight months.'[1]

He was disappointed to find that Bickerton had not yet arrived, and assumed, incorrectly, that the latter had decided to remain at Bombay due to the lateness of the season. To be on the safe side, however, he ordered the *Active* to cruise off Ceylon in order to warn Bickerton, if he did come, of the necessity of avoiding Trincomali. In giving his instructions to Captain Simon Mackenzie, he emphasised that his sole purpose was to warn Bickerton, and he was not to risk any engagement with an enemy warship.

Having made up his mind to leave for Bombay, Hughes informed Macartney of this, saying that he would sail as soon as the most urgent repairs had been completed, this, he said, could hardly be done before the arrival of the monsoon season. This information was very ill received; Macartney at once convened a meeting of the Committee to discuss the question. This produced a response which cannot have come as any surprise to Hughes. In a lengthy paper the Committee protested strongly against Hughes leaving the coast. Bickerton, they said, would shortly arrive. Having touched at Bombay he would have learned that Trincomali was in British hands but not that it had subsequently been taken by Suffren, so would assume that Hughes would winter there. But even if Bickerton did not come, Hughes should, said the Committee, remain on the Coromandel coast in order to protect the flow of provisions to Madras which would otherwise be at Suffren's mercy.

As for the immediate situation, the Committee suggested that Hughes should support Coote in his operations against Cuddalore. This, at least, Hughes was prepared to do, and he sent the swift sailing *Sceptre* and *Isis* to assist Coote's army. As has been seen, however, the operation against Cuddalore had already been

---

1   Richmond, *Navy in India*, p.283.

abandoned. Coote, though, was concerned for the safety of Negapatam, and the *Sceptre* and *Isis* on 20 September took 300 troops there by way of reinforcement.²

Once these ships were back in port, and with the army again in a position to commence operations, Macartney revived the project to strike a blow at Cuddalore. Coote was ready to undertake this provided that the squadron could support him for as long as it took to capture the place, writing:

> The cooperation of the squadron being the grand point upon which everything hinges, and whereof the late return of the army from, I may say, the gates of Cuddalore exhibits a very striking proof, I take it for granted that the Admiral having once embarked the assistance of the fleet towards the accomplishment of the object in view, will not, unless in the case of the most imminent danger, withdraw from the service until our united efforts have come to an issue.³

This was asking too much of Hughes. With the monsoon season rapidly approaching he could not possibly give an unconditional promise such as was sought. His squadron could only be reconditioned at Bombay. Only there were to be found the necessary resources, and he must sail for that port by 15 October. Before doing so he would have to water the squadron for a five-week voyage, so if he went to Cuddalore he must be back in Madras by 8 October. It was now 21 September; the army could not reach Cuddalore until 3 October. It was doubtful whether the business could be done in five days.

In any case the question which arose was whether it was wise at this point in time to contemplate another action against Suffren, who could be counted on to come to Cuddalore in support of the garrison. A close action, whatever its outcome, meant further heavy damage, and therefore to sail in that condition round Ceylon and up the Malabar coast was to invite disaster. This, Hughes told Macartney, was too much of a risk; the safety of all the Company's possessions in India depended on the squadron. To Coote, with whom he had almost always enjoyed a close and understanding relationship, he wrote:

> It is needless for me to point out to you, who are well informed, and have heretofore experienced the advantages of a squadron, how this total dependence arises. Very few men in this country but knew and felt that on the preservation of His Majesty's squadron depends the possession of the Company's possessions in it. Shall I, then, who command that squadron, be accessory to its ruin?⁴

Coote understood, and did not press further for the attack, assuring Hughes that he could always depend upon their cooperation.

---

2   Richmond, *Navy in India*, pp.288–289.
3   Richmond, *Navy in India*, p.289.
4   Richmond, *Navy in India*, pp.291–292.

The Committee did not immediately react to Hughes's letter and allowed two weeks to go by. Then, on 5 October, they exploded into action upon receiving a report that Suffren was in sight of Negapatam and evidently contemplating an attack. News also arrived that Bickerton was en route from Bombay, having sailed from there on 19 September.

The news of Suffren's appearance caused the Committee the gravest alarm, and a message was sent to Hughes demanding that he put to sea at once and attack the enemy. Hughes had by now had quite enough of this sort of thing. His patience with the Committee was exhausted, and he sent a terse reply refusing to comply with its request. The monsoon season was imminent, he had no port in which to effect repairs after an engagement, while Suffren had a secure port in Trincomali.

Not unexpectedly this provoked a response from the Committee which marked a new low in its relationship with the admiral. Reminding him that he had remained on the coast the previous year because of the importance he attached to Negapatam, the Committee suggested that if it now fell the whole of Tanjore and the Southern province might be lost. It repeated its previous arguments and asserted that Hughes had an ample choice of other bases. The Committee then moved on from argument to abuse:

> If the safety of His Majesty's ships were to be the sole or even primary object of His Majesty's commander, they should never meet the enemy at sea, or even go out of Bombay Dock. Ships of war have been on sundry occasions sunk designedly with a view to retarding the progress of the enemy, and when the safety of the British possessions on this coast depends on your remaining in this neighbourhood and your attacking immediately the enemy, the risk attending His Majesty's ships is not a sufficient reason for declining the service for which they were intended … We therefore have the right to call on you, Sir, in the name of our mutual sovereign and of the British nation to which all the territories in the possession of the East India Company are by Parliament declared to belong, and in the name of that Company (whose representatives you are by several Royal Charters *strictly charged and commanded to assist whenever thereunto required*) to give us that assistance which is in your power, and which we conceive to be essential to those interests which are committed to your and our care.[5]

The Committee went on at length to suggest that Hughes should take on board the bulk of the European troops now at Madras with a sufficient number of sepoys, proceed to attack Suffren, and then make for Trincomali, getting there before the enemy. The draughtsman of this remarkable letter (and Macartney must be presumed to have been in substantial part its author) added an unfortunate comparison between Hughes and Suffren, referring to the latter's statement that the value of his ships was nothing to the object for which they were sent to India and that he would keep them there as long as they were able to swim: 'It may be right to

---

5   Richmond, *Navy in India*, pp.293–294.

be taught even by a foe, and not to mistake the means for the end you were meant to answer, the defence of the British possessions which you seem willing to put to a great hazard rather than to put your ships to hazard.' The Committee said that they expected that once Hughes sailed for Bombay, the enemy would seek to burn or sink every vessel in the Madras roads and would effectively deprive the city of the grain upon which it depended. This would be followed by the loss of the whole Coromandel coast. Hughes's departure would be 'virtually to deliver the British possessions in India into the hands of the enemy.'[6]

In the course of this rant, the Committee threatened Hughes with an enquiry into his conduct. In his reply of 8 October, the admiral did not bother to reiterate in detail what he already explained as the situation of his squadron, since nothing had changed since his previous letter when he made clear that he was not going to invite an action with Suffren, on the verge of the monsoon season, without a secure port. The suggestion of an enquiry, however, prompted him to add that he would reserve what he would otherwise have communicated 'to that Enquiry with which you have so unhandsomely threatened me.'

That said, he went over to the attack, telling the Committee that the enquiry would find that it was responsible for the loss of Trincomali:

> Insignificant as you are in the scale of the natural and even the Company's interests, it will I believe be thought by all men highly unbecoming in you to attempt to hector or bully the commander-in-chief of His Majesty's forces by sea in this country into compliance with your selfish measures for the preservation of yourselves from dangers at the risk of the destruction of that force on which the whole of the British dominions in India greatly depend for preservation.[7]

Meanwhile Coote's health was now breaking down, and it was Major General James Stuart, designated as his successor in command of the British forces in the Carnatic, who made a rather more thoughtful approach to Hughes, writing on behalf of 85 merchants of Madras on 11 October to point out the problems that would arise if the grain convoy from Bengal was intercepted by the French. If this happened 'then the army he has now the honour to command and which is equal to any army by France and Hyder to be produced, in short the sheet anchor of India by land, must … be disbanded for want of rice only, and at the very time when the enemy will strike their stroke by land, he means the third week of December next.'[8]

Hughes was prepared to accept the force of this, and agreed to extend his stay until 20 October, in order to cover the arrival of the grain and rice convoy.

When reviewing this acerbic correspondence, Richmond, to be fair, did not automatically assume that Hughes was in the right. He analysed in considerable detail the various considerations that the admiral should take into account in deciding on the course of action to follow. He concluded that Hughes was entirely justified in the

---

6   Richmond, *Navy in India*, p.295.
7   Richmond, *Navy in India*, pp.297–298.
8   Cavaliero, *Admiral Satan*, p.198.

decision that he took; to remain on the open coast jeopardised India permanently and probably irrecoverably. Suffren could afford to take risks, with nothing to lose and everything to gain: 'Hughes had not only his squadron. He had India in his charge.'[9]

Whatever the pressure he might face to change his mind, Hughes was absolutely clear that his was the correct policy, and he would stick to it. His willingness to stay until 20 October proved, in the event, to be cutting it too fine. By 10 October the weather had become uncertain, and in the following days it became increasingly threatening. Watering was suspended to give priority to the unloading of the boats landing the grain. On the morning of 15 October the wind rose, and by noon it was blowing a gale; several ships had already parted their cables. At 2:00 p.m. Hughes made the signal to cut or slip. It was not a moment too soon. The intensity of the gale increased as the squadron clawed its way to the southward, and it continued to intensify as night fell. The *Superb* was especially badly affected; first its mizzen mast went over the side, followed by its main mast. Luckily, with the dawn, the fury of the gale abated, but the ship had seven feet of water in the hold, and the pumps could not keep up with the leaks.

The squadron had suffered severely; most of the ships were reduced to one anchor, and several had lost their topmasts. It was apparent that no return to Madras was possible. There, the gale had wrought fearful destruction, over 150 vessels having foundered, including all the rice vessels. Hughes detached his frigates for the protection of the coastal trade and, having shifted his flag to the *Sultan*, took the *Superb* in tow and began his long journey around Ceylon towards the Malabar coast en route for Bombay. It was of course necessary to give Ceylon a wide berth, but in spite of further gales the squadron succeeded in making its way to Anjengo, where it arrived on 25 November.

One of things that had particularly irritated Hughes in his correspondence with the Committee was having been compared unfavourably to his opponent, and he expressed his annoyance in a despatch which he sent to the Admiralty on 20 October:

> The compliments which the select Committee are pleased to pay Mr Suffren are far from unacceptable to me. I believe him all they say, able, active and sagacious, and, more, brave ... Yet they compliment Mr Suffren at my expense. That Mr Suffren expected to have effected a great deal more against His Majesty's squadron than he did is clear by his having dismissed and sent to France within these few months no less than eight of his captains.[10]

Hughes was evidently very well informed of Suffren's disciplinary problems.

It was at Anjengo that Hughes learned for the first time of Bickerton's movements. The Commodore had arrived at Madras escorting a convoy of 10 Company ships with troops, on 19 October. He did not linger, and at once set sail for Bombay, overtaking Hughes unseen at sea. Hughes, meanwhile, having paused at Anjengo, then moved on to Paniani, where Tipu was besieging a British force under Colonel McLeod. He left two frigates there to support the army. He was now very short of

---

9   Richmond, *Navy in India*, p.302.
10 Cavaliero, *Admiral Satan*, p.198.

water, and had 450 men suffering from scurvy, so he next went to Tellicherry. There, he landed his sick, and took on water. The coppered ships were watered first, and he sent these on to Bombay, with the *Magnanime* towing the *Superb*. He realised that so extensive were the repairs required by the squadron that Bombay would not be able to cope with so much work, so with the rest of his squadron he made his way to Goa with the *Sultan*, *Monmouth*, *Hero* and *Sceptre*. The Portuguese governor, Dom Federico de Souza, warmly welcomed Hughes, and made the facilities of his dockyard available.

Once the repairs to these ships had been completed, Hughes set off again to Bombay, which he reached on 17 January. There, he found the rest of his squadron which had in ones and twos arrived before him, together with Bickerton, with four ships of the line; these were the *Gibraltar*, *Cumberland*, *Defence* and *Inflexible*. The fifth ship, the *Africa*, had been sent to escort a convoy of troops to reinforce McLeod at Paniani. Bickerton's ships were also in need of repair following their lengthy journey, so the yards at Bombay were extremely busy, as Hughes prepared for the next campaign.

Meanwhile Suffren, like Hughes, had also had to face the difficult decision as to where he was to winter his squadron. His possession of Trincomali did not itself solve the problem. Several factors had to be taken into account, of which one of the most serious was the continuing lack of supplies at Trincomali. The Company had placed an embargo on the export of food to Ceylon, and such rice as was reaching the island came from Cochin, the Dutch settlement on the Malabar coast. Governor Falck was convinced that this would be a target for an imminent attack from Bombay. It was his wish that Suffren should winter there, where he could be more confident of the necessary supply of provisions, and where he would also find shipwrights to assist with his repairs.

For Suffren, however, the problem was in fact a lot more complex than it appeared to Falck. His original plan had been to winter at Achin, in Sumatra. Now that he had Trincomali, he had a port at which it might be possible to spend the winter, but it would not enable him to operate on the Malabar coast, as Falck proposed. It was plainly going to be difficult to ensure adequate provisions for the squadron at Trincomali. Of course, going to Achin meant that there could be no activity on the Malabar coast, but he could be confident of obtaining a ready supply of provisions there, as well as resources with which to refurbish his ships. From Achin, the prevailing winds after the end of the monsoon season were particularly favourable to a swift passage across the Indian Ocean to the Coromandel coast. This could not be said of Trincomali.

Finally, and perhaps most importantly, Achin had been designated as the rendezvous of the squadron with the convoy carrying Bussy and the troops intended to operate on the Indian mainland. If Suffren was not there to meet him, there was always the danger that the British might themselves go to Achin and take by surprise the Marquis's convoy. From Trincomali, Suffren had written to Castries to tell him of his anxiety:

> On all sides I see nothing but danger and uncertainty. However, if I get no other news I shall go there (Achin). I shall leave 2,000 troops here with

provisions and ammunition. I do not expect that the English will attempt its capture. The governor thinks he will be secure if he has time enough to work at the defences.[11]

On October 15, as Suffren lay off Cuddalore, the anticipated north-east gale burst on the Coromandel coast. Time was up, and he was more fortunate than Hughes in being able to leave the roadstead unscathed. The gale lasted only a short time, and he made his way to Achin, where he arrived on 2 November. Before departing he had written to Souillac to tell him of his intention to sail for his rendezvous with Bussy at Achin:

> I do not know whether I shall be able to reach the place; my position is most embarrassing. It would take a long time and it is unnecessary to go into details, but I see myself in a position in which it is necessary to guess what will occur but which I cannot do. Send me at Trincomali, as much in the way of munitions provisions and naval equipment. I leave here tomorrow.[12]

One of Suffren's major concerns was the potential effect on Hyder Ali of his departure from the coast. The Nawab was, however understanding of the necessity for Suffren's departure, as he told Piveron, who reported it to the admiral:

> I have great confidence in everything M. de Suffren says, and what you told me on his behalf has given me the deepest satisfaction and I believe it. Please God the moment has already arrived and that nothing will happen to upset our splendid projects, for I desire the glory of your nation as much as my own … Let him leave promptly, let him go and join M. de Bussy, let them return as soon as possible and we shall do great things. This will console me for the inaction in which I am forced to remain.[13]

Suffren's passage to Achin was trouble free. When he reached the northern tip of Sumatra, he sent the frigate *Fine* in to reconnoitre, just in case the British had indeed chosen this as their winter destination. The frigate examined the wide natural bay which would be the squadron's anchorage, and found there only the *Bellone* and the *Fortune*, which had made a faster crossing than the rest of the squadron. To ensure that the British had not found another anchorage nearby, Suffren now sent the *Fortune* to visit the rest of the archipelago. The *Fine* went to Kedah for rice, while the *Bellone* and the *Pulvériseur* went to Malacca for spars as well as rice. The commander of the latter, returning fully laden, encountered a convoy of five British East Indiamen, but concluded that he should not hazard his valuable cargo by attacking them. When he reported this, Suffren was far from pleased, telling him that he had read his log and that he had stained his flag.

---

11 Richmond, *Navy in India*, pp.313–314.
12 Roux, *Bailli de Suffren*, p.160n.
13 Cavaliero, *Admiral Satan*, pp.194–195.

Achin was in many respects ideal, as one French writer described: 'Achin is an excellent port for wintering, as much for the safety of the ships as for the supply of provisions which are in abundance there. Water is very easily procurable from the river ... It is not necessary to go high up to find sweet water. We have been permitted to buy wood from the Pulo Way.'[14]

On the other hand, the climate was not healthy, and the number of sick aboard the ships of the squadron soon increased. Suffren was, though, able by a tactful approach to the Sultan to overcome the latter's initial reluctance to be of assistance to the squadron, and he agreed to supply whatever was needed. In particular Suffren took the precaution of keeping his men aboard ship, to avoid any trouble with the local population. It was certainly necessary to keep on the right side of the Sultan, a difficult and touchy individual.

Work on the ships of the squadron made good progress. The condition of the *Vengeur* was however, so bad that it was essential that it be careened, and Suffren sent it back to Trincomali for the purpose. Without the availability of that port, he wrote later, he would have lost the ship.

On 24 November, Suffren received bad news when there arrived at Achin the *Duc de Chartres* carrying ammunition and provisions. Not only did its captain bring accounts of the naval defeats suffered by France in Europe and America; he also reported on the epidemic which had afflicted the convoy bringing Bussy's troops to the Ile de France, escorted by a squadron under Peynier. The news was uniformly bad. Not only were the troops decimated by the fever which swept through their ranks, but Bussy himself was gravely ill. The attempts to assemble a powerful military and naval force for operations in India had been seriously compromised.

The first instalment, under d'Aymar, which consisted of the *Saint Michel* and *Illustre*, with the frigate *Consolante* and the corvette *Victor*, had left Brest in November 1781, picked up Bussy at Cadiz, and then proceeded to Tenerife in the Canary Islands to await the next convoy under Soulanges. This, sailing with de Guichen from Brest, had been encountered by Rear Admiral Richard Kempenfelt on 17 December. He captured a large part of the convoy, and most of what was left of it returned to Brest, though two store ships carrying ammunition and heavy artillery made it to Tenerife. The third part of the force for India sailed with Peynier on 11 February. He had with him the *Fendant*, 74, *Argonaute*, 74, *Hardi*, 74 and *Alexandre*, 64, together with the frigates *Cleopatre* and *Chasseur*, escorting 35 ships carrying 2,500 men. The final instalment, again under Soulanges, left Brest on 19 April. It was intercepted by Vice Admiral the Honourable Samuel Barrington, who took two ships of its escort, and the rest returned to Brest.

When Peynier arrived at Port Louis, it was with a squadron of ships in very poor condition; the *Alexandre* was in such a bad state that it was useless and had to be burned. Thus out of the 10 ships which it was intended should reinforce Suffren, only five would now be available to him, and these not at once, due to their condition and the sickness of their crews. The loss of so large a part of his expected reinforcement would have mattered less to Suffren if it had been possible to persuade the Dutch

---

14 Sen, *French in India*, p.268.

squadron at Batavia to put to sea to join him in his campaign against the British in 1783. This squadron consisted of seven ships of the line under Schrymer, and together with Peynier's squadron would have given Suffren a commanding superiority over Hughes, even after Bickerton had arrived. As it was, however, the Dutch stoutly refused to leave harbour. It is possible that this refusal was due to a fear that the British were preparing an assault on Java and Sumatra, a suggestion that had formed part of the false instructions to Johnstone which had been leaked in 1781 at the time of the departure of his expedition to the Cape.

Pondering the gloomy information which had reached him, Suffren wrote to Bussy on 26 November. He was particularly concerned with the need to maintain Hyder's confidence, which was bound to be affected by news of the further delay in Bussy's arrival. An explanation must be given to the Nawab. He could tell him that the taking of Trincomali had altered Bussy's plans, but that he would soon arrive, or that the change was due to ensuring the meeting of the squadron with Bussy's army. In any event, Suffren felt that he must be seen to put in an appearance on the Indian coast as soon as possible, both to threaten the grain convoys to Madras and to reassure Hyder Ali. In his letter to Bussy he wrote: 'I shall go to the mouth of the Ganges to destroy the convoys which the enemy will despatch as early as he can to replace the losses suffered in the storm, and to try to capture some prizes to victual Cuddalore, Trincomali and the squadron.'[15]

He also suggested that, to save time, Bussy should make his way to Galle, rather than Achin, where he could receive up to date information as to the situation of the squadron. Suffren was extremely concerned that news of the sickness of Bussy's army and the consequent delay had already reached Cuddalore. There should have been, he thought, censorship to prevent this leaking out. In fact, there was a marked difference in the level of intelligence available to the two admirals. As the campaigning season approached, Suffren was fully aware that Hughes had gone to Bombay to refurbish his squadron; the disputes between the admiral and the Madras Committee were in the public domain. On the other hand, Hughes did not know where Suffren had gone for the winter, and the French commander had made every effort for it to appear that it had been to Trincomali that he had chosen to go.

---

15 Richmond, *Navy in India*, p.216.

17

Bussy

The news that had reached Suffren at Achin was almost uniformly depressing. On 30 November, pondering the setbacks which the French cause had suffered, he wrote to Mme de Seillans:

> I am very well, my dear friend, but this is the only good news I am able to send you. I fear that the misfortunes in Europe and America greatly affect our situation. A disastrous epidemic which M. de Peynier's squadron has suffered prevents everything. If I am able to return from India with honour it will be by the greatest good fortune. I was here expecting eight ships and as many as 1,000 men; but a despatch vessel has arrived here which tells me that one convoy has been taken and another has been held up by disease. In truth, it is too many misfortunes at once.[1]

It was entirely clear to Suffren that he was going to have to make the best of a bad job in his 1783 campaign. From one cause and another he was not going to have the ships that might have given him superiority over Hughes, and he had abandoned all hope of persuading the Dutch squadron at Batavia to join him. He was determined, nevertheless, to put in an appearance on the eastern coast of India as soon as he could. Once there he could, by a sustained assault on the Company's trade, deny to Madras the crucial food supplies on which the city depended. Hopefully, he would be able to make use of these supplies himself. The news of his activity would, he intended, serve as a reassurance to Hyder Ali that his French alliance was capable of yielding results. He determined to sail as soon as essential repairs had been carried out. The full refitting of the squadron could be completed when he arrived at Trincomali, where he could make use of the Dutch artificers. Accordingly, he sent a message to Governor Falck in Colombo asking him to arrange for the sending to the port of both carpenters and caulkers.

Suffren put to sea from Achin on 20 December, heading for the Orissa coast with 10 ships of the line; he despatched the *Petit Annibal* and the *Bellone* to the mouth of the Hooghly to operate directly against the Calcutta trade. These vessels arrived there on 8 January and were at once successful in taking a large number of prizes, capturing over 1,000 tons of rice which contributed to the squadron's own

---

1   Roux, *Bailli de Suffren*, p.167.

victualling. Meanwhile Suffren, with the rest of the squadron, arrived at Ganjam on the Orissa coast and anchored in the roadstead there.

On 11 January he enjoyed a stroke of good fortune, when the British frigate *Coventry* sailed during a dark night into the middle of the French squadron, having mistakenly taken it to be a convoy of East Indiamen. Completely surrounded in this way by the enemy, Captain William Wolseley realised at once that he had no chance of escape and bowed to the inevitable. It was a handsome prize; the *Coventry* was a coppered frigate and had been captured entirely undamaged. It was soon put to work under French colours, and on 18 January took its first prize, an 18-gun grab, and on 31 January snapped up a merchantman from Pegu.

Suffren had, however, missed the crucial Bengal convoy which brought desperately needed supplies to Madras. He had planned to undertake an operation against Vizagapatam but was obliged to give this up as impracticable because the surf there was running too high. In any case he was obliged to change his plans as a result of the intelligence which he had gained with the capture of the *Coventry*. Hyder Ali had died on 7 December, and the key question now which demanded an answer was whether Tipu Sultan would be driven by his father's extreme ambition and hatred of the British, and how far the French could count on his cooperation. Suffren did not know the present whereabouts of the army which Hyder Ali had sent into the Carnatic. He did know that Tipu was engaged on the Malabar coast defending his possessions there against the belated attack mounted from Bombay under the command of Brigadier General Richard Matthews. He was also, of course, aware that Hughes had been joined at Bombay by Bickerton's detachment and, a matter of immediate concern, that Bickerton had brought a substantial reinforcement to Madras on the occasion of his brief visit to the city in October. This last development meant that the French garrison at Cuddalore might well face an early attack.

In these circumstances, Suffren concluded that Cuddalore must be his first priority, and he abandoned his other operations and sailed there directly. The winds were against him, but he finally arrived on 6 February to find, thankfully, that no attack had yet materialised nor was apparently imminent. However, a substantial part of the garrison had marched off to join Tipu, and as a result Cuddalore was extremely vulnerable. Suffren sent an urgent letter to Tipu to plead for his return to the Carnatic as soon as possible.

Suffren was extremely discontented at Bussy's late arrival. Complaining to Castries of what he regarded as a totally avoidable delay, he wrote: 'They have waited to collect a little more provisions, without which we could have done very well, and complete the refit of the *Hardi*; as though two months more of the weather suitable for operations was not more essential than the addition of one ship!'[2]

For the moment there was nothing more he could do at Cuddalore, and he sailed for Trincomali where he intended to resume the refitting of his squadron. He arrived there on 23 February. Rather in the manner in which Hughes had been badgered by the presidencies of Madras and Bombay to operate in accordance with what each saw as its own most pressing needs, Suffren was also coming under pressure from

---

2 Richmond, *Navy in India*, p.329.

Tipu Sultan. (Public Domain)

various directions. He was in no doubt as to what should be his proper objective which, simply stated, was to bring about a British defeat in the Carnatic. Tipu, on the other hand, was apprehensive for the security of his possessions on the Malabar coast, and to Suffren's request that he return to the Carnatic he put forward the counter-proposal that the French squadron should be brought round to operate on the western coast.

On the other hand, Governor Falck, in Colombo, still saw as the immediate priority the defence of Cochin. For this, he too urged Suffren to come there with all or part of his squadron, suggesting that this would provide the opportunity to capture Tellicherry and Anjengo.

Suffren, though, would have none of these distractions. It was Cuddalore that was presently of crucial importance, and the sooner it could be reinforced by Bussy the better. So far as the western coast was concerned, he could not think of exposing his squadron to the risk of operating against a superior force with no base to fall back on, and there could be no question of dividing his force. For the moment, his most urgent priority was to ensure that all his ships were refitted. When departing from Cuddalore, he had left the *Saint Michel* and *Coventry* to cruise off Madras and brought the rest of the squadron back into Trincomali.

On his return there he encountered, as a prisoner of war, William Hickey, whose vivid description of Suffren has been previously quoted. Hickey was accompanied by the beautiful Charlotte Barry. They had been passengers abroad the *Rainha do Portugal* which had taken refuge in Trincomali after enduring a violent storm. The French naval officers made a considerable fuss of them; when he heard about them, Suffren entertained them to dinner aboard the *Héros*. His guests were not very impressed by what they saw of the French flagship. William Hickey was shocked by 'the scene of filth and dirt as I could not have believed had I not seen; it had more the appearance of an abominable pigsty than the inside of a ship of the line bearing an Admiral's flag!'³ He found the contrast with what he had seen of British men of war to be extremely striking; only the *Vengeur* and the *Flamand* were as clean and orderly as their antagonists. The capture of the *Rainha do Portugal* had provided another very substantial benefit. It was stripped of her copper, which was applied to the hull of the *Illustre*.

When the time came for the squadron to leave Trincomali Suffren, who had been much taken with William and Charlotte, released them, giving lavish farewell gifts (all of which had been taken from a prize in the Bay of Bengal). The couple embarked on the *Blake*, a small British prize. Later they were transferred to a Danish merchantman captured by the *Naiade*, aboard which Suffren thought that they would be more comfortable, and he released the vessel.

Bussy had finally embarked on the *Fendant* and sailed from Port Louis on 18 December. He paused for a week at the Ile de Bourbon, before setting his course for the agreed rendezvous with Suffren at Achin. He was not in an optimistic frame of mind, writing in his journal:

> At last I am embarking today at five in the afternoon, a convalescent, and yet much weak, from a cruel illness lasting for more than five months, which on several occasions appeared to carry me to the grave. It is certain that placed in my situation most other persons would not have proceeded further. But the confidence with which the King has honoured me, the noble dealings of the Ministers, and finally the importance which has been attached to the expedition entrusted to me have determined me to sacrifice the little health that I still retain and to start for India in spite of the paucity of my present resources ... In fact nearly all the 2,200 men I am taking with me have suffered from a pestilential malady which has completely wasted their vitality.[4]

Bussy looked forward gloomily to the length of the voyage he was to undertake and the possibility that the disease might again develop. When he arrived, he expected to find only 1,000 men awaiting him. The total forces available would then be far below the number originally stipulated, which had been fixed at 10,500. Nevertheless, his self-belief remained high:

> My situation presents a prospect sufficient to discourage all others except me, but my zeal has not been destroyed by the major obstacles I had to surmount since the moment of my departure from France, and I can see quite clearly, without being frightened, all the other obstacles which remain for me to face ... The principal one is to re-establish discipline among the troops who are in India.[5]

---

3   Cavaliero, *Admiral Satan*, p.210.
4   Sen, *French in India*, p.317.
5   Sen, *French in India*, pp.317–318.

By the time Bussy arrived at Achin, at the end of February, Suffren had long since sailed to commence operations on the Indian coast. On 2 March Bussy called a conference of the senior naval officers, who unanimously recommended that the convoy and its escort should proceed at once to Trincomali. This advice Bussy readily accepted, and the force put to sea immediately, and on 10 March the convoy of 32 transports carrying 2,500 men, escorted by Peynier's three ships of the line and a frigate finally sailed into the harbour of Trincomali.

Suffren was profoundly relieved. He at once put on his full-dress uniform to go on board the *Fendant* to call on Bussy. He remarked to William Hickey that he 'felt like a hog in armour, for so long a period had elapsed since he had been obliged to dress otherwise than in the lightest and thinnest clothing that he was really uncomfortable. But etiquette required his waiting upon the commander-in-chief properly equipped, even at the expense of his feelings.'[6] When he met Bussy, he was somewhat discouraged to see how far the passing years and his recent illness had withered the Marquis, but nonetheless he could now at last demonstrate to Tipu that, with his support, here was the man to lead the French forces to victory over the British.

Bussy's arrival did, however, have an immediate consequence for Suffren's command, since the general had been appointed as supreme commander of all the French forces in India, both by land and sea. When he had originally been consulted by the French government about the proposed despatch of an expedition to the Far East, Bussy had given it as his opinion that an overall command structure must be established, and Castries had been persuaded by this advice. The instructions issued in November 1781 announced that the King had decided to appoint Bussy 'to the command-in-chief of all the forces by land and sea in India.' Suffren, when he inherited the command of the squadron from d'Orves, made no secret of his disapproval of the arrangement, writing to Castries:

> According to M. Bussy's patent I am to be under his orders. I do not object except for the reason that no good to the service on land can come of it, though I can assure you that I will do my best to prevent harm from arising. Two possible conditions may exist: one in which a general at sea is acquainted with his profession, the other in which he is not. In the first case, why put him under the orders of someone who is ignorant of it? In the second, why leave him in command? For of what use will any orders be from someone more ignorant than himself? And who will in addition be on shore when he is at sea?[7]

Castries, who was perhaps not altogether surprised to have received this, replied patiently on 4 April 1783, setting out the reasoning behind the decision to appoint Bussy as commander-in-chief:

> If M. de Bussy has joined you, you will by now have seen that the authority over the forces at sea which the King has thought fit to give him relates only

---

6 Cavaliero, *Admiral Satan*, p.211.
7 Richmond, *Navy in India*, pp.397–398.

to the operations of the army, to which you will agree it was impossible not to subordinate those of the squadron. The principal object is the revolution against the English in India. The squadron must cooperate in this and, for that reason, is only an accessory to the operations on land. France has twice lost India on account of the immoderate desire to return to the islands, and, until yourself, no naval commander has had the strength to resist the demands. In view of this it is impossible to give authority, which does not subordinate everything to the operations on land, and to those that have the direction of those operations. Here, then, is more reason than enough to satisfy a fighting man such as yourself, and to convince him how necessary it was for the King to give the orders about which you write and which do not in any way deprive you of your immediate authority over and regulations of your ships.[8]

The desirability of appointing an overall commander-in-chief for a particular theatre of war or for some specific combined operations by the different services has been many times explored by historians. The principle of unity of command where both naval and military forces are to be employed has not always been followed; in general, historians have pointed to such instances having led to unfortunate results. In the present case the French government had to consider whether troops should be sent and, if so, how many. Could, in other words, a sufficiently powerful squadron be able to obtain by itself command of the sea, prevent British reinforcements, prevent the payment of her native armies, and thus enable the native princes on their own to destroy the British armies and reconquer the territories under British rule? The conclusion reached, on the basis of Bussy's advice, was that a substantial force of European troops would be necessary to achieve a revolution against the British in India. That being the case, it was considered that the appointment of an overall commander-in-chief was essential. How this would work out in principle remained to be seen.

Richmond, after a detailed analysis of the particular situation faced by Bussy and Suffren in 1783, concluded that 'the authority to command was not only useless but dangerous':

> Useless, becausee Bussy was necessarily ignorant of whether it was practicable for Suffren to work his way with his squadron from Trincomali in the face of a superior force of the whereabouts of which he had no information. Dangerous, because such an order given to a man physically brave but morally weak, might have been taken as binding, and an operation which would have ruined the squadron – and with it the army – might have been undertaken from lack of moral courage to disobey. The power which de Bussy needed was that of informing his colleague at sea of his needs. If the naval commander's orders from higher authority should be to cooperate to his utmost towards a common object, he could not abstain from giving

---

8 Richmond, *Navy in India*, p.398.

such help as it lay in his power to give without breach of his orders from the King. But whether he could throw in the provisions at all, and whether he should do so with a part only, were matters on which he, and he only, could possibly form a correct judgement.[9]

As soon as Bussy had arrived, Suffren set about the arrangements to despatch to Cuddalore the troops which he had brought. There was not a moment to lose. Suffren embarked the troops and the most essential artillery on board the fastest transports. He decided that only his seven coppered ships of the line should sail as an escort, as he later explained to Castries:

> If Hughes's squadron, composed of seventeen ships both stronger and better commanded than mine, should meet me, I should be forced to fight; the horrible slowness of my ships would make it impossible to take refuge in flight. On the other hand, by sailing with seven coppered ships the landing can be expedited before Hughes's arrival, and if he should be met he could be avoided.[10]

On 13 March the squadron and the convoy of transports departed from Trincomali and set off as fast as the winds allowed for the coast. They were fortunate and arrived at Porto Novo three days later. When the troops were put ashore there, working all through the night, they were then to march to Manjikuppam. The squadron anchored off Cuddalore, where the task of landing the most urgent artillery and heavy stores was begun. That operation took the best part of six days, with Suffren fretting that at any moment Hughes might put in an appearance. Finally, on 23 March, he was able to set sail for Trincomali, leaving Peynier with the *Fendant*, *Saint Michel*, *Cleopatre* and *Coventry* to cruise off Madras in the hope of intercepting a convoy of 11 East Indiamen which had left England in the previous September apparently escorted only by the 50-gun ship *Bristol*.

At Porto Novo Bussy learned that Tipu was still operating on the Malabar coast. He also received information that Hughes had been due to leave Bombay with 15 ships about the middle of February, which confirmed the need for haste in the disembarkation at Cuddalore, which would enable Suffren to return promptly to Trincomali. Before leaving, he promised Bussy that he would return with his squadron to meet Hughes if he should mount an attack on Cuddalore.

Bussy's pessimism had not lightened. He wrote in his journal: 'As regards our present situation on the Coromandel coast, it is such that I would not have undertaken the task of the re-establishment of our nation after peace with such a small number of troops as had been given me for waging war.'[11] He had little confidence in the reliability of Tipu Sultan, and the Dutch were proving unfriendly allies, refusing to pay the five million livres agreed upon in Paris on the grounds that they had no money and had already provided immense supplies to Suffren's squadron. This

---

9   Richmond, *Navy in India*, p.402.
10 Richmond, *Navy in India*, p.332.
11 Sen, *French in India*, p.320.

left him with insufficient funds to last more than four or five months. Once he had landed, Bussy confided to his diary his mounting concern at his exposed position. 'I am without allies, without provisions, without means of transport, and in a country devastated beyond imagination. I have only five millions to procure all those things as also to meet the other expenses necessary for an army; only the pay of the troops, apart from other normal expenses, will amount to nearly a million a month in spite of the reforms that I want to carry out.'[12]

Historians have not, in general, been kind to Bussy, treating him merely as a light of other days. Joseph Roux, for instance, wrote:

> The old governor of the Deccan, the military genius under Salabat, the illustrious lieutenant of Dupleix was now but an old man, gouty and worried, ignorant of the new politics and of the real situation of the belligerent powers. His talents and his proverbial enterprise had been lost during a repose of 22 years in the midst of his immense riches ... The vanity of this general was bound to have grave consequences which could not always be remedied by the genius of de Suffren.[13]

On the other hand, in Sen's view, the general condemnation of Bussy is unjustified, and not based on the facts. He suggested that Roux, as an admiring biographer of Suffren, 'deliberately painted Bussy black so that his own hero might shine all the more in contrast.'[14]

---

12 Sen, *French in India*, p.321.
13 Roux, *Bailli de Suffren*, p.177.
14 Sen, *French in India*, p.349.

18

Cuddalore

On his way back to Trincomali, Suffren wrote a despatch to Castries dated 23 March to report his situation which, in terms of the manning of his ships was particularly serious:

> I am proceeding to Trincomali where I will hasten the refit of the ships. I hope to refit completely, but a disquieting fact is the shortage of personnel. Supposing that the sick will soon return to duty, and taking men from transports and useless frigates, I will still be short of 1,200 men. During the thirteen months we have been in the Indies we have received no recruits. If the King wishes to maintain a fleet of fifteen to eighteen ships in the Indies, at least 3,000 men a year are required to keep the ships up to complement, especially if, as in the past year, there are four battles to be fought. The fleet is now well provided. We are only short of shot and spare top masts. More than anything, good ships of the line, coppered frigates and men are required.[1]

Suffren's trip north to Porto Novo and Cuddalore had been completed with little loss of time. During the return journey to Trincomali he was not so fortunate, dogged all the way by light and foul winds. By 10 April he was still some 20 miles short of his destination. It was at this point that the *Bellone*, scouting ahead of the squadron to the southward, signalled the siting of five sail; soon, this became 13, and then 23. There could be no doubt that, as Suffren had feared Hughes had arrived while the French squadron was still divided.

On this occasion fortune favoured the French. The squadron was not spotted by the British scouting vessels before night fell, and next day Suffren was able safely to bring his ships into the harbour at Trincomali. Hughes had thus narrowly missed an outstanding opportunity of destroying his enemy. It would perhaps be fairer to say that Suffren had deserved his luck by his speedy conduct of the operation to land Bussy and his troops in India, so that he was able, by the skin of his teeth, to return unscathed to unite his squadron.

It was clear, though, that he must immediately warn Peynier of the danger which he faced. He sent for *Lieutenant* Louis Villaret-Joyeuse, who one day would

---

1   Lacour-Gayet, *marine militaire* p.540.

command the French fleet in the next war, but who was now captain of the *Naiade*, instructing him to sail at once for Madras. Villaret-Joyeuse, perfectly aware of the danger which he faced, replied sardonically: 'Since you have singled me out for this honour, perhaps you could give me letters of introduction to both Lord Macartney and Admiral Hughes.' Suffren took the point, but the speedy *Naiade* was all he could spare. Villaret-Joyeuse sailed at once, but that night fell in with the 64-gun *Sceptre*. Under the light of the moon, he put up a brave and determined resistance for three and a half hours until, inevitably, he was obliged to strike. During the course of the engagement the *Naiade* had 34 men wounded, and the *Sceptre* 24.[2]

Although he had not received the intended warning, Peynier was fortunate. News that Hughes was in the offing soon reached him. Nevertheless, still hoping that he might snap up the convoy he was awaiting, he remained off the coast. Ultimately his mission failed when the convoy arrived under the escort of part of Hughes's squadron. Peynier had, however, nearly achieved a remarkable coup when on 14 March he encountered the Company's Indiamen *Resolution* and *Royal Charlotte*. The latter was carrying bullion and, among her passengers, Sir Eyre Coote. In the end the two Company ships got away and reached Madras, but the stress of the narrow escape caused Coote to suffer from a stroke, and he was taken ashore numbed and motionless on 24 March. Three days later, France's most potent enemy passed away.

Hughes had been three months at Bombay. The repairs to his ships had been put in hand at once. The work was considerable, since the damage sustained during the Battle of Trincomali had been accentuated by the gales experienced in October during his voyage. But neither the repairs nor the reprovisioning of the squadron had gone well. Notwithstanding the duty imposed on them by an Act of Parliament of 1782, the Presidency of Bombay, pleading inability, gave no assistance. Nothing was made available to the squadron without ready money paid for it and at that moment Hughes had none. The problem of revictualling his squadron was constant. When Hughes had finally left Bombay, he indented to Calcutta for supplies and was promised them at Madras by the end of June. To this he pointed out that not half of what was required could be found in Bengal, and even if it could, there was the problem of shipping it safely to Madras in the face of enemy cruisers. He pointed to a recent shipment of bread which had taken four months to make the passage, and most had been found to be spoiled on arrival. In further correspondence with the Presidency, Hughes became extremely angry and accused it of 'an attempt to ruin the Companies of the several Ships by holding up to him … partial supplies of Bread and other Articles.'[3] The business of watering was no less badly performed, due to an insufficiency of boats, which were invariably manned by slovenly crews. Meanwhile, the work of repairing and refitting the squadron had proceeded very slowly; the workmen in the yard were dilatory and supplies of food were not forthcoming.

Hughes, as usual, was not prepared to sail until his squadron was properly ready to do so. For the moment he could do little but fret about what was going on elsewhere. Gradually, though, he had begun to receive information, learning in January

---

2   Cavaliero, *Admiral Satan*, p.215.
3   Martin Wilcox, 'This Great Complex Concern; Victualling the Royal Navy on the East Indies Station, 1780-1815', *The Mariner's Mirror*, (2011) 97:2, pp.32–48.

that Suffren had gone to Achin, which meant that there was no immediate threat to Madras. Bussy, he heard, with four ships and many transports, had reached the Ile de France and was expected to sail in October, although with only 3,000 men. And from England there came news that Barrington had intercepted a French convoy bound for India. Overall, Hughes could feel that the situation was generally in hand, but, of course, the urgent need was to press on with the reconditioning of his squadron. He reported to London on 15 January:

> Nothing is so necessary or can so effectually answer that end (the protection of India) as a decided superiority at sea. I am now with every officer in the squadron exerting myself to the utmost to get fifteen ships of the line in a condition for sea, and shall then without a moment's delay proceed to the Coromandel coast to seek the enemy.[4]

Hughes had expected that he would be able to sail with his squadron from Bombay by the latter part of February, but the delays to the repairs, and the incomplete provisioning of his ships, meant that this was not possible. While he waited, the news which came in left him uncertain of the strategy he should employ when he was finally able to get to sea. Suffren's activity on the Orissa coast had not been expected, but at least it meant that his whereabouts were, for the moment, known. On the other hand, there was no information about the French army at the Ile de France which had been expected to sail in October. There had been a suggestion from the Cape that its objective might be Bombay, in which case it would be unwise for Hughes to sail to the Coromandel coast and leave the western coast without means of defence. Of one thing Hughes was certain and that was that it would be folly to divide the squadron.

The death of Hyder Ali was another factor in his assessment of his situation. So was the news that Stuart, with his army in Madras reinforced by 1,200 men from Negapatam, which had been abandoned, was now considered strong enough to move against Cuddalore. There was also encouraging news from Tanjore, where Colonel Ross Lang, the local British commander, was confident that he was secure there.

At last, on 20 March, the squadron was able to put to sea. It had been joined by those vessels which had been undergoing repairs at Goa. Hughes now concluded that it was late enough in the season to be safe to assume that Bussy would not appear on the Malabar coast, and he determined to make his way to the east; at this time, he was unaware of Bussy's arrival at Trincomali. As he sailed around the east coast of Ceylon, he had no information about Suffren's movements other than from a prize captured by one of his cruisers to the effect that the whole of Suffren's squadron was at Trincomali save for a detachment off Madras, information which was of course at that time incorrect. Having arrived off Trincomali, to find that Suffren was now safely installed there, he continued on his way to Madras, sending Captain Andrew Mitchell on ahead with the *Burford*, *Sultan*, *Africa*, *Eagle* and the *Active* frigate to deal with Peynier's detachment. Meanwhile the *Sceptre* had succeeded in capturing

---

4   Richmond, *Navy in India*, pp.335–336.

the *Naiade*. When Mitchell reached Madras, he met the convoy for which Peynier had been looking and shepherded it into Madras roadstead. He did not encounter Peynier, who accordingly returned unscathed to rejoin Suffren at Trincomali. Hughes, meanwhile, arrived with his main body at Madras on 13 April, where his most urgent task was to re-water and reprovision his squadron, having left Bombay incomplete in this respect. One way and another, the last few weeks had seen both French and British have narrow escapes, due principally to the lack on each side of sufficient scouting vessels.

One other disagreeable feature of Hughes's return to Madras was a resumption of his discordant relationship with Macartney and the Madras Committee. The dispute which arose between them on this occasion concerned the gold bullion that had reached the city aboard the *Royal Charlotte*. Hughes claimed to be entitled to it as payment for loans made on Coote's personal guarantee. Macartney, on the other hand, insisted that it should be applied to the needs of the Madras Presidency.

While Coote had been absent in Bengal, the Madras army had passed under the command of Major General James Stuart. To Warren Hastings in Calcutta, it had seemed essential that Coote should return to Madras to reassume command of the army, which is why he had prevailed on the still ailing Coote to take ship there. The general's untimely death left Stuart in command, but before he left Calcutta, Coote had written a paper setting out his views on the way in which the war was being conducted: 'As the best chance we yet have of rising superior to our enemies I must recommend the preservation and support of the army … And that you use your utmost endeavours to keep it ready for immediate service.' This had not been done. He also drew attention to the French presence in Cuddalore and the likelihood of it being reinforced, and the need to be as strong as possible at this, the decisive point. He complained that the Madras Committee had sought to break up the European forces by sending detachments elsewhere, which had meant that it was impossible to take advantage of Hyder Ali's death. He also protested at Macartney's decision to abandon Negapatam, which deprived the squadron of a convenient anchorage to windward.[5]

By the time Hughes reached Madras the decision had been taken to move against Cuddalore. Stuart wrote to the admiral on 19 April to seek his help:

> Our next campaign will, I trust, put an end to French consequence in India. The Army marches the day after tomorrow most undoubtedly, but our means of conveyance (in spite of three months foresight of this crisis) is *so very slender* and every attempt on our part, as I think, will fail, and we shall be in the disagreeable alternative of *starving*, or *disgracefully returning*, unless you, Sir, can assist us; not by detaching any thing considerable from your force while you have M. Suffrein to look to, but by taking in tow of his Majesty's ships all the vessels loaded with rice or military stores, and their provisions for the army, at the time you sail from hence.[6]

---

5 Richmond, *Navy in India*, pp.340–341.
6 Anon (ed.), *Letters from Major General James Stuart to Vice Admiral Sir Edward Hughes* (Place and publisher unknown, 1784), available at <https://books.google.co.uk/

Hughes replied at once, promising Stuart the protection of the squadron off Cuddalore. He told the general that the store ships were fully laden and could not be cleared until the watering of the squadron was finished, when it would immediately sail, and the boats would unload the store ships. In the meantime, he detailed the *Isis* and the *Active* under Captain Thomas Troubridge to cover the store ships. He added that the Committee had agreed with him 'that the operations of his Majesty's squadron to the southward will effectually prevent the enemy from interrupting the operations of the army against Cuddalore.' He could not promise that he would encumber the ships of his squadron with vessels in tow, but that every assistance could arise from his own plan of operations would be afforded to Stuart.[7] The general responded by reiterating his need for the towing of the supply ships and also expressing his opinion that the most effective support which Hughes could give was keeping Suffren in view. Stuart's plans had not been helped by the intervention of Macartney, who so worded the orders for the various British forces that only the minimum possible should be detached to join Stuart's army. One instance of this was an order by Macartney to Colonel William Fullarton, who had succeeded Lang in command of the Southern army, to conduct operations in the south rather than send troops to reinforce Stuart. Although Stuart was perhaps a difficult individual, this was an unforgivable step on the part of the government, but entirely consistent with the ceaseless interference which Coote had previously suffered.

In addition to Macartney's interference, Stuart also suffered from the mean-minded conduct of the Madras Committee in refusing to him coolies for the unloading and transport of rice from the ships to the camp, which meant that the troops had to do the work rather than their taking places in the ranks of the army. As a result, there were insufficient troops available to complete the investment of Cuddalore. Stuart, when he set off from Madras, had with him 2,945 European troops and 11,545 sepoys. He later received reinforcements increasing the number of his European troops to 3,500.[8]

Landing the army's stores was an extremely laborious process. There was a strong wind blowing which brought a heavy surf on the beach and many of the boats employed were soon knocked to pieces. In the end Troubridge had to go to Tranquebar to fetch more food and more boats. Stuart appreciated Troubridge's tireless efforts to keep the process going. He told him that he had sent additional working parties to expedite the landing, and that he thought 'every minute an hour that detains us from our destination.'[9]

Although the complete investment of Cuddalore had been delayed, the place could be isolated by a close blockade at sea, and it had originally been Hughes's intention to remain off the port with his entire squadron, so that he could be sure of meeting Suffren if he attempted to come to its relief. He changed his mind, however, when a false report arrived at Madras to the effect that Soulanges had arrived at the Cape with a force consisting of four French and six Dutch ships, and that he might now,

---

books?id=aAlgAAAAcAAJ>, pp.3–4.
7 Anon. (ed.), *Letters of Major General Stuart*, p.36.
8 Sen, *French in India*, p.349n.
9 Anon. (ed.), *Letters of Major General Stuart*, p.3.

with supplies for Suffren, be en route to Trincomali. It was a threat which Hughes did not feel able to ignore, and on 2 May, without completing his water, he sailed from Madras, his intention being 'to seek the enemy's squadron and if possible intercept their expected reinforcement.'[10] He left behind him a squadron to cooperate with the army, protecting its line of supply and assisting in landing the stores and other services required. This squadron consisted of the *Isis*, *San Carlos*, *Naiade*, *Chaser*, *Pondicherry*, *Minerva*, and *Harriet*.

Bussy, meanwhile, was reviewing his situation at Cuddalore. He was not impressed with the defensive qualities of the place. The walls were low, and there were 14 bastions, in poor condition, set far apart from each other. The force available to him consisted of 3,500 European troops, 3–400 native troops brought from the Cape, 4,000 French trained sepoys, and between 8–10,000 troops from Tipu's army under Sayyid Sahib, of poor quality. Bussy glumly noted in his diary: 'Our actual position on the Coromandel coast is such that I should not care to establish it even in time of peace.'[11] As has been seen, a particular anxiety was his financial position. The five million livres that he had brought with him might last him five months, but Suffren had to be paid for the rice he had landed in order to have funds to pay his own crews, while the troops at Cuddalore were owed arrears of pay. It was a bad time for the Marquis whose own health had not improved. He was suffering severely from gout, and he was incapable of riding a horse, so had to be carried in a litter.

Like Suffren, he sent urgent letters to Tipu appealing for assistance, and although promised some 35,000 men once Tipu had dealt with the threat from Matthews, which he was facing on the Malabar coast, Bussy doubted their early arrival. In the meantime, came news that Stuart was preparing to march on Cuddalore. Bussy, on 10 April, sent Suffren a message asking him to send without delay the munitions which it had not been possible to land at Cuddalore. He added that he needed 'food, wood, bullets – but above all food.' In reply, Suffren said that while the refitting of the squadron continued, he would not be in a position to leave Trincomali before 12 or 15 May. He was still uncertain about Hughes's strength: 'They tell me he has seventeen. That superiority is not enough to keep me shut in here, if you have need of me.'[12] He also requested that Bussy should lend him 1,500 troops to strengthen his crews. Meanwhile, in an effort to gather reliable intelligence, he sent out the *Coventry*, which sailed to Cuddalore and learned of the capture of the *Naiade*. It returned with information that Hughes had 18 ships of the line, that Coote had reached Madras with a large quantity of bullion, and that the *Bristol*'s convoy had arrived safely, bringing 600 troops.

At Cuddalore, Bussy was becoming increasingly apprehensive, and on 2 May he sent Suffren a positive order to come there at once. This reached the admiral on 12 May and was followed by another several days later. Bussy told Suffren that he could not reinforce the squadron from the garrison; it was insufficiently strong as it was. He urgently needed the support of the squadron: 'In consequence, Sir, you will sail as soon as possible with your fifteen ships: three things obliged me to give this order,

---

10 Richmond, *Navy in India*, pp.345–346.
11 Cavaliero, *Admiral Satan*, p.217.
12 Richmond, *Navy in India*, p.347.

the want of food, the lack of munitions and the pernicious effect that your absence cannot fail to have upon the spirits of our enemies, our allies and all the Asiatic peoples.'[13]

Here was the very situation that Suffren had feared might arise from the establishment of a unified command. When he received Bussy's order, he estimated that it would not be possible for the squadron to sail before 26 May. While his preparations were still not entirely complete, however, the British squadron was sighted off the port on the morning of 24 May. Hughes looked into the anchorage at Back Bay and concluded that Suffren's ships were moored in too strong a position to be attacked, and he disappeared to the southward. His movements perplexed Suffren. He could not tell whether Hughes had gone to pick up British reinforcements, or possibly to intercept those which Suffren was expecting from the Cape, or whether he was hovering off Ceylon with the intention of attacking Trincomali when Suffren put to sea. But he was himself bound to respond to Bussy's call for food and munitions.

He concluded that he should not obey Bussy's order in the way it was expressed. He told Castries, in a letter of 28 May, of what he had decided to do:

> Here then is the decision I took. Believing that with fifteen ships, only eight of which are coppered, I could not attack seventeen, all coppered and stronger than mine, and who have the wind of me which I cannot gain from them owing to their superior speed; and certain that they had left on 15 May with some frigates only blockading Cuddalore, I sent the *Fendant*, *Cleopatre* and *Coventry* to escort two transports laden with provisions and artillery. This I considered the best way to help Cuddalore without exposing Trincomali, which assures our existence in the southern seas, to the risk of loss. I considered that in not obeying M. de Bussy's order, given under different conditions, I should be carrying out his intentions.[14]

The convoy slipped out of Trincomali on the evening of 28 May. Although Hughes had left a frigate to keep watch on the port, she failed to spot the convoy, which safely arrived at Cuddalore on 1 June, landing its supplies and returning at once to Trincomali.

Hughes, meanwhile, had pursued his wild goose chase in pursuit of the non-existent Franco-Dutch squadron said to be en route from the Cape. In his haste to get to sea, he had left Madras without having completed the watering of his squadron, and it had become apparent to him that he must soon return to Madras to take on water. This, predictably, caused great alarm among the members of the Madras Committee. Enraged that Hughes would thereby not be able to support Stuart, they sent a characteristically intemperate message to the admiral:

> We trust that you will be able to water the squadron at such places and in the same manner as M. de Suffren did before Trincomali fell into his hands. By your coming to Madras operations to the southward would be

---

13 Richmond, *Navy in India*, p.348.
14 Richmond, *Navy in India*, pp.348–349.

exposed to imminent danger and the main object be defeated – as there is great reason to believe that so spirited and enterprising officer as M. Suffren would relieve Cuddalore the moment he knew that you returned from a station to the windward of that place.[15]

In setting off to look for the anticipated enemy reinforcements, Hughes had taken a risk, by preferring the possibility of meeting them rather than by remaining at Cuddalore where he could be certain of preventing any supplies reaching that port. He should have taken into account that the chance of intercepting the expected reinforcements was not great, because of the uncertainty of the time of their arrival. In taking this course he did not guess that Suffren might send supplies to Cuddalore in the way in which he did and was no doubt confident that the frigates which he had left would be adequate to deal with any attempt to supply the garrison. On this occasion, for once, the Madras Committee was right, and Hughes was wrong. If Hughes had not appeared off Trincomali, Suffren would have sailed with his whole squadron, and Hughes could have fought him in rather better circumstances than would prove to be the case three weeks later.

Hughes had gone as far south as Batticaloa. Having found nothing, he turned back to the north and took station off Trincomali on 1 June. Looking again into Back Bay, he noted that the French squadron had moved out of the inner harbour and appeared to be ready for sea. Once again, though, examining the position in which the French ships were anchored under the protection of the shore batteries, he concluded that it would be unwise to launch an attack. That night, Hughes received important information when two British seamen, prisoners in Trincomali, escaped in a canoe and told him of the departure of the *Fendant*'s convoy of store ships to Cuddalore. He set off at once, and on 3 June encountered the *Fendant* and *Coventry* returning to Trincomali. He chased them until, under cover of darkness, they escaped, and finally rejoined Suffren's squadron on 10 June. Hughes then continued his passage northward and cruised off Cuddalore for several days.

On 6 June Hughes had written to Stuart to express the hope that his operations were 'in a fair way;' he told him that his water, stores, and provisions would not last longer than the end of the month, and that for water it would be necessary to go to Madras. He added: 'Sorry I am to say, the late arrived ships under mine, are falling down apace with scurvy, which refreshments only can remove.'[16] On 10 June, by now off Porto Novo, he wrote again to Stuart to tell him that he had taken up that station to prevent any interruption should the French attempt it. He repeated his concerns about water and provisions; the *Bristol* and *San Carlos* had taken 605 particularly ill seamen to Madras. He received a reply from Stuart to his previous letter on 11 June, to the effect that he could take Cuddalore if Hughes would cover him for seven weeks: 'On the contrary, if the fleet goes to Madras, and Monsr Suffrein anchors off Cuddalore, with the means he will give to M. de Bussy, I fairly say to you, Sir Edward, I cannot succeed, speaking practically as a military man.'[17] He suggested

---

15 Cavaliero, *Admiral Satan*, p.223.
16 Anon. (ed.), *Letters of Major General Stuart*, p.38.
17 Anon. (ed.), *Letters of Major General Stuart*, pp.15–16.

that the squadron might water at Porto Novo, but when Hughes went to investigate the possibility he found both banks of the river there in the hands of large numbers of native troops. Seeking a possible alternative, he sent Troubridge in the *Active* to Tranquebar to see if sufficient water could be brought up in casks to extend his time at sea, but the wells there were found to be dry. To Stuart, therefore, the most that Hughes could promise was that he would remain off Cuddalore for as long, and in the best manner, he could. His situation was beginning to deteriorate rapidly. On 8 May he had 1,121 sick in the squadron, and the number was increasing daily.[18]

While Hughes's anxieties mounted at Cuddalore, Suffren had also had his problems. It was his intention as soon as he could to come to the aid of Bussy in Cuddalore. On 7 June the store ship, *Dromédaire*, which had formed part of the relief convoy, sailed into Back Bay with the news that the military campaign had begun. It also brought with her a fresh set of orders from Bussy expressly forbidding Suffren from risking the squadron by bringing it to Cuddalore. Bussy had changed his mind as a result of the news that Hughes had been seen off Trincomali. It now seemed to him that the British expedition against Cuddalore might be an elaborate trap to lure the French squadron to its destruction before the reinforcements which were expected came to join Suffren. A threat to the French army at Cuddalore, dependent as it was on support from the sea, must surely bring Suffren north. This, Bussy thought, would be fatal: 'A battle, with three ships less than the enemy, even admitting equal losses and injury aloft, would reduce us for the rest of the campaign to our land forces only, and consequently restrict us to very few operations.'[19] In sending this order Bussy was now hopeful that Tipu, who had been successful in his operations on the Malabar coast, might now be disposed to march to his assistance. Bussy followed this with a further order a fortnight later. The preservation of the squadron was, he said, of the highest importance, and he emphatically instructed Suffren to remain at Trincomali, limiting any action he took to containing the British squadron and thereby keeping Cuddalore open by sea. He was, Bussy told Suffren, not to leave Trincomali unless the defences were forced and the army had to shut itself in the walled town.

Thus, once again, Suffren was faced by orders from his commander-in-chief which he thought wrong and with which he was not disposed to comply. It was clear to him that he could not know of the situation at Cuddalore, or whether the defences had been driven in, and if news did reach him, it would be too late to do anything about it. To him, it appeared evident that Bussy was not in a position to judge the risks, and that it must be for him to decide the right course of action.

He convened a meeting of his captains, and explained the situation, telling them that he intended to put to sea as soon as possible with the object of attacking the British squadron:

> The critical state in which the King's affairs now find themselves demands that we all work together. Let us put far from us all misunderstanding that can prejudice success. Let us know that the honour of being French men

---

18 Richmond, *Navy in India*, p.353.
19 Richmond, *Navy in India*, p.354.

can outweigh the advantages that the enemy has over us. The army under
the walls of Cuddalore is lost unless we go to its rescue. Perhaps the glory of
saving it is reserved for us. We ought at least make the attempt.[20]

To Suffren's considerable satisfaction his captains unanimously agreed with him. Munitions and food were hastened aboard the ships of the squadron and on 11 June they put to sea. It was a brave mission, in which the odds were heavily against the French. They were sailing with 15 ships of the line to attack Hughes, who had 18, and the condition of their ships was far from good. One was leaking very badly, and another found that its pumps were constantly in use. Only eight of the ships were coppered, while so far as Suffren knew all the British ships were. Many of his ships had been constantly at sea for three or four years, while Hughes would have been able to dock some at least of his at Bombay. Suffren's crews were some 25 percent short of a full complement. He could not know of course that the extent of the scurvy in the British squadron had left it in an even worse state.

As he sailed north, with the real prospect of fighting Hughes for a fifth time, Suffren had in his mind another order which he had received and of which he did not approve, but this was one which he felt obliged to obey. Based on the experiences of de Grasse in the West Indies, a letter was issued in the King's name announcing that, in the future, commanders of squadrons consisting of more than nine ships should, when attacking in line, go on board a frigate 'from whence it will be more easy for them to observe the enemy's movements and direct the movements considered most proper for the squadron under their command, and to hasten their execution.' Suffren found the rigidity of this order disagreeable, as he grumpily observed to Castries:

> I shall conform to it so far as I consider it a value to the good of the service. The spirit of this order would be but poorly complied with if in putting it into execution the commander-in-chief should not give that example which a commander must show on those occasions in which he is able to command from his own ship quite as well as from elsewhere.[21]

He had always regarded the setting of an example as a key part of a commander's functions, and this prompted him to circulate a note to his captains observing that only an order from the King could prevent him from sharing the dangers of the action with them.

This, it might be supposed, was not an unreasonable message to send. Caron, however, takes Suffren to task for responding so negatively to the directive in what he considers to be 'a strange attitude, reflecting a very narrow vision of what constitutes command, and an inability to learn lessons from experience; the Bailli had no real awareness that the art of command requires other qualities than that of physical courage alone.'[22] An alternative view might perhaps be that throughout his career

---

20 Lacour-Gayet, *marine militaire*, p.544.
21 Richmond, *Navy in India*, p.367.
22 Caron, *Mythe de Suffren*, p.409.

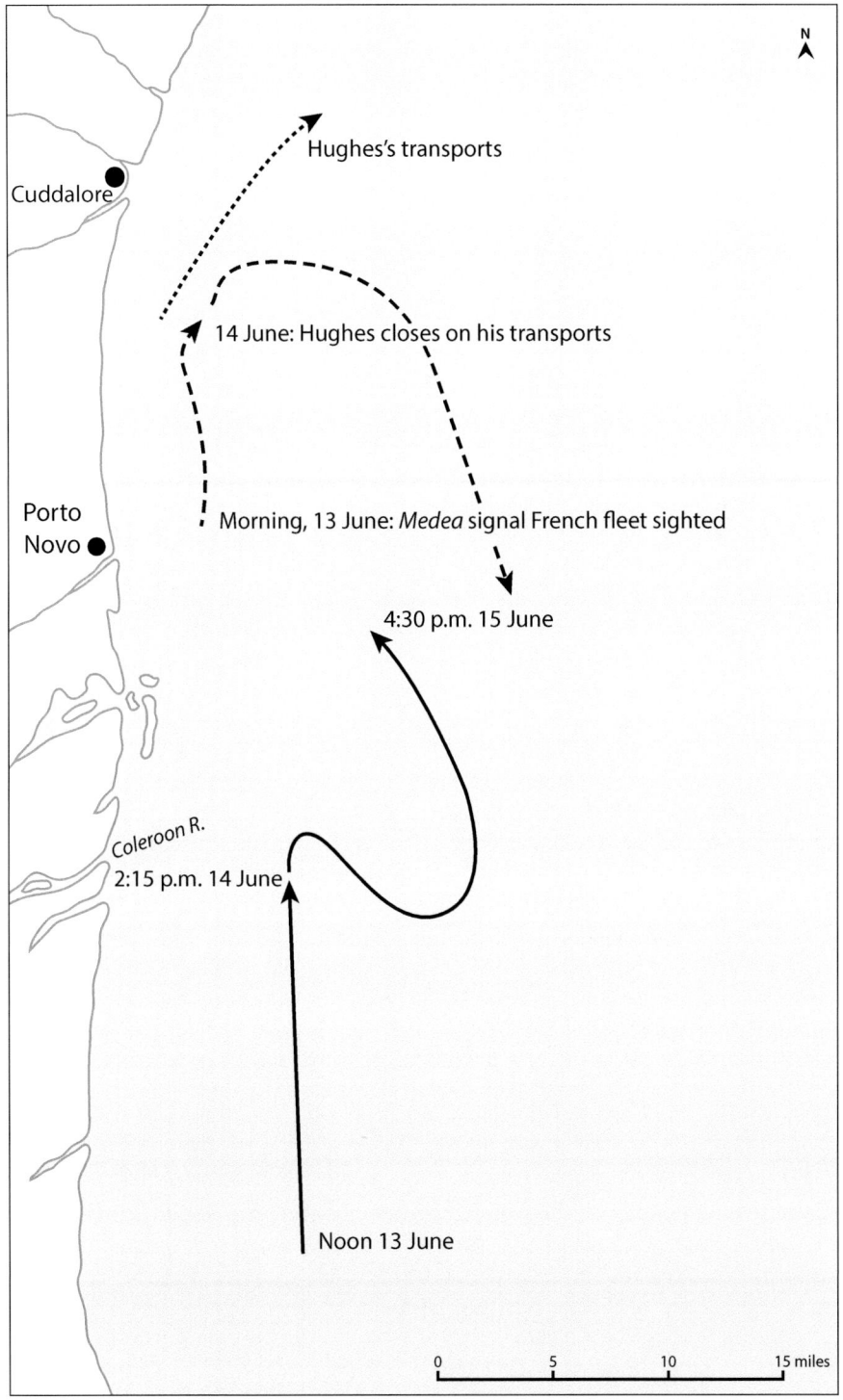

Cuddalore, 13-15 June, based on a map in Cavaliero, *Admiral Satan*.

Suffren had demonstrated an instinctive grasp of what his command responsibilities actually entailed, and that in the light of past experience he used every means to keep his captains up to the mark.

Suffren had been thinking over the problem of getting his ships into action in the way he wanted. Before he left Trincomali he issued his 'Order of Battle No 3' which provided for his five most powerful ships – the 74-gun *Fendant*, *Argonaute*, *Héros*, *Illustre* and *Annibal* – to be massed in the rear, while the *Saint Michel*, 60, *Petit Annibal*, 50, and *Consolante*, 40, which were his fastest coppered ships, were to double on the British rear and attack to leeward. In this way eight ships would concentrate their fire on five of the enemy, while the seven remaining ships, six 64s and one 50, would engage at long range the 13 British ships ahead of the rear. This order of battle could only apply if the French held the weather gauge. To succeed, this manoeuvre would depend on surprise, with the French intention concealed long enough for the ships to get into the required positions, and on the effectiveness of the fire concentrated on the British rear. As always, time would be the decisive factor, and close action would be essential.

The winds were favourable, and Suffren arrived on 13 June. The British scouting frigate, the *Medea*, signalled that morning that sails were visible to the southward, subsequently identifying them as 15 ships of the line with three frigates. Hughes was not surprised, having predicted the early arrival of the French in a letter to Stuart of two days previously. He was no doubt relieved to see that Suffren had not received any reinforcements, so his numerical superiority was assured. Meanwhile he had heard from Stuart in a letter of 11 June of his intention to drive the French into the boundaries of the fort, which he hoped he would be able to do in not many days; next day Stuart confirmed that the assault would begin at dawn on 13 June.

It was Hughes's intention that if the French came, he should engage them to windward. Only in this way, he considered, could he win the kind of decisive victory necessary once and for all to ensure the safety of the British position in India. When Suffren was sighted on 13 June, Hughes's transports were still unloading supplies for the army, some nine miles north of his own position. He had three choices as to what to do: he could make sail and head for Suffren, who was about 23 miles to the south; he could close on his transports to make sure that they were able to complete their offloading; or he could stay where he was. The wind was south south-east. If he made sail at once, he would have to steer due east, as the current would carry him northward, opening the way to Cuddalore to the enemy, who could fall on his unprotected transports. It was his belief that this was Suffren's intention, so to put to sea would give his enemy what he wanted. He opted to close his transports, as the safest option, and moved his squadron six miles nearer to them.

Once Hughes had completed his move northward, Suffren himself anchored, since he wished to retain the weather gauge. Next day he closed on the British in the formation dictated by his Order of Battle No 3. The wind, now light, was between west south-west and south-west. In fact, the current was pushing the French northwards, and he had difficulty regaining his anchorage. Hughes watched him, and waited to see what his enemy did next. He told Stuart on the afternoon of 14 June that after coming down very cautiously Suffren seemed to be retreating again. Hughes was in an optimistic frame of mind. He ended his letter: 'They expect reinforcements; so do we; yet I think with you, this is the finishing stroke of the French, and will raise your fame to a high pitch, as it will justify merit.'[23] Stuart, meanwhile, reported that he had as he had hoped been able to drive the French into the walled town. During intense fighting in which both sides lost heavy casualties, Bussy had suffered a setback which might have been avoided if Sayyid Sahib had come to his support instead of remaining inactive some 15 miles off. It had been Bussy's first thought to renew the action next day, but he changed his mind because he had lost a large number of transport oxen and because he judged that he should not risk his small army against a superior force. During the night of 13/14 June he brought his entire army within the walls of Cuddalore.[24] The place was scarcely defensible; only Suffren's appearance could save it.

Writing to Stuart next day, Hughes told him that Suffren continued at anchor to the south of the River Coleroon, and that he had seen no movement since. The position he had taken up himself appeared to be 'the best post I can take for the protection of the army, and the several ships and craft that attend it; therefore cannot myself take the advantage yet of Porto Novo, for the benefit of water and refreshments for our people.'[25] He added that Suffren seemed at a loss what to do but concluded that it seemed that he wished to get into Cuddalore. In fact, Suffren was by no means at a loss. He intended to attack, but only when the wind served. He had, obedient to the Royal command, transferred to the *Cleopatre* in anticipation of an engagement, re-embarking aboard the *Héros* at nightfall.

Next day he returned to the *Cleopatre* and got his squadron under way northwards in a light westerly wind. He again signalled for Order No 3. By noon the two squadrons were some nine miles apart. The wind had steadily worked round to the south-east. Hughes, seeing the French approaching in line abreast, weighed anchor at 3:00 p.m., forming line on course east north-east close hauled, and ordering his transports to move northwards. The wind now began to fail. At 4:30 p.m. the two squadrons, just out of range, were passing each other on opposite tacks, with Suffren having kept his wind. But by the time the range closed he concluded that it was too late to launch an attack.

That night Hughes, still hoping that he could get to the eastward next day and thus gain the weather gauge, remained to seaward. This meant, however, that at dawn on 17 June the French squadron was now between the British and Cuddalore. Suffren had, during the night, communicated with Bussy and learned of the military situation. Bussy told him that if he could, after a successful action, come in to take up the sick and wounded, he, Bussy, would try to cooperate with Tipu in an effort to save Cuddalore. This was followed by the news that Tipu could not be counted on. Suffren had asked for 1,500 men to reinforce his squadron. The hard pressed Bussy, to his very great credit recognising that only at sea lay his salvation, agreed to help, although the most he could spare was 1,200. Suffren got the news of this reinforcement during the afternoon of 17 June, and he saw his chance. The 1,200 men might make all the difference, and the manoeuvres of the squadron meant that

---

23 Anon. (ed.), *Letters of Major General Stuart*, pp.46–47.
24 Sen, *French in India*, pp.357–358.
25 Anon. (ed.), *Letters of Major General Stuart*, p.47.

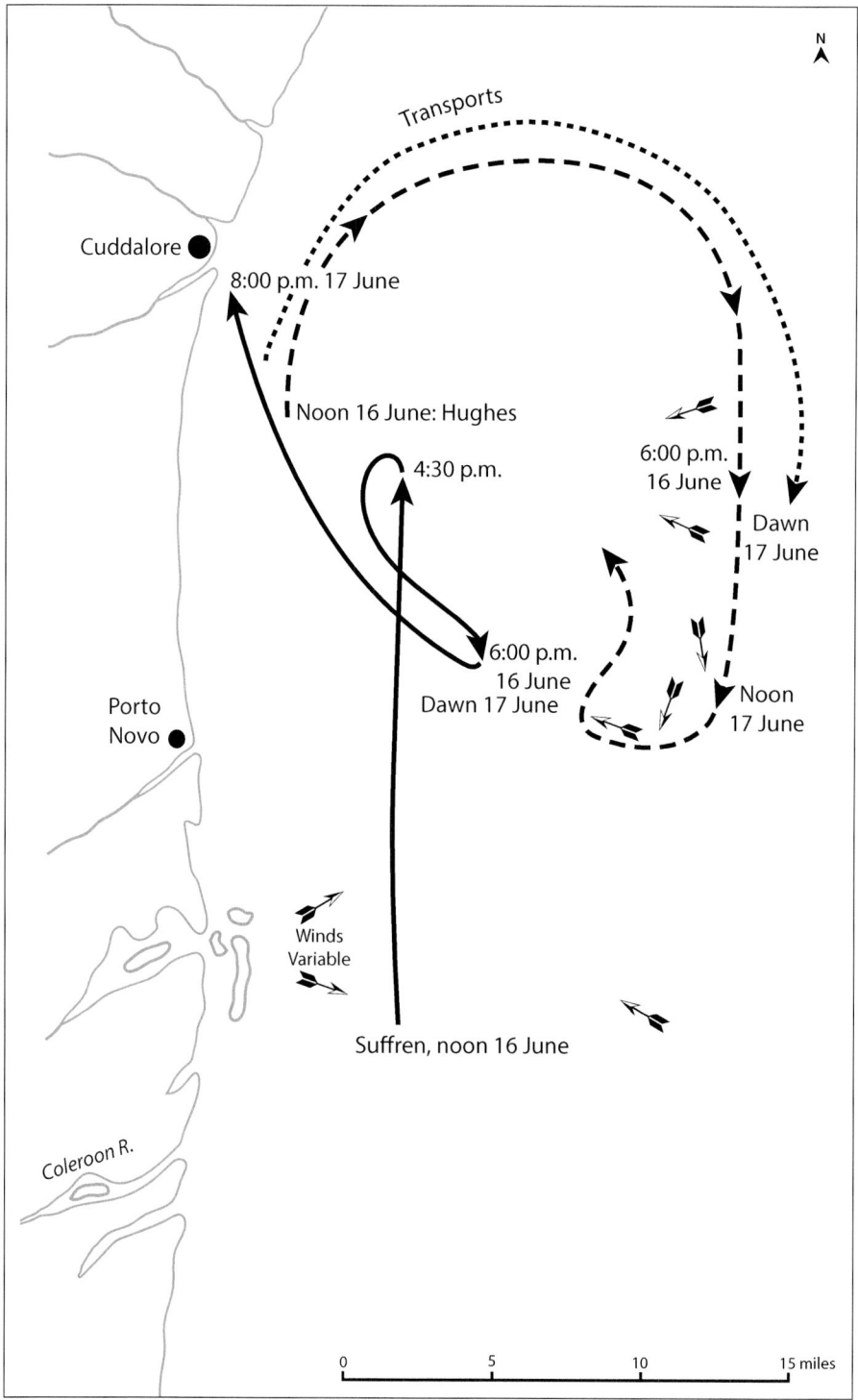

Cuddalore, 16-17 June, based on a map in Cavaliero, *Admiral Satan*.

he would be able to get in to pick them up. That evening, the usual sea breeze which might have enabled Hughes to interfere, had failed to materialise, and Suffren ran into the anchorage and collected the crucial reinforcement.

On the morning of 18 June, the tactical positions of the squadrons had been effectively reversed, with Suffren off Cuddalore and Hughes out at sea to the east. The wind, though, was now blowing from the west north-west. Hughes tried so far as he could to beat up for the French against the light offshore wind but made little progress. Suffren weighed anchor but he too moved hardly at all, and night fell with the two squadrons still well apart. On the following day the wind remained feeble, and quite insufficient to enable Suffren to attack. One French account of the proceedings read:

> From 3 o'clock there were so many puffs from the sea, so many from the shore; half the ships of the squadron had one breeze, half had another. It would have been dangerous for us to attack in such weather, for it was necessary with our inferior forces to come into action in good order and with a wind on which we could depend.[26]

Hughes, in his subsequent despatch, described his frustration in the days following 17 June: 'From this time to the 20th I was continually employed in endeavouring to get the wind of the enemy: which, however, I was never able to effect, from the extraordinary variables of the winds, that often brought part of the two squadrons within a random shot of each other.'[27]

In these ineffectual manoeuvres, Hughes had been counting on the sea breeze coming in as it usually did, but in this he was to be disappointed. To the surprise of all observers, it ceased completely. Hughes calculated on the morning of 20 June, as he surveyed the relative positions of the two squadrons, that he would simply have to make the best of the wind which was now steadily blowing offshore from the north-west by northward. At noon, he formed line on a bearing north-east and south-west, and prepared for battle. If the wind did come around, he would have the position he wanted, but it never did. At 2:00 p.m., as he recorded, Hughes brought to, since the enemy were 'showing a disposition to engage', and prepared to receive them.

Suffren bore down with the offshore breeze, but it was so light that it took him four hours to cover the dozen miles which separated the squadrons. At 3:15 p.m., as he neared the enemy, Suffren decided not to adopt his Order No 3. His speed was so slow in the light wind that surprise was impossible, and he adopted Order No 1, which contained no special features. There was to be no concentration of force in any part of his line, and nor did he employ a fast division in the way in which he had previously contemplated. It may be that this entirely orthodox mode of attack was justified not only by the lack of surprise, but by the fact that he had so considerably reinforced his gun crews. He was now approaching 1,202 enemy guns with a total of 1,018 in his own squadron, but they would be better manned than on previous occasions. And, unknown to him, he was facing an enemy whose own crews had

---

26 Richmond, *Navy in India*, p.363.
27 Ekins, *Naval Battles*, p.196.

been savagely reduced by scurvy, so that Suffren enjoyed a considerable superiority in manpower.

At 1:00 p.m. Suffren had gone on board the *Cleopatre* again and from her quarterdeck was obliged to endure the frustration of not being directly involved in the battle. The first ranging shot was fired by the *Sphinx*, at the head of the French line. Forty-five minutes later the *Cleopatre*, sailing abreast of the French van, signalled for the squadron to open fire at pistol shot range. He warned the 40-gun *Consolante* not to engage the British heavy ships except at long range, and his fire ship to be ready to attack when ordered to do so. Aboard the *Cleopatre*, Suffren cruised along the line, urging his ships to close with the enemy. With the exception of the *Artésien* and *Consolante*, at the rear of the line, they all did so. The distribution of the British superior numbers meant that the 50-gun *Flamand* came under fire from two 64s, the *Inflexible* and *Exeter*, suffering heavy casualties, among whom was her commander, Perrier de Salvert. Succeeding to the command, *Lieutenant* Trublet took her temporarily out of the line. As usual, the *Héros*, under Moissac, engaged the *Superb*. The two ships hammered each other ferociously, both sustaining a considerable number of casualties. In fact it was the *Fendant*, third in line, and opposed by the 80-gun *Gibraltar*, that suffered the greatest loss of all the French ships, while among the British ships it was the *Sceptre* which sustained the greatest number of casualties in a prolonged duel with the *Saint Michel*.

As the battle wore on, and the light began to fail, the *Fendant*'s mizzen mainsail caught fire when a barrel of grenades exploded. The *Gibraltar*, edging in to take advantage of this, was thwarted by the *Flamand*. Still the broadsides continued to blaze until, as darkness fell, the two squadrons drew apart. Whatever Suffren might have felt about his subordinates on previous occasions, he could not complain this time; his captains had pressed home their attack with courage and great determination. It was not a battle in which either admiral was able to display any skilful tactics; it was a remorseless pounding which lasted until the coming of night brought it to an end at about 7:00 p.m.

The French had lost a total of 102 men killed and 376 wounded; the British losses were much the same, at 103 killed and 429 wounded. Among the French dead, though, were Dupas, the captain of the *Ajax*, as well as Perrier de Salvertt, and Dieu, who had been responsible for preserving the *Sévère* at Negapatam. The *Superb* had suffered particularly badly, her maintop being smashed. The *Gibraltar* and *Isis* each had seven to eight feet of water in their holds, while the *Defence* was unable to make sail. The *Héros*, once again, was badly cut about in her rigging, but had not suffered in her hull, and no French ship was incapacitated.

Hughes laconically described the aftermath of the battle: 'At daylight, I made the signal, and wore with the squadron, and brought to repair the damages, with the ships' heads towards the land; several of the ships much disabled in their hulls, masts and rigging, the *Gibraltar* and *Isis* in particular; the enemy's Squadron not in sight.'[28]

---

28 Ekins, *Naval Battles*, p.196.

During the night the strong current carried the French squadron northwards almost abreast of Pondicherry, a considerable way up the coast from Cuddalore, where Suffren anchored. When the British came in sight, Suffren was still to windward, and for a moment he contemplated cutting his cables and giving chase to Hughes. He later explained his reasons for not pursuing this idea:

> The reasons for which I did not do so were (1) that I was too short of cables to make the sacrifice, (2) that Cuddalore was besieged, and that I had 1,200 of the garrison on board, (3) that the enemy had a great advantage in speed and that chasing it to the NNE might take me so far that I should not be able to regain the coast, while it would have been quietly at Madras; for at this season of the year ships which sail badly do not get back to the coast if they once leave it. I therefore steered for Cuddalore, anchored there on the 23rd, and landed the detachment I had embarked on the 24th together with 1,000 men of the squadron.[29]

Suffren watched as Hughes sailed by; the British subsequently anchored off the ruined fort of Alemparve.

Next morning Hughes sent for Commodores Bickerton and King to seek their views as to what to do next, bearing in mind that the squadron was suffering so severely from scurvy which had made such a rapid progress, and from the number of wounded and lost in action, as well as the prevailing scarcity of water. In the light of the squadron's present circumstances, it was not a difficult decision, and it was agreed to proceed immediately to Madras. Accordingly, he weighed within two hours and proceeded there, anchoring in the roadstead on 25 June.

The two squadrons had fought another indecisive battle. Suffren, though, could be justly satisfied with what he had achieved. He had saved Cuddalore and had done so by sailing to attack a superior force in defiance of positive orders not to do so, and had much the best of the complex manoeuvres which had preceded the battle. In this he had been assisted by the unexpected behaviour of the wind, while in giving more than he got in the battle itself he had had the benefit of the fearful epidemic of scurvy that had assailed his enemy. Suffren, therefore, had earned the tumultuous welcome which he received when he went ashore at Cuddalore. His native servants carried him triumphantly through the decorated streets of the town to bring him to Government House, where Bussy greeted him as the army's saviour.

Ashore, Stuart was disappointed, but he remained hopeful. Macartney had effectively attempted to ruin the expedition by going behind his back to order Fullarton, in the south, to remain there. Stuart overrode those instructions, and Fullarton responded to Stuart's request by marching north. He was three days short of Cuddalore when news came that the preliminaries of peace between France and Britain had been signed in Europe on 20 January. As soon as Hughes heard of this, when he reached Madras, he sent Captain Erasmus Gower in the *Medea* to Suffren to give him the news.

---

29 Richmond, *Navy in India*, p.375.

19

Conclusion

It had been agreed between France and Britain that with the coming of the peace both admirals on the East Indies station should be recalled, and that the respective squadrons should be scaled down. Suffren was relieved to hear of the peace treaty, as he told Castries on 23 July, and looked forward to returning home: 'I await your orders with impatience. I hope they will allow me to leave. Certain things have so disgusted me that only war has made them bearable.'[1] He wrote again in September reflecting on what peace would mean:

> I have no doubt the peace will bring about many changes but I hope they will be effected and consolidated before I return, for those who have been consulted up to now have ideas so different from mine that I should not wish to be associated with them. There have been some very stupid adventures, but if the general officers had been good and well supported this war would not have lasted two years, we should have saved 500 millions and 50,000 men, and secured an honourable peace.[2]

In August, the frigate *Hermione* had arrived with the news of Suffren's promotion to the rank of *lieutenant-général* (the equivalent of vice admiral). He had previously been elevated by the Knights of Malta to the status of Bailli Grand Cross, a title by which he came widely to be known. Suffren openly enjoyed the high regard in which he was now so widely held, writing to Mme de Seillans on 13 September:

> The consideration in which I am held in India is almost unbelievable: verses, songs, letters etc. but beware! The least thing could change cheers into hisses ... I do not know, as no one has written to tell me, the letters from the Minister being lost, how I am regarded in France, and how the public has taken my early promotion; but in India, in Madras above all and in the Iles de France and Bourbon I am infinitely more regarded than I deserve. If I visit the Ile de France they will go mad, if their enthusiasm is not restrained.[3]

---

1 Chevalier, *Histoire de la marine Francaise*, p.480.
2 Cavaliero, *Admiral Satan*, p.240.
3 Roux, *Bailli de Suffren*, pp.179–180.

He went on to make clear his pride in what he had achieved at Cuddalore:

> You will have learned of my promotion to *chef d'escadre* in March 82 and in March 83 to *lieutenant-général*. Now I tell you in the sincerity of my heart and for your own ear alone that what I have done since then is worth infinitely more than what I had done before. You know the capture and battle of Trincomali; but the end of the campaign, and that which took place between the month of March and the end of June, is far above anything else done in the navy since I entered it. The result has been very advantageous to the state, for the squadron was endangered and the army lost.

He finally left Trincomali on 6 October sailing with the *Héros, Annibal, Ajax, Artésien, Illustre* and *Sphinx*. Peynier remained behind with a squadron consisting of the *Fendant, Argonaute, Brillant, Saint Michel, Coventry* and *Bellone*. When Suffren arrived at the Ile de France he did indeed receive the reception he had foretold. Perhaps somewhat less expected was the tribute that awaited him when he called at the Cape on his way home. There, Commodore Sir Richard King was at anchor with 10 of Hughes's ships of the line. They, together with some Russian vessels, were dressed overall in honour of Suffren, and the officers came on board the *Héros* to congratulate him in person on his promotion. Suffren was greatly touched by this evidence of the regard in which he was held by his erstwhile enemies. He sailed for Toulon on 3 January 1784.

Once back in France, he was greeted by the adulation of the general public, while the King readily accepted the advice of Castries as to the importance of properly rewarding the admiral who had done so much to restore the navy's reputation. Castries submitted to the King a memorial in which he wrote:

> It is only the steadfastness of this general officer which brought the last successes; it is to these examples that we must look for the energy and obedience that gave us victory in the last battle; it is by his conduct both clear-sighted and vigorous that showed the princes of India as well as of Europe that the English were not invincible and that for the first time their Empire could be defeated. He has proved that your nation does not lack men to lead it. It is principally to him that the superiority of the French navy is recognised in the opinion of all Europe.[4]

In considering the rewards that should be granted to Suffren, Castries wrote that the most powerful argument for granting them was the King's determination to have a vigorous navy. Castries recommended not only the promotion to *lieutenant-général*, but also Suffren's admission to the orders of Saint Esprit and Saint Michel. He did not, however, recommend that he be made a *maréchal de France*, to Suffren's disappointment.

---

4   Lacour-Gayet, *marine militaire*, p.555.

Suffren returned to Provence in July 1785, where the whole population received him with acclaim, and he was able to be with his beloved cousin. He was, however, not destined for a long life; on 7 December 1788 he suffered a sudden attack of apoplexy and died next day. He was buried in the Hospitaller's church of Saint Marie.

Hughes did not get away from India as soon as his long-time opponent. He took most of his squadron around to the Malabar coast in October 1783 to relieve Mangalore, besieged by Tipu's forces. On 9 November he suffered a grievous blow when in a gale the *Superb* dragged her anchor in Tellicherry roads, fouled the *Sultan* and struck a sandbank; she quickly broke up, but save for one man all her crew was rescued. Hughes was profoundly upset, saying that he 'would have given all he was worth to have had his ship safe and sound again.'[5]

Hughes's departure from India was further delayed when Sir Peter Parker, who had been appointed to succeed him, was lost at sea when the *Cato* went down with all hands and it was not until November 1784 that he was able to transfer the command to his senior captain, Andrew Mitchell. He finally returned to Spithead on 16 May 1785 after an absence of six years. His return did not inspire the extravagant adulation that had greeted Suffren, but his achievements were understood, and were recognised by a vote of thanks in the House of Commons. In his reply to this mark of respect, Hughes wrote:

> Although I found it impossible to ruin the French naval force in this country, every exertion in my power was made for that purpose consistent with the preservation of His Majesty's squadron on which the fate of the national possessions in this country greatly, if not wholly, depend. I have, however, with the assistance of the brave men who served with me, been able effectually to disappoint and defeat all their designs of conquest in this part of the world.[6]

Hughes did not go to sea again, but on 1 February 1793 received a well-deserved promotion to the rank of Admiral of the Blue. While in India he had amassed a considerable fortune, estimated to be worth £40,000 a year. Hughes was a generous man and gave away a large part of his fortune to various deserving charities, as well as helping friends in need. One such was Lord Sandwich, to whom he lent £14,000 after the end of the war and a further £10,000 without security in 1784. He had taken Sandwich's son, who later became Admiral Robert Montague, with him to the East Indies. Hughes, after his return to England, retired to his estate at Luxborough in Essex, where he died on 17 February 1794.

Hughes and Suffren had a profound respect for each other. Suffren had made his feelings known to William Hickey when he met him at Trincomali, at which time the squadrons had met three times:

> It has been my fate to be opposed to him in three different hard-contested battles, in every one of which Sir Edward Hughes in my humble opinion

---

5   Cavaliero, *Admiral Satan*, p.244.
6   Richmond, *Navy in India*, p.379.

gave positive proofs that he possessed consummate skill and abilities equal to any man's I have ever had to deal with in my profession. His manner and general conduct, too, has uniformly been that of a brave and gallant officer, blended with the mild and benevolent disposition of a truly philanthropic citizen of the world … A braver man does not exist.[7]

Hughes had acknowledged a similar admiration for Suffren in the course of his painful correspondence with Macartney and the Madras Select Committee, and in his conversation with William Hickey.

History has not so much been unkind to Hughes as having paid less attention to him than perhaps his qualities deserved. He has inspired no biographies; and whereas the French navy has almost always possessed a ship named after Suffren, there has never been a ship bearing the name of Hughes in the Royal Navy.

Among historians who have analysed the Suffren-Hughes campaigns, Mahan rated Hughes as a journeyman, whose ability was substantially below that of his opponent, observing that he had apparently all the technical accomplishments of the seaman's profession, 'would probably have commanded a ship equally well with any of his captains, but shows no trace of the qualities needed of a general officer.' He considered Hughes to be 'lacking in enterprise, and giving no token of tactical skill or *coup d'oeil*.' Reviewing the five battles in which they met, Mahan concluded that 'it is probable that Hughes's self-confidence had been badly shaken by his various meetings with Suffren.'[8] This is a view which has been shared by other commentators.

Suffren's only English biographer, Roderick Cavaliero, was somewhat more generous in his assessment of Hughes, summing up his natural gifts as 'duty, humanity, courage and dignity, if not genius', and this is a judgement with which it is hard to disagree.[9] The difficulties which Hughes faced were not the same as those faced by Suffren. The toxic relationship with the civil authorities, and his awareness of the wider responsibilities that he bore on his shoulders certainly contributed to the defensive approach which generally characterised his strategic and tactical thinking. Inevitably Hughes has been overshadowed not just by the extraordinary and vivid personality and abilities of his opponent, but also by comparison with the very many British naval leaders of history who have made a greater impact on their times. In the course of the worldwide conflict between France and Britain, the Indian Ocean was a sideshow, albeit a very important one; neither side could readily spare large numbers of ships of the line to contest the command of the sea there.

Naturally, Suffren's life and career has inspired a huge literature, which in France continues to grow. It is of course not surprising that many French historians have treated him extremely favourably, most being in no doubt that he ranks extremely highly among the leading admirals of French naval history. It must be conceded, though, that in some instances their assessment of his qualities is perhaps unduly favourable.

---

7   Cavaliero, *Admiral Satan*, pp.242–243.
8   Mahan, *Influence of Sea Power*, p.464.
9   Cavaliero, *Admiral Satan*, p.247.

One of the most balanced of the French historians who have studied the campaigns in the Indian Ocean is Georges Lacour-Gayet. In his history of the French navy during the reign of Louis XVI, he wrote:

> The opinion of France, of England and of Europe immediately placed Suffren in the first rank of the great seamen; the study of his campaigns in the Indies, from Praya to Trincomali can only confirm this judgment. Activity, rapidity, energy, spirit of initiative and decisiveness, forethought in all things, firmness in assuming responsibility, and heroism, all these qualities of a commander Suffren possessed to an outstanding degree.[10]

Among twentieth century historians Raul Castex devoted an entire book to Suffren's battle against Johnstone at Porto Praya, using it to illustrate his own tactical and strategic principles. A more recent historian, Philippe Masson, in his essay on Suffren in *The Great Admirals*, remarked of him that 'there is no doubt that the man was steeped in arrogance and ambition and thirst for fame.' However, he still finds him entitled to a place in the front rank of French admirals, though not occupying the first place. He acknowledges his enormous talent, his energy, tenacity, flair for improvisation and his strategic genius.[11]

It is against this background that it is necessary to consider one of the most recent studies of Suffren, by François Caron, to which reference has previously been made in the preceding chapters. Published in 1996, his book is entitled *Le Mythe de Suffren*, a title that makes clear its author's objective, which is to expose what he regards as the unjustified extent of Suffren's reputation. Caron accordingly sets out to undertake a comprehensive demolition of practically every aspect of Suffren's professional life and career. Coming from the pen of such a distinguished historian, the indictment must be accepted as carrying considerable weight. Nevertheless, with all due respect to his lengthy and detailed analysis, it is not entirely unreasonable to suggest that he does perhaps somewhat overstate his case, going out of his way to find fault when none really exists, or where the facts are explained otherwise than by shortcomings on Suffren's part.

When he comes to sum up his examination of Suffren's career, Caron does not mince words, observing that 'one is only able to conclude that if the Chevalier Suffren displays an indisputable courage and an incomparable tactical *coup d'oeil*, his performance when all is said and done is very ordinary and extremely disappointing.' He goes on to add that some historians put this down to deception on the part of the Ministry: 'Perhaps, but it does not affect at all the image of the Bailli in the eyes of the general public.'[12] His conclusion amounts to a powerful denunciation of a popular hero. If it does not entirely efface the opinions of such as Georges Lacour-Gayet, quoted above, it is because of the relentlessly one-sided nature of his analysis.

---

10 Lacour-Gayet, *marine militaire*, p.551.
11 Philippe Masson, 'Suffren', in Jack Sweetman (ed.), *The Great Admirals* (Annapolis: Naval Institute Press, 1997), p.189.
12 Caron, *Mythe de Suffren*, p.459.

Mahan, writing at the end of the nineteenth century, concluded that the honours heaped on Suffren were well-deserved:

> They were the tribute paid to his unyielding energy and genius, shown not only in actual fight but in the steadfastness which held to his station through every discouragement, and rose equal to every demand made by recurring want and misfortune. Alike in the general conduct of his operations and on the battlefield under the fire of the enemy, this lofty resolve was the distinguishing merit of Suffren.[13]

Mahan added, though, that he expected too much of his captains: 'He had the right to expect more than he got, but not that ready perception of the situation and that firmness of nerve which, except for a few favourites of nature, are the result only of practice and experience.'

Suffren possessed a remarkable and overpowering personality, which perhaps in many respects was not agreeable. He was certainly a bully and, invariably convinced of the correctness of his judgement, always ready to blame others for his setbacks. Account must always be taken of the extremely adverse conditions in which he was operating. He was dependent on subordinates, some of whom inexcusably let him down. Far from home, for most of the time he had no proper base. It is perhaps not altogether surprising that the passion and arrogance in his nature should have divided opinion among historians. In spite of all his faults, nevertheless, it is possible to agree with Mahan that he was indeed a great man.

It may be appropriate to end this survey of the campaigns in the Indian Ocean of 1782–1783 by considering the spirited debate which took place in the course of 1927 between two distinguished British admirals, both well respected historians, in the pages of *The Mariner's Mirror*. George A Ballard had just published a history of naval warfare in the Indian Ocean entitled *Rulers of the Indian Ocean*, in which he devoted a chapter to the campaigns of Suffren and Hughes.[14] In this he offered a number of comments on the battles which took place and in particular upon the two admirals. He followed this with an essay published in *The Mariner's Mirror* in that year entitled 'The Last Battlefleet Struggle in the Bay of Bengal', in which he developed a number of the opinions which he had previously expressed. This provoked Sir Herbert Richmond to publish a response in the next issue of *The Mariner's Mirror* under the title 'The Hughes-Suffren Campaigns', in which he challenged some of Ballard's conclusions. The latter responded with a further essay, entitled 'Hughes and Suffren', defending his position. After that, the matter rested, until 1931 when Richmond published his magisterial history *The Navy in India 1768–1783*, in which he was able to enlarge on the opinions he had previously expressed.

This was certainly a conflict between two undoubted heavyweights. Ballard had reached a number of conclusions with which Richmond strongly disagreed, and the latter wrote that 'throughout his description of the campaign Admiral Ballard weights the scales against Hughes.' It was in the descriptions of the Battle of

---

13 Marne, *Influence of Sea Power*, p.465.
14 G.A. Ballard, *Rulers of the Indian Ocean* (London: Duckworth, 1927).

Cuddalore that Ballard did, in Richmond's view, the gravest injustice to Hughes's reputation. It was Ballard's opinion that by the end of the four battles of 1782 Hughes was 'a tired man' and that at Cuddalore he 'fought almost like a man resigned to defeat.' A passage in Ballard's essay to which Richmond took particular exception compared the performance of the two commanders:

> In a fifth and last battle (Suffren) attacked so fiercely – and in such good order – that he knocked the British Admiral squarely off the stage; who was in retreat by nightfall a beaten man. With the remarkable personal tribute to his credit of having compelled the retirement of a hostile fleet superior to his own in every respect but leadership, the great Frenchman reached the culminating exploit of his career.[15]

Richmond completely rejected the suggestion that Hughes was 'a beaten man', or that his return to Madras was a retreat, pointing out that Hughes 'took no less than five days to cover a distance of about 90 miles with fair winds and a northerly current to help him. This has the appearance of an uncommonly leisurely retreat.'[16] Richmond considered that Ballard's account of the battle of Cuddalore was the most 'inaccurate and misleading account of the battle ever written.' Richmond concluded his essay by observing that, in the absence of compelling evidence to counter established facts, he considered it right to describe Ballard's description of the events as inaccurate, 'and his comments upon Hughes's conduct unjustified.'

This prompted a fresh broadside from Ballard. He protested against the suggestion that he was 'apparently disinclined to allow Hughes credit for anything', and he stoutly defended himself against the charge that his description of Cuddalore was 'inaccurate and misleading;' he claimed that Richmond's narrative only served to prove that his own account 'was a fundamentally accurate summary.' One passage in Richmond's essay he found incomprehensible, which was where he suggested that he did not recollect a case of a decisive victory having been obtained by a fleet in the lee berth, and he drew attention to Rodney's victory at Les Saintes in 1782. In standing up for the views he had expressed, Ballard insisted that there was ample material for independent investigation, and he had no sources of information not available to other people.

No punches had been pulled in this instructive and vigorous debate between Ballard and Richmond, and it perhaps illustrates the difficulty in arriving at a conclusive and balanced judgement on Suffren and Hughes as they struggled for mastery in the Indian Ocean. The immediate objectives which they pursued were determined by the complex politico-military situation in which they found themselves. Suffren's task required him to adopt an offensive strategy entirely consistent with his personality. Hughes, on the other hand, was obliged to stand on the defensive; this, too, accorded with his own instincts. Neither was able to achieve a decisive

---

15 Ballard, 'The Last Battlefleet Struggle in the Bay of Bengal', *The Mariner's Mirror*, (1927) 13:2, p.141.
16 Richmond, 'The Hughes-Suffren Campaigns', *The Mariner's Mirror*, (1927) 13:3, p.236.

victory, but this in the context of sea fighting in the eighteenth century was not surprising.

It may be that Suffren's reputation has been to a certain extent overblown by some French historians. It may also be the case that Hughes has not been given sufficient credit for what he did achieve. Nevertheless, by the end of the campaign Suffren had demonstrated the greater boldness, determination and tactical skill. He was always ready to innovate and almost always ready to attack. For his part Hughes never felt able to depart from the orthodoxy of the time, nor could he escape the defensive pressures created by his situation.

Appendix

The Two Squadrons 1782–1783

Battle of Sadras 17 February 1782

Monmouth	64	*Héros* (Suffren)	74
Burford	70	*Orient*	74
Eagle	64	*Sphinx*	64
Worcester	64	*Vengeur*	64
Superb (Hughes)	74	*Annibal* (Tromelin)	74
Hero	74	*Sévére*	64
Isis	50	*Petit Annibal*	50
Monarca	70	*Bizarre*	64
Exeter (King)	64	*Ajax*	64
		Artésien	64
		Brillant	64
		Flamand	60

Battle of Provedien 12 April 1782

Exeter (King)	64	*Vengeur*	64
Sultan	74	*Artésien*	64
Eagle	64	*Petit Annibal*	50
Burford	70	*Sphinx*	64
Monmouth	64	*Héros* (Suffren)	74
Superb (Hughes)	74	*Orient*	74
Monarca	70	*Brillant*	64
Magnanime	64	*Sévére*	64
Isis	50	*Ajax*	64
Hero	74	*Annibal* (Tromelin)	74
Worcester	64	*Flamand*	60
		Bizarre	64

Battle of Negapatam 6 July 1782

Hero	74	Flamand	60
Exeter (King)	64	Annibal (Tromelin)	74
Isis	50	Sévére	64
Burford	70	Brillant	64
Sultan	74	Héros	74
Superb (Hughes)	74	Sphinx	64
Monarca	70	Artésien	64
Worcester	64	Petit Annibal	50
Monmouth	64	Vengeur	64
Eagle	64	Bizarre	64
Magnanime	64	Orient	74
		Ajax (took no part)	64

Battle of Trincomali 3 September 1782

Exeter (King)	64	Artésien	64
Isis	50	Sévére	64
Hero	74	Saint Michel	60
Sceptre	64	Orient	74
Burford	70	Brillant	64
Sultan	74	Petit Annibal	50
Superb (Hughes)	74	Héros (Suffren)	74
Monarca	70	Illustre	74
Eagle	64	Flamand	50
Magnanime	64	Ajax	64
Monmouth	64	Annibal (Tromelin)	74
Worcester	64	Bizarre	64
		Consolante	40
		Vengeur	64

Battle of Cuddalore 20 June 1783

Defence	74	Sphinx	64
Isis	50	Brillant	64
Gibraltar (Bickerton)	80	Fendant	74
Inflexible	64	Flamand	50
Exeter (King)	64	Ajax	64
Worcester	64	Petit Annibal	50
Africa	64	Argonaute	74
Sultan	74	Héros (Suffren)[1]	74
Superb (Hughes)	74	Illustre	74

---

1   Suffren transferred his flag to the frigate *Cleopatre* during the battle.

Monarca	70	Saint Michel	60
Burford	70	Vengeur	64
Sceptre	64	Sévére	64
Magnanime	64	Annibal	74
Eagle	64	Hardi	64
Hero	64	Artésien	64
Bristol	50	Consolante	40
Monmouth	64		
Cumberland	74		

Bibliography

Anon (ed.), *Correspondence with Vice Admiral Sir Edward Hughes* (place and publisher unknown, 1784)
Ballard, G.A., 'Hughes and Suffren', *The Mariner's Mirror*, (1927) 13:4, pp.348–356
Ballard, G.A., 'The Last Battlefleet Struggle in the Bay of Bengal', *The Mariner's Mirror*, (1927) 13:2, pp.125–144
Ballard, G.A., *Rulers of the Indian Ocean* (London: Duckworth, 1927)
Barnes, G.R. and Owen, J.H. (eds), *The Private Papers of John, Earl of Sandwich* (London: Navy Records Society, 1936)
Barry, Quintin, *Crisis at the Chesapeake* (Warwick: Helion & Co, 2021)
Barry, Quintin, *From Ushant to Gibraltar* (Warwick: Helion & Co, 2022)
Beatson, Robert, *Naval and Military Memoirs of Great Britain from 1727 to 1783* (London: J. Strachan, 1804)
Black, J.R. and Woodfine, P. (eds), *The British Navy and the Use of Naval Power in the Eighteenth Century* (Leicester: Leicester University Press, 1988)
Bonner-Smith, D. (ed.), *The Barrington Papers* (London: Navy Records Society, 1941)
Caron, Francois, *Le Mythe de Suffren: La campagne dans l'Inde 1781-1783* (Vincennes: Service Historique de la Marine, 1996)
Cary, L.H.S.C., 'Trincomali', *The Mariner's Mirror*, (1931) 17:1, pp.20–23
Castex, Raoul, *La Manoeuvre de la Praya* (Paris: L. Fournier, 1912)
Castex, Raoul, *Les idées militaires de la marine du XVIIIe siècle* (Paris: Le Fournier, 1911)
Cavaliero, Roderick, *Admiral Satan* (London: I B Tauris, 1994)
Charnock, John, *Biographia Navalis* (London: Faulder, 1798)
Chevalier, E., *Histoire de la marine Francaise* (Paris: Hachette et Cie, 1902)
Clowes, William Laird, *The Royal Navy: A History from the Earliest Times* (London: Sampson Low Marston and Co, 1898)
Corbett, Julian S. (ed.), *Fighting Instructions 1530-1860* (London: Navy Records Society, 1905)
Corbett, Julian S. (ed.), *Signals and Instructions 1776-1794* (London: Navy Records Society, 1908)
Creswell, John, *British Admirals of the Eighteenth Century* (London: George Allen and Unwin, 1972)
Dull, Jonathan R., *The French Navy and American Independence* (Princeton: Princeton University Press, 1975)
Fabel, R.F.A., *Bombast and Broadsides* (Birmingham: University of Alabama Press, 1987)
Graham, Gerald S., *The Politics of Naval Supremacy* (Cambridge: Cambridge University Press, 1965)
Hamilton, C.I., *The Making of the Modern Admiralty* (Cambridge: Cambridge University Press, 2011)
James, W.M., *The British Navy in Adversity* (London: Longmans Green & Co, 1933)
Jenkins, E.H., *A History of the French Navy* (London: Macdonald and Jane's, 1973)
Keay, John, *The Honourable Company* (London: Harper Collins, 1991)

Kennedy, Paul M., *The Rise and Fall of British Naval Mastery* (London: Macmillan, 1983)
La Varende, Leon, *Suffren et ses ennemis* (Paris: Les Editions de Paris, 1948)
Lacour-Gayet, Georges, *La marine militaire de France sous le règne de Louis XVI* (Paris: Honore Champion, 1905)
Laughton, John Knox, *Studies in Naval History* (London: Longmans, Green and Co, 1887)
Laughton, Sir John (ed.), *Letters and Papers of Charles, Lord Barham* (London: Navy Records Society, 1908)
Lavery, B. (ed.), *Shipboard Life and Organisation 1731-1815* (Aldershot: Navy Records Society, 1998)
Low, C.R., *History of the Indian Navy 1613-1863* (Delhi: Manas Publications, 1965)
Macdougall, Philip, 'British Seapower and the Mysore Wars of the Eighteenth Century', *The Mariner's Mirror*, (2011) 97:4, pp.299–314
Mackesy, Piers, *The War for America 1775-1783* (London: Longmans Green & Co, 1964)
Mahan, A.T., *Major Operations of the Navies in the American War of Independence* (London: Sampson Low Marston & Co, 1913)
Mahan, A.T., *The Influence of Sea Power upon History* (Boston: Little, Brown & Co, 1890)
Malleson, G.B., *Final French Struggles in India and on the Indian Seas* (London: W.H. Allen & Co, 1878)
Marcus, G.J., *A Naval History of England* (Boston: Little, Brown & Co, 1961)
Masson, Philippe, 'Pierre-Andre de Suffren de Saint-Tropez', in Jack Sweetman (ed.), *The Great Admirals* (Annapolis: U.S. Naval Institute, 1997)
Pernoud, Regine, *La Campagne des Indes: Lettres inédites du Bailli de Suffren* (Mantes: Petit Mantaise, 1941)
Richmond, Sir Herbert, 'The Hughes-Suffren Campaigns', *The Mariner's Mirror*, (1927) 13:3, pp.219–237
Richmond, Sir Herbert, *The Navy in India 1763-1783* (London: Ernest Benn, 1931)
Rodger, N.A.M., *The Command of the Ocean* (London: Allen Lane, 2004)
Rodger, N.A.M., *The Insatiable Earl* (New York: WW Norton & Co, 1993)
Rodger, N.A.M., *The Wooden World: An Anatomy of the Georgian Navy* (London: Collins, 1986)
Roux, Joseph Siméon, *Le Bailli de Suffren dans l'Inde* (Marseille: Barlatier Feissat, 1862)
Rutherford, G., 'Sidelights on Commodore Johnstone's Expedition to the Cape, Part II', *The Mariner's Mirror*, (1942) 28:4, pp.290–308
Sen, S.P., *The French in India 1763-1816* (Delhi: Munshiram Manoharlal, 1971)
Talbott, John E., *The Pen and Ink Sailor* (London: Frank Cass, 1998)
Tunstall, Brian, Nicholas Tracy (ed.), *Naval Warfare in the Age of Sail* (London: Conway Maritime Press, 1990)
Wilcox, Martin, 'This Great Complex Concern: Victualling the Royal Navy on the East Indies Station, 1780-1815', *The Mariner's Mirror*, (2011) 97:2, pp.32–48
Willis, Sam, *The Struggle for Sea Power* (London: Atlantic Books, 2015)

General Index

d'Aché, *Chef d'Escadre* Comte 35, 39–40, 52
Achin 51, 175–179, 182–183, 189
d'Albert de Rioms, *Capitaine de Vaisseau* François Hector 16–17, 20–22, 66
Alms, Captain James 93, 118, 124
Anjengo 42, 93, 98, 118, 148, 174, 181
Arcot 41, 47, 54
d'Aymar, *Capitaine de Vaisseau* Louis-Esprit 148–149, 155, 163, 177

Baillie, Lieutenant Colonel William 47, 54
Barbados 17
Barrington, Rear Admiral Samuel 17–20, 177, 189
Bassein 31, 50
Batavia 63, 65, 88, 133, 137, 178–179
Batticaloa 34, 117, 128, 130–131, 133, 138, 149, 152, 154–155, 194
Bengal 31–35, 42, 88, 90–91, 115, 117–118, 132, 173, 180, 182, 188, 190, 209
Bickerton, Commodore Sir Richard 150–151, 159, 168, 170, 172, 174–175, 178, 180, 203
Bombay 30–31, 34, 39, 42, 44–45, 47–50, 53–54, 88, 93, 118, 151, 154, 168–175, 178, 180, 185, 188–190, 196
Boscawen, Vice Admiral Edward 13, 28, 75
Boston 16, 44
Braithwaite, Colonel John 42, 113, 118
Brest 13–14, 31–32, 44, 64–65, 67–68, 70, 72, 132–133, 177
Bussy, Charles Joseph Patissier, Marquis de 33, 35, 131–133, 147–151, 169, 175–187, 189, 192–195, 199, 203
Byron, Vice Admiral John 16–21

Cadiz 13, 22–23, 28, 132, 177
Calcutta 10, 31, 34–35, 42, 47, 113, 153, 179, 188, 190

Calicut 34, 48
Canada 12–13
Canary Islands, the 133, 177
Cape of Good Hope, the 23, 46–47, 55–59, 61–69, 72–76, 81–88, 91, 93, 133, 150–151, 178, 189, 191–193, 205
Cape Verde Islands, the 73, 75–76, 81, 150
Carnatic, the 33–34, 41–42, 46–47, 49–50, 53, 89, 95, 113, 118, 120, 148, 168–169, 173, 180–181
Cartagena 13, 26
Castries, Marquis de 23–24, 63–69, 72–73, 75, 83, 86, 88, 94–95, 107, 109, 111, 114–115, 117, 127, 130–132, 138, 144–145, 166, 168, 175, 180, 183, 185, 187, 193, 196, 204–205
Ceylon 55, 59, 90–91, 96–97, 102–103, 115, 119–121, 131–133, 135, 138, 148, 151, 164, 170–171, 174–175, 189, 193
Chaffault, *Chef d'Escadre* Louis-Charles du 15, 28
Chandernagore 31, 33, 35–36
Chilleau, *Capitaine de Vaisseau* Charles Louis du 46, 66, 96, 109, 130, 135, 145
Clive, Robert 33, 35
Cochin 118, 175, 181
Compagnie des Indes, the 33, 35–36, 38, 66
Conflans, *Vice-Amiral du Ponant* Comte de 13, 28
Coote, Lieutenant General Sir Eyre 35, 48–54, 89–92, 98–99, 118, 136, 151, 153–154, 167–168, 170–171, 173, 188, 190–192
Cornwall, Captain Frederick 11–12
Coromandel Coast, the 31, 35, 39–40, 46–47, 49, 51–53, 55, 88, 90–91, 93, 97, 115, 117–118, 131, 136, 146, 149, 152, 168, 170, 173, 175–176, 185, 189, 192
Cruickshank, Captain John 26, 28

Cuddalore 34, 41, 49, 51–54, 117, 133, 135, 138, 143–144, 146–153, 155, 158, 167–168, 170–171, 176, 178, 180–181, 185, 187, 189–201, 203, 205, 210

Duchemin, *Maréchal de camp* Pierre 93, 96, 99, 112, 114–115, 117–118, 132, 135–136
Dupleix, Joseph-François 33, 35–36, 186

East India Company, the 30–33, 36–38, 42–46, 48–50, 52, 55, 57–59, 61, 63, 89–90, 92–93, 98, 113, 120, 168–169, 171–173, 175, 179, 188
d'Estaing, *Vice-Amiral* Comte 15–21, 23, 44, 64, 66, 129

Falck, Iman Willem 120, 132, 135, 156, 168, 175, 179, 181
Ferrol 22, 28
Forbin, *Capitaine de Vaisseau* Chevalier de 66, 78, 96, 109, 123, 130, 144
Fort Ostenburg 92, 156
Fullarton, Colonel William 57, 61, 191, 203

Galle 34, 77–78, 86, 93–94, 96, 103, 109, 115, 120, 127–128, 133, 148–149, 166, 178
Ganjam 34, 180
Gell, Captain John 92, 142
Gibraltar 13, 15, 22, 46, 61, 64–65, 68
Gorée 45, 66–67
Grasse, *Lieutenantgénéral des Armées Navales* François-Joseph-Paul de 13, 23, 64–65, 67–68, 70, 72, 196
Grenada 19–21
Guadalupe, 17, 21
Guichen, *Capitaine de Vaisseau* Luc Urbain du Bouëxic de 15, 132–133, 177

Hastings, Warren 42–43, 47–48, 113, 190
Hawke, Rear Admiral Edward 12, 28
Hickey, William 10, 32, 83–84, 137, 165, 181, 183, 206–207
Howe, Vice Admiral Lord Richard 16–17, 61
Humberstone, Lieutenant Colonel Thomas Frederick Mackenzie 57, 148
Hyder Ali 31, 42–44, 46–54, 59, 63, 88–91, 93, 95, 99, 111–112, 114–115, 117–118, 120, 132–133, 135–137, 144, 147–149, 154, 156, 167–169, 173, 176, 178–180, 189–190

Ile de Bourbon (Réunion) 39, 56, 67, 182
Ile de France (Mauritius) 23, 25, 31, 35, 37, 39–40, 42, 45–47, 49, 51, 53, 56, 59, 62–63, 65–66, 69, 72, 87–89, 91, 93, 96, 99, 110, 115, 117, 131–133, 137, 146, 156, 159, 166, 168, 177, 189, 204–205

Java 65, 178
Johnstone, Commodore George 22, 57–65, 67–68, 70–77, 79–88, 91, 93, 148, 178, 208

Kandy 34, 120
Kempenfelt, Rear Admiral Richard 133, 177
King, Commodore Sir Richard 108–109, 203, 205
Knights of Malta, the 9, 12–13, 204
Knowles, Commodore Charles 26, 28

La Clue, *Chef d'Escadre* Comte de 13, 17
Lang, Colonel Ross 189, 191
Lestock, Rear Admiral Richard 11–12
Lorient 46, 66
Louisbourg 13, 26, 28

Macartney, Lord George 89–91, 118, 120, 136–138, 152–153, 170–172, 188, 190–191, 203, 207
Macdowall, Captain Hay 155–156
Madras 30, 33–36, 38–43, 45, 47–49, 51–52, 54, 89, 91, 93, 96–98, 102, 104, 115, 117–121, 132, 146, 148, 150–154, 156, 158, 164, 167–168, 170–174, 178–181, 185, 188–194, 203–204, 207, 210
Mahé 42, 45
Mahratta Confederacy, the 31, 50, 89
Malabar Coast, the 42, 48, 88, 93, 98, 120, 148–149, 151, 171, 174–175, 180–181, 185, 189, 192, 195, 206
Mangalore 34, 53, 169, 206
Martinique 12, 17–19
Mathews, Vice Admiral Thomas 11–12
Matthews, Brigadier General Richard 180, 192

Mauritius, see Ile de France
Medows, Major General William 61–62, 65, 79, 86–87, 93, 98, 118
Mitchell, Captain Andrew 189–190, 206
Motte, *Chef d'Escadre* Comte Dubois de la 13
Motte, *Chef d'Escadre* Jean Guillaume Toussaint Picquet 13, 19, 23, 66
Munro, Colonel Sir Hector 54, 91
Mysore 34, 42, 114, 136–137

Negapatam 41, 46–47, 55, 90–93, 97, 103–104, 114, 117, 119, 129–130, 134–136, 138–139, 141–143, 147, 150–151, 153, 168, 171–172, 189–190, 202

Orissa Coast, the 179–180, 189
d'Orves, *Capitaine de Vaisseau* Jean-Baptiste Thomas, comte 25, 45–47, 50–53, 69, 72, 75, 87, 94–97, 110, 112, 132, 145, 183

Paniani 174–175
Pasley, Captain Thomas 70, 72–73, 79, 84–85
Pollilur 47, 54, 91
Pondicherry 33–36, 38–42, 47, 49, 51, 102–103, 112, 136, 167–168, 203
Poona 34, 42, 50, 53
Port Louis 42, 45, 51, 88, 93–95, 115, 117, 131, 133, 145, 177, 182
Porto Novo 41, 54, 112–115, 117–118, 120, 185, 187, 194–195, 199
Porto Praya 70–71, 73–74, 76, 82–84, 93, 99, 101, 112, 118, 208
Provedien 114, 116, 122, 128, 130, 133, 136, 140

Quiberon Bay 28, 66, 144

Réunion, see Ile de Bourbon

Sadras 41, 98, 100, 112–114, 117, 119, 121
Saint Kitts 19, 21
Saint Lucia 17, 19, 21
Saint Vincent 19, 22
Salvert, *Lieutenant de Vaisseau* Éléonor Jacques Marie Stanislas de Perrier de 96–97, 99, 101–102, 125, 145, 202
Sandwich, John Montagu, 4th Earl of 29, 57, 63, 65, 206
Sartine, Antoine de 14–15, 21–23, 37, 49
Sayyid Sahib 192, 199
Seven Years War, the 14, 28, 33, 35–38
Souillac, François de 47, 51–52, 63, 69, 93, 102, 111, 113–115, 131–132, 136–138, 144, 147, 166, 176
Stuart, Major General James 173, 189–195, 198–199, 203
Sumatra 51, 96, 115, 175–176, 178

Tellicherry 34, 48, 53, 175, 181, 206
Tipu Sultan 167, 174, 180–181, 183, 185, 192, 195, 199
Toulon 10–11, 13–15, 21–22, 26, 65, 205
Tranquebar 41, 103, 115, 133, 138, 191, 195
Trincomali 30, 34, 55, 89–93, 97, 99, 101–104, 115, 117–122, 127–129, 133, 135, 138, 140, 146, 149–159, 164–165, 167–170, 172–173, 175–185, 187–190, 192–195, 198, 205–206, 208
Tromelin, *Capitaine de Vaisseau* Bernard de 93–94, 96, 103–104, 107, 109–112, 126, 128, 130, 140, 142, 145, 163, 166
Tronjoly, *Chef d'Escadre* Jean-Baptiste-François Lollivier de 39–40, 42, 45, 47, 51–52
Troubridge, Captain Thomas 191, 195

Vellore 41, 118
Vernon, Vice Admiral Edward 26, 31, 39–40, 42, 45
Villaret-Joyeuse, Lieutenant Louis 96, 187–188

Wandewash 35, 41, 50, 91
Watt, Captain James 141, 144

Index of Ships

British

Actaeon 45
Active 62, 71–72, 74, 84–85, 87, 91, 170, 189, 191, 195
Africa 150, 175, 189

Belleisle 44, 46
Bristol 150, 185, 192, 194
Burford 26, 44, 49, 106, 123, 126, 130, 134, 140–142, 162–164, 189

Chaser 115, 192
Colombo 34, 63, 119–120, 132, 156, 168, 179, 181
Coventry 39–40, 50, 154, 180
Cumberland 26, 150, 175

Defence 150, 175, 202
Diamond 26
Diana 62, 71, 73–74, 77–78, 87

Eagle 44, 49, 106, 109, 123, 134, 138, 140–142, 162–164, 189
Essex 60, 64, 206
Exeter 44, 49, 105–109, 117, 123, 126, 134, 140, 142, 157, 161–164, 202

Fortitude (EIC) 64, 77–78, 146

Gibraltar 150, 175, 202
Glatton (EIC) 39–40

Hannibal 87, 96, 116
Hero 62, 70–71, 74, 77, 79, 87, 106, 118, 125, 134, 140–143, 175
Hinchinbrook (EIC) 77, 83, 118

Infernal 62, 71, 73–74, 78, 80, 83, 87
Inflexible 150, 175, 202

Isis 17–18, 62, 71, 74, 77–80, 87, 100, 103, 106, 118, 125–126, 130, 134, 140–141, 160–162, 170–171, 191–192, 202

Jason 62, 71, 74, 79, 82, 84–85, 87
Jupiter 62, 70–74, 77, 79, 83, 87

Lark 26, 28, 59, 72, 84, 87

Magnanime 96, 115, 118–119, 123, 134, 140, 164, 175
Marlborough 11, 26
Medea 150–151, 154, 197–198, 203
Monarca 91–92, 106, 109, 123–124, 126, 134, 139–143, 162–163
Monmouth 20, 62, 73–74, 77–80, 87, 93, 103, 106, 116, 118, 123–126, 128–130, 133–134, 140, 152, 158, 161–162, 164, 175

Naiade 192
Namur 11, 28
Nymph 44, 55

Prince of Wales 18, 20
Pulicat 41, 50, 91, 97

Rattlesnake 84, 87
Resolution 146
Resolution (EIC) 70, 188
Ripon 39, 46
Romney 62, 70–71, 74, 79–80, 82, 87
Royal Charlotte (EIC) 188, 190

Salisbury 29–30
San Carlos 70, 192, 194
Sartine 49
Sceptre 133, 150–152, 158, 170–171, 175, 188–189, 202
Seahorse 30, 39–40, 103

Somerset 28–29
Suffolk 20, 26
Sultan 96, 115, 140–142, 162, 165, 175, 189, 206
Superb 32, 44, 52, 106–112, 116–117, 123–126, 134, 139–140, 142, 150, 162–165, 174–175, 202, 206

Terror 62, 71, 73–74, 78, 87

Valentine 39, 64

Warwick 26, 28
Worcester 44, 50, 106, 109, 122, 126, 134, 140–142, 161, 164

French

Ajax 46–47, 52, 96, 106–107, 110, 116, 122–123, 125–127, 134, 139, 142–145, 161–163, 166, 202, 205
Alexandre 133, 177
Annibal 65–66, 74, 76–78, 80, 82–84, 86–88, 93–94, 96, 106–107, 109–110, 116, 122–124, 126, 130, 134, 140–142, 162–163, 198, 205
Argonaute 133, 177, 198, 205
Artésien 65–66, 71–72, 74–78, 80, 86, 96, 104, 106–107, 116, 122–123, 125, 130, 133–135, 140, 142, 145, 160–161, 202, 205

Bellone 96, 115, 133, 139, 145, 154, 159, 168, 176, 179, 187, 205
Bizarre 10, 52, 96, 106, 116, 122–123, 130, 134, 140, 162–163, 166, 168
Brillant 39, 52, 93, 96, 106–108, 116, 122–124, 134, 140–143, 145–146, 161, 205
Brisson 39, 67, 119

Chasseur 131, 133, 177
Cleopatre 133, 177, 185, 193, 199, 202
Consolante 52, 132, 148–149, 160–161, 164, 166, 177, 198, 202
Coventry 180–181, 185, 192–194, 205

Diligente 95–96, 128

Elephant 47, 168
Expédition 52, 131

Fantasque 15–16, 20, 129
Fendant 44, 133, 177, 182–183, 185, 193–194, 198, 202, 205
Fine 69, 93, 96–97, 101, 120, 125, 127, 133, 176
Flamand 45, 52, 93, 96, 101, 106–110, 116, 122–123, 130, 134, 140–141, 143, 145, 157, 162–163, 182, 202
Fortune 65–66, 72, 74, 78, 80, 83–84, 86, 88, 93, 96, 176

Hardi 133, 177, 180
Héros 65, 71, 74, 77–78, 80–81, 83–85, 96, 101, 105–107, 110–112, 116, 122–126, 134, 141–142, 161–166, 168, 181, 198–199, 202, 205

Illustre 132–133, 148, 161–163, 165–166, 168, 177, 182, 198, 205

Lezard 132, 155

Marseille 9, 22

Naiade 182, 188, 190, 192

Orient 52, 96, 106–107, 116, 122–127, 134, 140, 161, 165, 168

Petit Annibal 87, 96, 106–107, 109, 122–124, 134, 140, 160, 165, 179, 198
Pourvoyeuse 39, 96, 103, 145–146
Pulvériseur 96, 131, 146, 176

Sagittaire 16, 20
Saint Michel 132, 148, 160–161, 163, 177, 181, 185, 198, 202, 205
Sartine 39–40, 49
Sévére 46, 52, 106, 122–123, 140–145, 161, 202
Sphinx 44, 65–66, 71, 73–74, 76–80, 83, 86, 96, 106–107, 116, 122–124, 126, 130, 133–135, 140–141, 202, 205
Subtile 39, 52, 96
Sylphide 63, 96, 139, 146

Union 14, 67

Vengeur 65–66, 74, 76–78, 80, 96, 106–107, 116, 122–123, 125–126, 130, 134, 142, 145, 160–161, 164, 168, 177, 182

From Reason to Revolution – Warfare 1721-1815

http://www.helion.co.uk/series/from-reason-to-revolution-1721-1815.php

The 'From Reason to Revolution' series covers the period of military history 1721–1815, an era in which fortress-based strategy and linear battles gave way to the nation-in-arms and the beginnings of total war.

This era saw the evolution and growth of light troops of all arms, and of increasingly flexible command systems to cope with the growing armies fielded by nations able to mobilise far greater proportions of their manpower than ever before. Many of these developments were fired by the great political upheavals of the era, with revolutions in America and France bringing about social change which in turn fed back into the military sphere as whole nations readied themselves for war. Only in the closing years of the period, as the reactionary powers began to regain the upper hand, did a military synthesis of the best of the old and the new become possible.

The series will examine the military and naval history of the period in a greater degree of detail than has hitherto been attempted, and has a very wide brief, with the intention of covering all aspects from the battles, campaigns, logistics, and tactics, to the personalities, armies, uniforms, and equipment.

Submissions

The publishers would be pleased to receive submissions for this series. Please email reasontorevolution@helion.co.uk, or write to Helion & Company Limited, Unit 8 Amherst Business Centre, Budbrooke Road, Warwick, CV34 5WE.

Titles

1. *Lobositz to Leuthen: Horace St Paul and the Campaigns of the Austrian Army in the Seven Years War 1756-57* (Neil Cogswell)
2. *Glories to Useless Heroism: The Seven Years War in North America from the French journals of Comte Maurés de Malartic, 1755-1760* (William Raffle (ed.))
3. *Reminiscences 1808-1815 Under Wellington: The Peninsular and Waterloo Memoirs of William Hay* (Andrew Bamford (ed.))
4. *Far Distant Ships: The Royal Navy and the Blockade of Brest 1793-1815* (Quintin Barry)
5. *Godoy's Army: Spanish Regiments and Uniforms from the Estado Militar of 1800* (Charles Esdaile and Alan Perry)
6. *On Gladsmuir Shall the Battle Be! The Battle of Prestonpans 1745* (Arran Johnston)
7. *The French Army of the Orient 1798-1801: Napoleon's Beloved 'Egyptians'* (Yves Martin)
8. *The Autobiography, or Narrative of a Soldier: The Peninsular War Memoirs of William Brown of the 45th Foot* (Steve Brown (ed.))
9. *Recollections from the Ranks: Three Russian Soldiers' Autobiographies from the Napoleonic Wars* (Darrin Boland)
10. *By Fire and Bayonet: Grey's West Indies Campaign of 1794* (Steve Brown)
11. *Olmütz to Torgau: Horace St Paul and the Campaigns of the Austrian Army in the Seven Years War 1758-60* (Neil Cogswell)
12. *Murat's Army: The Army of the Kingdom of Naples 1806-1815* (Digby Smith)
13. *The Veteran or 40 Years' Service in the British Army: The Scurrilous Recollections of Paymaster John Harley 47th Foot – 1798-1838* (Gareth Glover (ed.))
14. *Narrative of the Eventful Life of Thomas Jackson: Militiaman and Coldstream Sergeant, 1803-15* (Eamonn O'Keeffe (ed.))
15. *For Orange and the States: The Army of the Dutch Republic 1713-1772 Part I: Infantry* (Marc Geerdinck-Schaftenaar)
16. *Men Who Are Determined to be Free: The American Assault on Stony Point, 15 July 1779* (David C. Bonk)
17. *Next to Wellington: General Sir George Murray: The Story of a Scottish Soldier and Statesman, Wellington's Quartermaster General* (John Harding-Edgar)
18. *Between Scylla and Charybdis: The Army of Elector Friedrich August of Saxony 1733-1763 Part I: Staff and Cavalry* (Marco Pagan)

19	*The Secret Expedition: The Anglo-Russian Invasion of Holland 1799* (Geert van Uythoven)	37	*Québec Under Siege: French Eye-Witness Accounts from the Campaign of 1759* (Charles A. Mayhood (ed.))
20	*'We Are Accustomed to do our Duty': German Auxiliaries with the British Army 1793-95* (Paul Demet)	38	*King George's Hangman: Henry Hawley and the Battle of Falkirk 1746* (Jonathan D. Oates)
21	*With the Guards in Flanders: The Diary of Captain Roger Morris 1793-95* (Peter Harington (ed.))	39	*Zweybrücken in Command: The Reichsarmee in the Campaign of 1758* (Neil Cogswell)
22	*The British Army in Egypt 1801: An Underrated Army Comes of Age* (Carole Divall)	40	*So Bloody a Day: The 16th Light Dragoons in the Waterloo Campaign* (David J. Blackmore)
23	*Better is the Proud Plaid: The Clothing, Weapons, and Accoutrements of the Jacobites in the '45* (Jenn Scott)	41	*Northern Tars in Southern Waters: The Russian Fleet in the Mediterranean 1806-1810* (Vladimir Bogdanovich Bronevskiy / Darrin Boland)
24	*The Lilies and the Thistle: French Troops in the Jacobite '45* (Andrew Bamford)	42	*Royal Navy Officers of the Seven Years War: A Biographical Dictionary of Commissioned Officers 1748-1763* (Cy Harrison)
25	*A Light Infantryman With Wellington: The Letters of Captain George Ulrich Barlow 52nd and 69th Foot 1808-15* (Gareth Glover (ed.))	43	*All at Sea: Naval Support for the British Army During the American Revolutionary War* (John Dillon)
26	*Swiss Regiments in the Service of France 1798-1815: Uniforms, Organisation, Campaigns* (Stephen Ede-Borrett)	44	*Glory is Fleeting: New Scholarship on the Napoleonic Wars* (Andrew Bamford (ed.))
27	*For Orange and the States! The Army of the Dutch Republic 1713-1772: Part II: Cavalry and Specialist Troops* (Marc Geerdinck-Schaftenaar)	45	*Fashioning Regulation, Regulating Fashion: Uniforms and Dress of the British Army 1800-1815 Vol. II* (Ben Townsend)
28	*Fashioning Regulation, Regulating Fashion: Uniforms and Dress of the British Army 1800-1815 Volume I* (Ben Townsend)	46	*Revenge in the Name of Honour: The Royal Navy's Quest for Vengeance in the Single Ship Actions of the War of 1812* (Nicholas James Kaizer)
29	*Riflemen: The History of the 5th Battalion 60th (Royal American) Regiment, 1797-1818* (Robert Griffith)	47	*They Fought With Extraordinary Bravery: The III German (Saxon) Army Corps in the Southern Netherlands 1814* (Geert van Uythoven)
30	*The Key to Lisbon: The Third French Invasion of Portugal, 1810-11* (Kenton White)	48	*The Danish Army of the Napoleonic Wars 1801-1814, Organisation, Uniforms & Equipment: Volume 1: High Command, Line and Light Infantry* (David Wilson)
31	*Command and Leadership: Proceedings of the 2018 Helion & Company 'From Reason to Revolution' Conference* (Andrew Bamford (ed.))		
32	*Waterloo After the Glory: Hospital Sketches and Reports on the Wounded After the Battle* (Michael Crumplin and Gareth Glover)	49	*Neither Up Nor Down: The British Army and the Flanders Campaign 1793-1895* (Phillip Ball)
33	*Fluxes, Fevers, and Fighting Men: War and Disease in Ancien Regime Europe 1648-1789* (Pádraig Lenihan)	50	*Guerra Fantástica: The Portuguese Army and the Seven Years War* (António Barrento)
34	*'They Were Good Soldiers': African-Americans Serving in the Continental Army, 1775-1783* (John U. Rees)	51	*From Across the Sea: North Americans in Nelson's Navy* (Sean M. Heuvel and John A. Rodgaard)
35	*A Redcoat in America: The Diaries of Lieutenant William Bamford, 1757-1765 and 1776* (John B. Hattendorf (ed.))	52	*Rebellious Scots to Crush: The Military Response to the Jacobite '45* (Andrew Bamford (ed.))
36	*Between Scylla and Charybdis: The Army of Friedrich August II of Saxony, 1733-1763: Part II: Infantry and Artillery* (Marco Pagan)	53	*The Army of George II 1727-1760: The Soldiers who Forged an Empire* (Peter Brown)

54 *Wellington at Bay: The Battle of Villamuriel, 25 October 1812* (Garry David Wills)
55 *Life in the Red Coat: The British Soldier 1721-1815* (Andrew Bamford (ed.))
56 *Wellington's Favourite Engineer. John Burgoyne: Operations, Engineering, and the Making of a Field Marshal* (Mark S. Thompson)
57 *Scharnhorst: The Formative Years, 1755-1801* (Charles Edward White)
58 *At the Point of the Bayonet: The Peninsular War Battles of Arroyomolinos and Almaraz 1811-1812* (Robert Griffith)
59 *Sieges of the '45: Siege Warfare during the Jacobite Rebellion of 1745-1746* (Jonathan D. Oates)
60 *Austrian Cavalry of the Revolutionary and Napoleonic Wars, 1792–1815* (Enrico Acerbi, András K. Molnár)
61 *The Danish Army of the Napoleonic Wars 1801-1814, Organisation, Uniforms & Equipment: Volume 2: Cavalry and Artillery* (David Wilson)
62 *Napoleon's Stolen Army: How the Royal Navy Rescued a Spanish Army in the Baltic* (John Marsden)
63 *Crisis at the Chesapeake: The Royal Navy and the Struggle for America 1775-1783* (Quintin Barry)
64 *Bullocks, Grain, and Good Madeira: The Maratha and Jat Campaigns 1803-1806 and the emergence of the Indian Army* (Joshua Provan)
65 *Sir James McGrigor: The Adventurous Life of Wellington's Chief Medical Officer* (Tom Scotland)
66 *Fashioning Regulation, Regulating Fashion: Uniforms and Dress of the British Army 1800-1815 Volume I* (Ben Townsend) (paperback edition)
67 *Fashioning Regulation, Regulating Fashion: Uniforms and Dress of the British Army 1800-1815 Volume II* (Ben Townsend) (paperback edition)
68 *The Secret Expedition: The Anglo-Russian Invasion of Holland 1799* (Geert van Uythoven) (paperback edition)
69 *The Sea is My Element: The Eventful Life of Admiral Sir Pulteney Malcolm 1768-1838* (Paul Martinovich)
70 *The Sword and the Spirit: Proceedings of the first 'War & Peace in the Age of Napoleon' Conference* (Zack White (ed.))
71 *Lobositz to Leuthen: Horace St Paul and the Campaigns of the Austrian Army in the Seven Years War 1756-57* (Neil Cogswell) (paperback edition)
72 *For God and King. A History of the Damas Legion 1793-1798: A Case Study of the Military Emigration during the French Revolution* (Hughes de Bazouges and Alistair Nichols)
73 *'Their Infantry and Guns Will Astonish You': The Army of Hindustan and European Mercenaries in Maratha service 1780-1803* (Andy Copestake)
74 *Like A Brazen Wall: The Battle of Minden, 1759, and its Place in the Seven Years War* (Ewan Carmichael)
75 *Wellington and the Lines of Torres Vedras: The Defence of Lisbon during the Peninsular War* (Mark Thompson)
76 *French Light Infantry 1784-1815: From the Chasseurs of Louis XVI to Napoleon's Grande Armée* (Terry Crowdy)
77 *Riflemen: The History of the 5th Battalion 60th (Royal American) Regiment, 1797-1818* (Robert Griffith) (paperback edition)
78 *Hastenbeck 1757: The French Army and the Opening Campaign of the Seven Years War* (Olivier Lapray)
79 *Napoleonic French Military Uniforms: As Depicted by Horace and Carle Vernet and Eugène Lami* (Guy Dempsey (trans. and ed.))
80 *These Distinguished Corps: British Grenadier and Light Infantry Battalions in the American Revolution* (Don N. Hagist)
81 *Rebellion, Invasion, and Occupation: The British Army in Ireland, 1793 -1815* (Wayne Stack)
82 *You Have to Die in Piedmont! The Battle of Assietta, 19 July 1747. The War of the Austrian Succession in the Alps* (Giovanni Cerino Badone)
83 *A Very Fine Regiment: the 47th Foot in the American War of Independence, 1773–1783* (Paul Knight)
84 *By Fire and Bayonet: Grey's West Indies Campaign of 1794* (Steve Brown) (paperback edition)
85 *No Want of Courage: The British Army in Flanders, 1793-1795* (R.N.W. Thomas)
86 *Far Distant Ships: The Royal Navy and the Blockade of Brest 1793-1815* (Quintin Barry) (paperback edition)

87	*Armies and Enemies of Napoleon 1789-1815: Proceedings of the 2021 Helion and Company 'From Reason to Revolution' Conference* (Robert Griffith (ed.))	102	*Olmütz to Torgau: Horace St Paul and the Campaigns of the Austrian Army in the Seven Years War 1758-60* (Neil Cogswell) (paperback edition)
88	*The Battle of Rossbach 1757: New Perspectives on the Battle and Campaign* (Alexander Querengässer (ed.))	103	*Fit to Command: British Regimental Leadership in the Revolutionary & Napoleonic Wars* (Steve Brown)
89	*Waterloo After the Glory: Hospital Sketches and Reports on the Wounded After the Battle* (Michael Crumplin and Gareth Glover) (paperback edition)	104	*Wellington's Unsung Heroes: The Fifth Division in the Peninsular War, 1810-1814* (Carole Divall)
90	*From Ushant to Gibraltar: The Channel Fleet 1778-1783* (Quintin Barry)	105	*1806-1807 – Tsar Alexander's Second War with Napoleon* (Alexander Ivanovich Mikhailovsky-Danilevsky, trans. Peter G.A. Phillips)
91	*'The Soldiers are Dressed in Red': The Quiberon Expedition of 1795 and the Counter-Revolution in Brittany* (Alistair Nichols)	106	*The Pattern: The 33rd Regiment in the American Revolution, 1770-1783* (Robbie MacNiven)
92	*The Army of the Kingdom of Italy 1805-1814: Uniforms, Organisation, Campaigns* (Stephen Ede-Borrett)	107	*To Conquer and to Keep: Suchet and the War for Eastern Spain, 1809-1814, Volume 1 1809-1811* (Yuhan Kim)
93	*The Ottoman Army of the Napoleonic Wars 1798-1815: A Struggle for Survival from Egypt to the Balkans* (Bruno Mugnai)	108	*To Conquer and to Keep: Suchet and the War for Eastern Spain, 1809-1814, Volume 2 1811-1814* (Yuhan Kim)
94	*The Changing Face of Old Regime Warfare: Essays in Honour of Christopher Duffy* (Alexander S. Burns (ed.))	109	*The Tagus Campaign of 1809: An Alliance in Jeopardy* (John Marsden)
94	*The Changing Face of Old Regime Warfare: Essays in Honour of Christopher Duffy* (Alexander S. Burns (ed.))	110	*The War of the Bavarian Succession, 1778-1779: Prussian Military Power in Decline?* (Alexander Querengässer)
95	*The Danish Army of the Napoleonic Wars 1801-1814, Organisation, Uniforms & Equipment: Volume 3: Norwegian Troops and Militia* (David Wilson)	111	*Anson: Naval Commander and Statesman* (Anthony Bruce)
		112	*Atlas of the Battles and Campaigns of the American Revolution, 1775-1783* (David Bonk and George Anderson)
96	*1805 – Tsar Alexander's First War with Napoleon* (Alexander Ivanovich Mikhailovsky-Danilevsky, trans. Peter G.A. Phillips)	113	*A Fine Corps and will Serve Faithfully: The Swiss Regiment de Roll in the British Army 1794-1816* (Alistair Nichols)
97	*'More Furies then Men': The Irish Brigade in the service of France 1690-1792* (Pierre-Louis Coudray)	114	*Next to Wellington: General Sir George Murray: The Story of a Scottish Soldier and Statesman, Wellington's Quartermaster General* (John Harding-Edgar) (paperback edition)
98	*'We Are Accustomed to do our Duty': German Auxiliaries with the British Army 1793-95* (Paul Demet) (paperback edition)	115	*King George's Army: British Regiments and the Men who Led Them 1793-1815, Volume 1* (Steve Brown)
99	*Ladies, Wives and Women: British Army Wives in the Revolutionary and Napoleonic Wars 1793-1815* (David Clammer)	116	*Great Britain and the Defence of the Low Countries, 1744-1748: Armies, Politics and Diplomacy* (Alastair Massie)
100	*The Garde Nationale 1789-1815: France's Forgotten Armed Forces* (Pierre-Baptiste Guillemot)	117	*Kesselsdorf 1745: Decision in the Fight for Silesia* (Alexander Querengässer)
101	*Confronting Napoleon: Levin von Bennigsen's Memoir of the Campaign in Poland, 1806-1807, Volume I Pultusk to Eylau* (Alexander Mikaberidze and Paul Strietelmeier (trans. and ed.))	118	*The Key to Lisbon: The Third French Invasion of Portugal, 1810-11* (Kenton White) (paperback edition)

- 119 *Not So Easy, Lads: Wearing the Red Coat 1786–1797* (Vivien Roworth)
- 120 *Waging War in America: Operational Challenges of Five Armies* (Don N. Hagist (ed.))
- 121 *Sailors, Ships and Sea Fights: Proceedings of the 2022 'From Reason to Revolution 1721–1815' Naval Warfare in the Age of Sail Conference* (Nicholas James Kaizer (ed.))
- 122 *Light Troops in the Seven Years War: Irregular Warfare in Europe and North America 1755–1763* (James R. McIntyre)
- 123 *Every Hazard and Fatigue: The Siege of Pensacola 1781* (Joshua Provan)
- 124 *Armies and Wars of the French East India Companies 1664-1770: European, Asian and African Soldiers in India, Africa, the Far East and Louisiana* (René Chartrand)
- 125 *Suffren Versus Hughes: War in the Indian Ocean 1781-1783* (Quintin Barry)
- 126 *The Russian Patriotic War of 1812: The Russian Official History* Vol.1 (Modest Ivanovich Bogdanovich, trans. Peter G.A. Phillips)
- 127 *The King and His Fortresses: Frederick the Great and Prussian Permanent Fortifications 1740-1786* (Grzegorz Podruczny)
- 128 *A Swedish Soldier in the Napoleonic Wars: The Memoirs of Carl Magnus Hultin* (trans. Erik Faithfull)